LIVING ON THE EDGE

Research in Social Work series

Series Editors: Anna Gupta, Royal Holloway, University of London, UK and John Gal, Hebrew University of Jerusalem, Israel

Published together with The European Social Work Research Association (ESWRA), this series examines current, progressive and innovative research applications of familiar ideas and models in international social work research.

Also available in the series:

Migration and Social Work
Edited by Emilio José Gómez-Ciriano, Elena Cabiati and Sofia Dedotsi

When Social Workers Impact Policy and Don't Just Implement It
By John Gal and Idit Weiss-Gal

The Origins of Social Care and Social Work
By Mark Henrickson

Social Work Research Using Arts-Based Methods
Edited by Ephrat Huss and Eltje Bos

Critical Gerontology for Social Workers
Edited by Sandra Torres and Sarah Donnelly

Involving Service Users in Social Work Education, Research and Policy
Edited by Kristel Driessens and Vicky Lyssens-Danneboom

Adoption from Care
Edited by Tarja Pösö, Marit Skivenes and June Thoburn

Interprofessional Collaboration and Service User Participation
Edited by Kirsi Juhila, Tanja Dall, Christopher Hall and Juliet Koprowska

The Settlement House Movement Revisited
Edited by John Gal, Stefan Köngeter and Sarah Vicary

Social Work and the Making of Social Policy
Edited by Ute Klammer, Simone Leiber and Sigrid Leitner

Research in Social Work series

Series Editors: Anna Gupta, Royal Holloway, University of London, UK and John Gal, Hebrew University of Jerusalem, Israel

Forthcoming in the series:

Social Work and Social Innovation

Edited by Jean-Pierre Wilken, Anne Parpan-Blaser, Sarah Prosser, Suzan van der Pas and Erik Jansen

Find out more at:

policy.bristoluniversitypress.co.uk/
research-in-social-work

Research in Social Work series

Series Editors: Anna Gupta, Royal Holloway, University of London, UK and John Gal, Hebrew University of Jerusalem, Israel

---

International Editorial Board:

Find out more at:

policy.bristoluniversitypress.co.uk/
research-in-social-work

LIVING ON THE EDGE

Innovative Research on Leaving Care and Transitions to Adulthood

Edited by
Samuel Keller, Inger Oterholm,
Veronika Paulsen and Adrian D. van Breda

First published in Great Britain in 2024 by

Policy Press, an imprint of
Bristol University Press
University of Bristol
1–9 Old Park Hill
Bristol
BS2 8BB
UK
t: +44 (0)117 374 6645
e: bup-info@bristol.ac.uk

Details of international sales and distribution partners are available at policy.bristoluniversitypress.co.uk

The open access research in this book was supported by funding from ZHAW Zurich University of Applied Sciences, VID Specialized University and NTNU Social Research.

British Library Cataloguing in Publication Data
A catalogue record for this book is available from the British Library

ISBN 978-1-4473-6629-4 paperback
ISBN 978-1-4473-6630-0 ePub
ISBN 978-1-4473-6631-7 ePdf

Cover design: Bristol University Press
Front cover image: iStock/Mordolff
Bristol University Press and Policy Press use environmentally responsible print partners.
Printed and bound in Great Britain by CPI Group (UK) Ltd, Croydon, CR0 4YY

FSC
www.fsc.org
MIX
Paper | Supporting
responsible forestry
FSC® C013604

Contents

List of figures and tables

Figures

Tables

Notes on contributors

Ingri-Hanne Brænne Bennwik (she/her) is Lecturer and PhD student at the Faculty of Social Studies at VID Specialized University in Oslo, Norway. Her research is mainly oriented towards professional practice in the intersections between disability and leaving care. She is currently a member of the coordinator-team in CoRiT (Community of Researchers in Transition) and an executive committee member of INTRAC (International Research Network on Transitions to Adulthood from Care).

Jenna Bollinger (she/her) has a Master's in Forensic Psychology from the University of New South Wales and a PhD from Monash University, Australia. She has worked in out-of-home care in different capacities since 2012 and is currently Director of Psychology and Clinical Services for Knightlamp Consulting. She conducts a variety of assessments, including therapeutic assessments for out-of-home care, forensic assessments and parenting capacity assessments in the context of the child protection system.

Sue Bond (she/her) is Senior Lecturer at the University of Johannesburg, South Africa. Her research focus is on the circular relationship between possible selves and resilience in care-experienced young people and how these contribute to their journey through and after care. She is a member of the INTRAC steering group and conference committee.

Róisín Farragher (she/her) is a care-experienced young person currently working in policy development in Ireland. She has several international publications in the areas of family and family relationships, grounded theory, reflexivity and insider research. She has been part of INTRAC for several years and is part of a number of other international organisations.

Catherine Flynn (she/her) is an experienced academic at Monash University, Australia, acknowledged for her research and expertise at the intersection of justice and social work, with a particular focus on the implications for children and families of justice policies and interventions. She has supervised a number of PhD students whose research has focused on the processes to improve transitioning from out-of-home care.

Laura García-Alba (she/her) is Postdoctoral Researcher at the Family and Childhood Research Group, University of Oviedo, Spain. Her research focuses on supporting the transition to adulthood from childcare through the development and evaluation of life-skills development tools for young people in residential care. She has participated in INTRAC's activities since 2019.

Petra Göbbels-Koch (she/her) completed her PhD in Social Work at Royal Holloway, University of London, United Kingdom. Her PhD project looked at the occurrence and influencing factors of suicidal ideation among people with care experience in England and Germany. She holds a degree in social work (BA) and psychosocial counselling and mediation (MA) from the Hochschule Niederrhein. Her research interests include mental health, out-of-home care, and the transition from care to adulthood.

Federica Gullo (she/her) PhD in Education and Psychology, is Researcher in the Family and Childhood Research Group, at the University of Oviedo, Spain. She collaborates on various national and international projects and focuses her research on topics related to the transition to adulthood from care, especially on care-leavers' needs, the interventions carried out to support them, their results, and their satisfaction with the received benefits.

John Paul Horn (he/him/his) is Assistant Professor of Social Work at California State University – East Bay, United States. His scholarship focuses on structural barriers to emerging adulthood development in the educational and child welfare systems. He is a care-experienced person and is active in providing mentorship to care-experienced students as they pursue graduate and professional degrees in the United States.

Samuel Keller (he/him) is Senior Researcher and Lecturer at the Department of Social Work, Zurich University of Applied Sciences, Switzerland. His research interests and recent projects are on concepts of child wellbeing, transitions and participation in the fields of residential care, (unaccompanied) refugee children and adoption. His preferred qualitative methods are based on biographical, participatory and subject-oriented approaches as well as on visual methodologies.

Berni Kelly (she/her) is Professor of Disability Studies and Social Work at Queen's University Belfast in Northern Ireland and current member of the Executive Committee of INTRAC. Her research focuses on the intersections of childhood disability and alternative care, including the transitional experiences of disabled care-leavers. She has published widely on supporting disabled young people leaving care and participatory research with disabled youth and care-experienced young people.

Philip Mendes (he/him) is Professor of Social Work at Monash University, Australia. His research examines the policy, practice and legislative factors that inform pathways and outcomes for care-leavers. He is the author or co-author of 13 books including *Young people leaving state out-of-home care: A* *research-based study of Australian policy and practice* (2011), and *Young people transitioning from out-of-home care: International research, policy and practice* (2016).

Malose Samuel Mokgopha (he/him) is a child and youth care practitioner and Director at Kids Haven, a child and youth care centre in Benoni, South Africa. His main work centres around facilitating the transition of young people from care into adulthood.

Anne-Kirstine Mølholt (she/her) is Associate Professor at Aalborg University, Department of Sociology and Social Work, Denmark. Her research focus is within the field of leaving care and young people's experiences of aftercare and everyday life. Additionally, she explores ethical perspectives of conducting research among young people in vulnerable positions. She has been part of INTRAC since 2014.

Wendy Mupaku (she/her) is a PhD student at the University of Johannesburg, South Africa, and a clinical social worker by profession. A member of INTRAC and the African Network of Care-Leaving Researchers, her research focuses on the preparation of disabled care-leavers for the transition out of care. She published the first article in South Africa on the transitional journey during the COVID-19 pandemic.

Inger Oterholm (she/her) is Professor of Social Work at VID Specialized University, Oslo, Norway. Her research is focused on the institutional context of support for young people leaving care in transition to adulthood and the differences in logics and support between child and adult services. She has been part of INTRAC since 2010.

June Paul (they/them) is Assistant Professor in the Social Work Department at Skidmore College, United States. Their research examines programmes and policies in child welfare, juvenile justice, and other social service settings with a particular focus on advancing strategies for providing more equitable and effective care and services to LGBTQIA+ youth and families. June is currently a member of INTRAC.

Veronika Paulsen (she/her) is Professor in Child Welfare at the Norwegian University of Science and Technology (NTNU), Department of Social Work, and Research Professor at NTNU Social Research, Norway. Her main research field is in leaving care and transition to adulthood, children and young people's participation and child welfare interventions. She has for many years been a member of the international research network INTRAC.

Jade Purtell (she/her) is Postdoctoral Research Fellow at Monash University, Australia, with a transdisciplinary focus on participatory research methodology and youth participation in policy-making processes. Her PhD study was on care-leavers and early parenting in the Department of Social Work and Jade is now working in the Department of Human Centred Computing on participatory information governance in out-of-home care.

Annie Smith (she/her) is Adjunct Professor in the School of Nursing at the University of British Columbia, Canada, and has been the Executive Director of the McCreary Centre Society since 2006. Annie has conducted a range of participatory action research projects with care-leavers and is a co-founder of the society's Youth Research Academy.

Adrian D. van Breda (he/him) is Professor of Social Work at the University of Johannesburg, South Africa. His research centres on the resilience processes that facilitate the transition of young people from care towards adulthood. He is well published in the international literature on resilience and leaving care. He is currently the Chair of INTRAC.

Marcela Losantos Velasco (she/her) is Coordinator at the Research Institute of Behavioural Sciences at the Universidad Católica Boliviana 'San Pablo', Bolivia. Her research focuses on various aspects of the lives of children who have lost parental care. Her work has been recognised by the National Academy of Sciences, which awarded her the Marie Curie distinction in 2018, and she was named researcher of the year in 2021.

Jacinta Waugh (she/her) is Teaching Fellow and Researcher in the Department of Social Work at Monash University, Australia, where she completed her PhD thesis on the influence of informal relationship on the lives of young people leaving out-of-home care. Her professional interest and research expertise are working with disadvantaged young people, social capital and resiliency and exploring new ways of applying theoretical concepts to social conditions. Jacinta is a member of INTRAC.

Acknowledgements

Acknowledgement of funding

The editors wish to acknowledge, with grateful thanks, funding provided to make this book open access. Open access funding was provided by:

- ZHAW Zurich University of Applied Sciences, Switzerland
- VID Specialized University, Oslo, Norway
- NTNU Social Research, Norway

Acknowledgement of reviewers

This book underwent multiple levels of review. First, the book proposal was blind-reviewed by experts in the field. Second, each chapter was double-blind peer-reviewed by experts in the field. And third, the complete book manuscript was single-blind peer-reviewed by a subject expert. All reviewers provided exceptionally helpful feedback, all of which was carefully considered and acted on by the authors and editors.

The editors therefore wish to acknowledge and thank the following individuals who assisted with reviewing the book chapters:

- Anna Chalachanová (VID Specialized University, Norway)
- Annemiek Harder (Erasmus University Rotterdam, the Netherlands)
- Eavan Brady (Trinity College Dublin, Ireland)
- Emily Munro (University of Bedfordshire, United Kingdom)
- Gerald P. Mallon (Silberman School of Social Work, Hunter College, United States)
- Ingrid Höjer (University of Gothenburg, Sweden)
- Jan Storø (Oslo Metropolitan University, Norway)
- Jannike Kaasbøll (NTNU, Norway)
- Jim Wade (University of York, Honorary Research Fellow, United Kingdom)
- John Devaney (University of Edinburgh, United Kingdom)
- John Pinkerton (Queen's University Belfast, United Kingdom)
- Jorge del Valle (University of Oviedo, Spain)
- Kelly Devenney (University of York, United Kingdom)
- Kwabena Frimpong-Manso (University of Ghana, Ghana)
- Leah P. Cheatham (University of Alabama, United States)
- Mandi MacDonald (Queens University Belfast, United Kingdom)
- Maren Zeller (Eastern Switzerland University of Applied Sciences, Switzerland)

- Mariana Incarnato (Latin American Network of Care Leavers, Argentina)
- Mary Elizabeth Collins (Boston University School of Social Work, United States)
- Robbie Gilligan (Trinity College Dublin, Ireland)
- Sarojini Naidoo (University of Johannesburg, South Africa)
- Stian H. Thoresen (NTNU Social Research, Norway)
- Sue Bond (University of Johannesburg, South Africa)
- Tehila Refaeli (Ben Gurion University, Israel)
- Thomas Gabriel (Zurich University of Applied Sciences, Switzerland)
- Yvonne Sjöblom (University of Gävle, Sweden)

Foreword

Mike Stein
Department of Social Policy and
Social Work, University of York

Research evidence concerning the poor outcomes of young people leaving care led in 2003 to the setting up of the International Research Network on Transitions to Adulthood from Care (INTRAC), bringing together for the first time researchers from Europe, the Middle East, Australia, Canada and the United States – and later from Asian, African and South American countries.

Since it began, INTRAC has provided an opportunity for its members to reach beyond a parochial understanding of young people's transitions from care to adulthood, by sharing research findings and exploring their implications for policy, practice and theory, contributing to a growing body of publications. From the outset, a lively and dynamic development within INTRAC has been the contribution of PhD researchers who established the Community of Researchers in Transition (CoRiT). It is they who have been the driving force behind this book.

Living on the Edge is ground-breaking in many ways: first, in giving voice to new researchers from many countries, including the Global South, who have often struggled to be heard; second, in exploring new and hitherto unresearched questions and topics; and third, in doing this with the use of innovative methodologies and challenging theoretical perspectives.

The introductory chapter sets the context by detailing the arguments for a shift from the current centre ground of the 'leaving care' knowledge bank – which has laid the empirical and conceptual foundations – to the 'edge'. Whilst acknowledging these earlier building blocks, the authors suggest to avoid embracing the new will not only result in recycling existing approaches – 'Haven't I heard that before somewhere?' – it also contributes to legitimising the status quo, and by implication limits the parameters of inquiry.

Enabling young people from care to experience normative transitions to adulthood – gradual, supported and extended – has been an ongoing challenge in the construction of leaving-care law, policy and practice. The difficulties of achieving this in relation to the diverse and often neglected groups of care-leavers 'living on the edge' – who are often diminished or missing in larger general samples of care-leavers – is detailed in the four chapters in Part I of this book.

These chapters give voice to accelerated, insecure and at times damaging and desperate transitions: to the uncertain adult futures of unaccompanied migrant young people in Spain as they seek permission to remain in order to be entitled to much needed aftercare services; to Bolivian youth rescued from the streets but returning to the streets on leaving care; to the recognition of 'street family' support in South Africa and the need to replicate positive networks in care; and finally to the homophobic and transphobic discrimination and victimisation experienced by LGBTQIA+ young people from care.

The application of established methodologies has set the scientific bar high in terms of rigour, replication, reliability and results – the four R's. However, by living in a traditional methodological comfort zone, more problematic questions in researching care-experienced groups are often overlooked, as explored in the 'edgy' chapters in Part II of the book.

How to address power imbalances in the research process, including practical ways to reduce stigma, tokenism and re-traumatisation from the perspective of care-experienced and non-care-experienced researchers. How to bridge the gap between the individual experiences of care-leavers and the institutional practices that shape their experiences, by applying 'institutional ethnography'. How to ensure sampling, recruitment and fieldwork methods can meet the needs of disabled care-leavers; and drawing on care-leavers' experiences of early parenting, how to balance rigour and empowerment, whilst avoiding tokenism and re-traumatisation.

Sixteen years ago, I concluded my paper reflecting on the 'Poverty of theory' by suggesting that 'linking empirical and theoretical work has the potential to enhance our understanding of aging out of care issues, as well as the theoretical foundations of practice' (Stein, 2006: 431). The chapters in the third and final part of this book build upon earlier work in contributing to new conceptual knowledge.

We read of: a 'habitus of instability' to explain how care-leavers' life choices are limited by unstable experiences – which connects with an exploration of the features of 'stability' in residential care; how sociological theory and leaving-care research contributes to a better understanding of the higher risk of suicidal ideation and behaviour among care-leavers and its implications for improving prevention; and of the positive impact of 'informal social capital' on care-leaver transitions. It is welcome that many of the chapters in Parts I and II are also theoretically and conceptually underpinned, and, as recognised in the concluding chapter, that there is potential for further exploration from the social, political and behavioural sciences.

Living on the Edge makes an important and original contribution to our understanding of contemporary care-leaving. It does so by capturing a symmetry between researchers starting their careers, the 'edgy' contributions contained within this volume and the lives of the many care-experienced young people moving on to adulthood in different contexts, circumstances and cultures. Finally, as I mentioned at the outset, this book has come about due to the commitment determination and skills of early-career researchers. The future of care-leaving research is in very good hands.

Reference
Stein, M. (2006) 'Young people aging out of care: The poverty of theory', *Children and Youth Services Review*, 28(4): 422–434. doi: 10.1016/j.childyouth 2005.05.005

Introduction: Moving towards the edge

Samuel Keller, Inger Oterholm, Veronika Paulsen
and Adrian D. van Breda

Introduction

Research on leaving residential and foster care and transitioning towards young adulthood has been burgeoning in recent years. A solid foundation of knowledge about care-leaving processes and outcomes has been laid, albeit largely in a few Global North countries. This knowledge foundation has edges that have been neglected, even overlooked. Young people leaving care are, in many ways, 'on the edge', as they transition between childhood and adulthood, care and independence, school and work. This book aims to shed light on these aspects of leaving care, by reporting about on-the-edge research. The book addresses edgy topics regarding specific groups of care-leavers, methods and theories, rather than keeping to the mainstream research topics. The authors of the chapters in this book are themselves 'on the edge' – emerging from their postgraduate studies and starting the journey towards the ranks of 'established researchers'. Many of these on-the-edge researchers bring a fresh, critical and innovative perspective on leaving care. This book illuminates not only marginalised facets of leaving care and care-leaving research, but also looks forward towards the future, anticipating where leaving care and care-leaving research might go over the coming years.

Balancing on the edge to ensure relevant knowledge for the future

Leaving-care research has contributed significantly to the field of out-of-home or alternative care (including residential and foster care) by raising the first-hand experiences of children and young adults. Care-leaving research was and is responsible for evidence-informed arguments, for the participatory creation of perspectives and for identifying opportunities for quality improvement. This growing field of scholarship consistently advances the voices and needs of young people transitioning out of the care system into young adulthood. Leaving-care scholars have often been closely engaged with practice, care-leaver associations and advocacy groups, working to translate research into real-world improvements to the lot of young people exiting state care. For this book, we construct leaving care as 'living on the edge'.

Young people transitioning out of care towards independence, out of school towards work, or out of adolescence towards adulthood are on the edge between these phases. 'Living on the edge' speaks to the liminality inherent in youth transitions and leaving-care transitions. Furthermore, living on the edge speaks to the precarity experienced by many care-leavers between dependent care and independent adulthood, who lack the social capital and resources to transition into stable education, employment and family life, and who are at risk of marginalisation and social exclusion.

Recent publications on leaving care have tended to focus on challenges that care-leavers face in the transition to adulthood and their outcomes in adulthood. Many publications have presented results from single research projects, international comparisons or on changes in policy and practice. These were very important sources that often prompted changes to the law, practice and conditions of growing up in and leaving care in many countries. But once a discourse has been established, it always risks recycling and reproducing similar themes and topics, methods, perspectives and ethics – system theories name it 'autopoiesis' or a self-referential system.

However, in a rapidly changing world, various new questions arise for which previous answers are not always sufficient. That is why our aim with this book is to make known and encourage researchers around the globe to dare to do 'research on the edge'. To facilitate such a fresh angle on the edges of the leaving-care field, the authors selected to work on this book are part of an international research network on leaving care, come from around the globe, have different experiences in practice and research, and mostly have either recently finished their PhD or are still working on it.

Research on leaving care is burgeoning, because those who provide services to and research young people in care have increasingly realised that the end point of care is the transition out of care into young adulthood. In essence, the success of child welfare is judged by how young people do after they have left care. Consequently, there is a growing interest about aftercare among all those working in, teaching and researching child welfare. At the same time, there is the emergence of new experiences, sensitive questions and issues, and new knowledge, which the current books on leaving care do not adequately address.

This book intends to develop and connect an experience- and methodology-based store of international research knowledge, questions and answers to make an innovative contribution to an important dialogue about the next steps in leaving-care scholarship. This dialogue 'on the edge' between past, present and future has the aim of influencing future researchers and research, future policy makers and policies, as well as future concepts of leaving care. As it is designed and internationally coordinated by the next generation of scholars, it will support care-leavers, scholars and practitioners to shape the future development of high-quality care and leaving care through accessible and innovative knowledge transfer.

Leaving care – as a specific concept of structural, processual and/or individual transitions from care to adulthood – has been in focus and widely studied in several countries, is still emerging in many countries, and is not studied at all in others, particularly in the Global South. This unevenness in research across the globe informs this publication: how can we reflect on learnings, on gaps and on child- and practice-oriented futures of leaving-care research internationally? We address these questions by inviting emerging leaving-care researchers with diverse ranges of experiences and countries of origin to write about their most important cutting-edge methodological, theoretical, ethical and political learnings, as well as about their imagination for the future. In summary, following our idea of 'edgy' topics in the field of leaving-care research, the authors of this book are not reproducing existing (albeit important) knowledge, but developing so-far under-researched paths on overlooked care-leavers using creative research methods and fresh theories.

This book presents recent innovative and edgy international leaving-care studies to create future scenarios of research and practice that is on the edge, by presenting and discussing the following three themes:

- *Part I: Groups of care-leavers living on the edge*: the way we consider groups of care-leavers with specific needs or types of transitions who may have been overlooked in the research to date.
- *Part II: Methods of care-leaving research*: addressing power imbalances, using existing methods mindfully and raising critical questions about taken-for-granted methods.
- *Part III: Theory and conceptualisation of leaving care*: theoretical frameworks that shed new and provocative light on our understanding of leaving care.

This publication avoids merely presenting, comparing and discussing the latest results and implications of care-leaving research. While this is important, it is already being done by many publications. This book aims to explore themes on the edge. It draws on the work of emerging scholars, from around the world, studying under-researched groups (such as care-leavers with a street-connected history who go back onto the streets), using innovative methodologies (such as institutional ethnography) and exploring the use of innovative theories and conceptualisations of leaving care (such as the concepts of stability versus instability among care-leavers).

The global network behind this publication

When aiming to generate new insights, on new stages, by new actors – when aiming to be cutting-edge and innovative – we need to have a promising pool of interesting and interested researchers, who are willing to recognise and define various edges: edges between enabling and labelling specific groups by research, the edges within innovative or underutilised methods, and the edges when doing theoretical reflections that lead to conceptualisations of leaving care (as set out in the three parts of this book). The idea of this book is a result of several meetings and discussions in the PhD care-leaving research network CoRiT (Community of Researchers in Transition).[1] The CoRiT network aims to establish a forum for research and knowledge dissemination about care-leavers' situation, capacities and support needs during their transition from care.

The CoRiT network is an offspring from the already established INTRAC (International Research Network on Transitions to Adulthood from Care) that brings together internationally leading researchers in the field of leaving care.[2] The pioneer work of leaving-care research was carried out mainly by a small number of members of INTRAC. As the field of care-leaving has grown, so has INTRAC, which now (in March 2023) has 331 signed-up members representing 47 countries around the globe, from (in descending order of membership) Europe, North America, Oceania, Asia, Africa and South America. INTRAC hosts an annual Global INTRAC meeting, which sometimes runs as a standalone symposium or connected to an existing conference (such as the EUSARF[3] conference).

CoRiT members constitute the next generation of care-leaving scholars – they are on the edge of becoming established and picking up where the original INTRAC members, many of whom are retiring, left off. Thus, the CoRiT network aims to expand the opus of research it has inherited from the first generation of care-leaving scholars, by setting it in relation to challenges in our contemporary and anticipated future society, such as issues of migration and the consequences of a more globalised world. Further, we identify a great need for continuous work on improving policy and translating research into practice. It is also crucial to develop an even more reflexive stand in the field and thus also to focus on research methods and methodological issues.

Members from CoRiT have presented several symposia together at conferences like the European Conference of Social Work (ECSWR) and the European Scientific Association on Residential & Family Care for Children and Adolescents (EUSARF). Through those presentations and intense discussions, we realised that many of the CoRiT members are interested in research concerning care-leavers who are in an especially vulnerable situation and/or care-leavers who meet other or additional challenges in the transition to adulthood (compared to care-leavers in general). Much of the research on care-leavers until now has had a broad focus and tends to treat care-leavers as a homogeneous group, leading to young people with specific profiles or challenges being overlooked. Recent reviews of care-leaving research find that much of the research is focused on policy, programmes and services that target care-leavers in general, and there is also much research on transition markers and outcomes, which often draws on large data sets. Less research is focused on sub-populations and specific challenges, and there is also limited research on youth participation. We thus concluded that these are topics that researchers 'on the edge' – the next generation – could have the unique potential to address.

From the middle towards the edges: overview of the book

This book moves from the middle of often well-established care-leaving research topics towards the edges. It sets out the authors' concept of the 'edge' and 'edgy' in connection with care-leavers' resources and needs, emerging researchers, specific groups, creative methods and innovative theory. 'On the edge' in the title speaks to the liminality inherent in leaving-care transitions and to the precarity experienced by many care-leavers. But it also speaks to the status of recent developments in research and practice or to evolving questions, methods and paradigms, thanks to the next generation of researchers. The book is structured in three parts: Groups, Methods and Theories.

Part I: Groups of care-leavers living on the edge

Unaccompanied minors usually become familiar with 'living on the edge' at a young age, when they start their migratory process as minors and move towards a journey in which they cross multiple borders at geographical and legal levels. However, after turning 18, they are treated as adult migrants and depend on the immigration law. But still, the transition to adulthood remains one of the less studied life periods of this group of young people, at both national and international levels. That's why Laura García-Alba and Federica Gullo (Spain) aim to explore, through a mixed-methods approach, the profiles, needs and experiences of transitioning to adulthood of this especially vulnerable group in comparison with non-unaccompanied-migrant care-leavers in Spain.

Marcela Losantos Velasco (Bolivia) was disturbed by the fact that in Bolivia, 97 per cent of street-connected children who entered care programmes left care before reaching adulthood to return to the street for a variety of reasons. She observed through her extensive practice experience that this was common also when formerly street-connected young people aged out of care. Thus, her research aims to understand what leads young adults with a street past to transition back onto the streets when they aged out of care. This chapter explores the factors that drove five street-connected looked-after young adults back to the streets. Considering the findings, the author questions if there are real possibilities for social integration, after a street-connected and care history, for young adults who have lived for many years at the margins of society or within institutional walls.

Sam Mokgopha, Adrian van Breda and Sue Bond (South Africa) also conducted research with and on former street-involved children in South Africa. They used a social-ecological construction of resilience to interpret findings. One main finding expands the normative concept of family: children build family-like connections when living in the streets. The chapter underlines the relevance of recognising, naming, celebrating and advancing such resilience processes when working with children with a street-involved history while in care and leaving care. Following these findings, attention should be given to enable these children to recognise the care setting as a safe and collaborative 'family' of supportive relationships, similar to what they formed on the streets.

Further, we know that LGBTQIA+ youth are disproportionally represented in foster care. In addition to experiencing mistreatment and victimisation at home, school and within their communities, they report experiences of homophobic and transphobic discrimination and victimisation from peers and professionals within child welfare system. But as there are still very few studies that explore the outcomes of LGBTQIA+ former foster youth, June Paul (United States) discusses three theoretical frameworks/perspectives to understand and improve the lives of LGBTQIA+ youth leaving foster care. They include minority stress theory, life course theory, and an anti-oppressive practice perspective.

Part II: Methods of care-leaving research

Ingri-Hanne Brænne Bennwik and Inger Oterholm (Norway) understand the process of leaving care as a complex balancing act between the young person's own agency and ruling relations from a wide range of service organisations. In contrast to much research on leaving care that ignores this complexity and focuses on either individual or organisational factors, this chapter uses institutional ethnography to establish a connection between individual experiences of leaving care and institutional practices that shape these experiences. Drawing on two studies on leaving care in Norway, the findings illustrate the importance of including the institutional conditions to understand the support given to care-leavers and their experiences of this support.

While research on care-leaving is growing globally, for disabled youth this is an emerging field of study, and little is known about how to design studies to recruit and involve disabled care-leavers. When disabled care-leavers reach the age of majority, they often have a dual experience of ageing out of both child welfare services and children's disability services. Therefore Wendy Mupaku (South Africa), Ingri-Hanne Brænne Bennwik (Norway) and Berni Kelly (United Kingdom) aim to highlight the methodological issues encountered by the authors as they engaged disabled youth leaving care in qualitative research in Norway, South Africa and Northern Ireland – three countries, each with different policies. The chapter presents a thematic discussion of the challenges and methodological issues identified across the three countries and offers guidance to inform future care-leaving research that is more inclusive of disabled youth. Whilst the primary focus is on research with disabled care-leavers, the discussion also has relevance to the ongoing advancement of leaving-care research more widely to ensure it is inclusive of the heterogeneous experiences of care-leavers.

To improve the engagement of hard-to-reach cohorts generally, Jade Purtell (Australia) suggests in her chapter the use of trauma-informed research designs. She starts with her experiences carrying out a PhD project concerning care-leaver early parenting in the state of Victoria, Australia. The aim of the chapter is to explore ways that low-resource research can be carried out to ensure minimum risk of tokenism or re-traumatisation, while maximising reach and impact. Her reflections have led to the development of an adaptive participation model to assist in research and consultation design.

Róisín Farragher (Ireland), Petra Göbbels-Koch (United Kingdom), John Paul Horn (United States) and Annie Smith (Canada) notice that while much of leaving-care research has been addressing a wide range of issues, it seems to be slowly shifting towards exploring caring relationships and the relationship between 'the researcher' and 'the researched'. The authors use case studies from different countries to examine transnational strategies for addressing power imbalances, bias and disempowerment in the research process from the perspective of both care-experienced and non-care-experienced researchers. Their chapter on addressing the power imbalance present in research with care-leavers, also provides practical advice for those engaging care-experienced people in research.

Part III: Theory and conceptualisation of leaving care

Although placement instability has been found to correlate with problematic outcomes in several areas, including mental health, criminal behaviour and sexual behaviour, existing empirical literature has not found close links between placement stability and positive outcomes. Jenna Bollinger (Australia) criticises operationalisations that use continuity of a placement as a factor of stability as this considers neither the care-leaver's internal experience of the placement nor the many moving parts in residential care. Her examination of stability in residential care is based on semi-structured interviews with eight care-leavers in New South Wales, Australia. The essential elements of stability based on their experiences include a consistent care team, consistent rules within the house, a sense of safety within the placement and a perception that the staff genuinely care for the wellbeing of the young people. The young people's relationships were the main drivers of them feeling stable.

Anne-Kirstine Mølholt (Denmark) also explored the facets of instability in the lives of young people who have been in out-of-home care. She draws on the concept of a habitus of instability, by stressing that the young people's actions, strategies and perceptions of self are based on their uncertain and unstable circumstances. Her qualitative longitudinal study conducted in Denmark with eight care-leavers focuses on their everyday life. The findings point to different ways of how the care-leavers position themselves in relation to experiences of instability, for example, when they changed educational status, living arrangements and circle of friends.

However, extreme experiences of instability can have dramatic consequences: care-experienced young people are considered to be at higher risk of experiencing suicidal thoughts and attempting suicide. Previous research on this topic has largely neglected considering existing theories of suicide to explain the elevated risk among this group. Petra Göbbels-Koch (United Kingdom) brings together the two fields of theoretical suicidology and leaving-care research. She wonders if theories – specifically, Joiner's Interpersonal-Psychological Theory of Suicide – can help to better understand the elevated risk of suicidal ideation and behaviour among care-leavers. The results highlight the relevance of a theoretical understanding of young people's experiences in the context of leaving care. The author discusses how far the practical application of theories of suicide could inform guidelines for suicide prevention tailored to care-experienced young people.

Overall, leaving-care literature emphasises that developmental and environmental resources are critical for helping care-leavers navigate transitional difficulties. However, these resources are not always obtainable by formal systems of support. In seeking to examine how informal social resources may assist in a gradual transition for care-leavers, Jacinta Waugh, Philip Mendes and Catherine Flynn (Australia) have developed an overall conceptual and analytical framework of how social capital and social support interact to provide these resources. For this, they interviewed eight care-leavers and six nominated informal support people in Victoria, Australia. The main findings of the study are that informal social capital and social support can be valuable for all care-leavers. They are more accessible and continuous than formal social capital and social support and help develop resilience and positive self-identity.

From the edges into the future

In the conclusion, the editors – Samuel Keller (Switzerland), Inger Oterholm (Norway), Veronika Paulsen (Norway) and Adrian van Breda (South Africa) – bring together and analytically discuss the key learnings from each part of the book (groups, methods and theory) as well as from the book overall. We consider which edges we learned about in the book and where will they lead us. On this basis, we imagine the future of care-leaving research that we referred to earlier in this Introduction, but which is not much visible in the individual chapters: What do we imagine going forward? What are the 'edges' that are still sharp? What specific groups with specific needs or vulnerabilities could be overlooked or re-stigmatised by practice or research, such as LGBTQIA+ or Indigenous peoples? What methodological paradigms can we expect to change because of greater numbers of care-experienced researchers, participative collaboration with care-leavers in research and the emerging of new or neglected research designs? How might these changes result in research that is more strongly theory-driven, increasing leaving-care discourses in the Global South and to new interdisciplinary perspectives in theories and concepts (for example, anthropology, sociology, youth studies). The conclusion ends with a specific focus on the meaning of global research and practice exchange (Global South and North), of children's and young people's perspectives and of self-critical reflections.

We wish our readers many provocative insights and edgy thoughts that, in alliance with care-experienced young people and their supporters, inspire your further thinking, further critical self-reflection, further research and further action concerning developments in policy and practice in the field of childcare, leaving care, child protection and child services all around the globe.

Notes

[1] https://globalintrac.com/corit/
[2] https://globalintrac.com/
[3] European Scientific Association on Residential & Family Care for Children and Adolescents

PART I

Groups of care-leavers living on the edge

Unaccompanied migrant youth leaving care in Spain: how their journeys differ from those of other care-leavers

Laura García-Alba and Federica Gullo

Introduction

The arrival of unaccompanied migrant[1] young people (UMYP) in Europe has received growing attention from the field of child welfare services since the 2000s. These young people usually become familiar with 'living on the edge' at a young age when they start their migratory process as minors and arrive in a foreign country without the protection of an adult person. This is the first milestone of a journey determined by crossing multiple borders at geographical, legal and personal levels.

European policy advocates for effective protection and integration of UMYP into society (Council of Europe, 2019). However, the transition to adulthood still constitutes a particularly vulnerable 'crossing' period for them in which they face several additional challenges, such as migratory experiences, lacking social support, or dealing with cultural and language barriers (Sirriyeh and Ní Raghallaigh, 2018). Moreover, UMYP usually navigate ambivalent migratory policies regarding their access to alternative care and support, especially after becoming of age (Gimeno-Monterde et al, 2021).

This phenomenon is particularly relevant for Southern European countries that serve as an entry point to the continent (UNHCR, 2020). Among them, Spain has become one of the main gateways for UMYP from the Maghreb and Sub-Saharan Africa (Gimeno-Monterde and Gutiérrez-Sánchez, 2019) seeking to find better opportunities to improve their socioeconomic conditions (Alonso-Bello et al, 2020), sometimes even encouraged by their own families (Calzada, 2007). Although their number is difficult to quantify since not all of them are identified (UNICEF, 2019), their increasing arrival is having a strong impact on the Spanish child welfare system. In fact, the number of looked-after UMYP increased by 18 per cent in 2019 alone, reaching 11,490 cases and being almost exclusively boys (93.91 per cent; Observatorio de la Infancia, 2020).

In Spain, migrant unaccompanied underage youth are eligible for the same services as any other unprotected minor (Act 26/2015), being mostly placed in residential care (Bravo and Santos, 2017). However, their possibilities of legally remaining in the country after turning 18 are conditional on fulfilling the demanding criteria for obtaining or renewing their residence permit (accreditation of enough financial resources, one-year employment contract), according to immigration law (Organic Act 4/2000). These legal obstacles put a lot of pressure on UMYP to become independent and find a job to avoid becoming illegal (Gonzales, 2011).

However, despite the consensus about the additional challenges and barriers that UMYP face to become independent adults and the impact of this phenomenon in childcare services, the transition to adulthood remains one of the less-studied life periods of this group at an international level (Salmerón-Manzano and Manzano-Agugliaro, 2018). This is even more pronounced in Spain, where studies have been limited to the use of small, local samples and tend to address specific areas such as educational experiences (González-García et al, 2017), employability skills (Alonso-Bello et al, 2020), personal wellbeing (Manzani and Arnoso-Martínez, 2014) or childcare policies (Gimeno-Monterde et al, 2021).

Therefore, this chapter aims to explore the profiles, needs and transitional experiences of UMYP in Spain. We will focus on depicting their pathways from care to independence, describing their psychosocial adjustment in terms of personal wellbeing, self-esteem and perceptions of readiness for independent living. We will also describe the supports received during their transitions compared to those of other care-leavers. The chapter will use a quantitative analysis approach using data from semi-structured interviews and standardised tests to provide evidence about key areas towards the transition to adulthood of UMYP in contrast with a comparison group. Two groups of care-experienced young people participated in this study. The first group comprises 101 adolescents living in children's homes and preparing for leaving care, while the second is composed of 141 care-leavers involved in aftercare services. The groups include both UMYP and non-UMYP with similar characteristics (age, gender, and so on), which serve as comparison groups. To the best of our knowledge, this study will be the first one to include this comparative perspective with a sample from several regions of Spain. The discussion of findings in the light of previous research will identify major challenges and opportunities. It will draw implications for policy and practice in the field of supporting UMYP's journeys from care to independence as they navigate the liminal space between laws, evolutionary stages and international borders.

Study's research questions

Specifically, this study is guided by the following exploratory research questions:

- Do UMYP show lower levels of personal wellbeing, self-esteem and independent living skills than other care-leavers without this background?
- Are the wellbeing, self-esteem and independent living skills impacted differently after leaving care?
- To what extent are their backgrounds and profiles different to those of other care-leavers?
- To what extent do their backgrounds and profiles influence their psychosocial adaptation?

Method

Participants

The sample was composed of 242 male care-experienced young people aged 14–25 (M = 18.08; SD = 1.77) living in Spain. Among them, 101 were adolescents living in residential care and preparing for leaving care (RC group), aged 14–18 (M = 16.55, SD = 0.74), of whom 66 per cent were UMYP. These adolescents were evaluated before using Planea Program, a web-based independent living skills programme for young people in residential care (Del Valle and García-Alba, 2021). The second group was composed of 141 youths that were receiving aftercare services (AC group) for their transition to adulthood (48.2 per cent UMYP), aged 18–25 (M = 19.17, SD = 1.45). The reason for selecting only male participants was due to the lack of female UMYP in residential facilities in Spain, where they only account for 6.8 per cent (Observatorio de la Infancia, 2020). UMYP mainly came from North Africa. Young people in the comparison groups came from families living in Spain, being either Spanish or having a migratory background.

Instruments

Standardised instruments

Self-esteem scale (RSES; Rosenberg, 1965). This is one of the most used instruments for the assessment of self-esteem. It includes ten items with a four-point Likert scale (1 = 'strongly disagree', 4 = 'strongly agree'). Scores vary from 10 to 40, high self-esteem being attributed to those scoring 30 or more. The scale's internal consistency in this study was acceptable in the present study (α = 0.75; Cronbach, 1951).

Personal Wellbeing Index (PWI; Cummins et al, 2003). This instrument included seven items in its original version, which assessed the satisfaction with different areas of life using a ten-point Likert scale (0 = 'completely dissatisfied', 10 = 'completely satisfied'). We used the version developed by Casas et al (2012), adapted for Spanish population. We followed the recommendation by Cummins and Lau (2005) and included items to measure satisfaction with the family and the facility in which they live. The total score was calculated on the seven original items of the scale, and converted to a 0–100 scale to facilitate comparisons and interpretation, considering 70–80 as normal scores (Cummins et al, 2003). The additional items were analysed qualitatively. Moreover, the Overall Life Satisfaction (OLS) item was included to measure satisfaction with life globally, as Campbell et al (1976) suggested. In the current study, the reliability coefficient of this scale was very good (α = 0.84; Cronbach, 1951).

Planea Independent Life Skills Assessment Tools (PLANEA, García-Alba et al, 2021, 2022b). This is a self-reported scale developed from the framework of the Planea Program (Del Valle and García-Alba, 2021) to assess the perceived level of independent living skills. It is made up of three subscales with a four-point Likert scale (1 = 'nothing', 4 = 'a lot') that measure the perceived ability of young people to perform tasks related to being autonomous in different domains of everyday life, including taking care of oneself and one's home (Self-Care and Well-Being, SCWB), making simple arrangements in the community (Daily Arrangements and Organizational Skills, DAOS), and being financially independent to maintain a home (Employment and Accommodation, EA). The total score represents a global score in Independent Living Skills (ILS). Cronbach's alpha in this study showed similarly high levels both for the total scale (α = 0.94) and for the subscales (0.81 ≤ α ≤ 0.89; Cronbach, 1951).

Semi-structured interview

An in-depth semi-structured interview was conducted with young people in the AC group (*n* = 141) to gather information about their trajectories through and after care, including the experiences of abuse and neglect in their families, the path through different care placements, school and work, their health and risk behaviours, social support, and help received for their transition from care to independent living. Participants' answers were transcribed and translated into quantitative categorical variables to analyse them through quantitative methods.

Procedure

Participants in the RC group were administered the standardised instruments as part of a baseline assessment conducted when they started using the Planea

Program with their key educator. This tool is implemented in one of the biggest regions of Spain as the primary resource for preparation for leaving care and life skills development in children's homes. The participants in this group were adolescents who registered in Planea Program's platform from June 2019 to August 2021 and completed this assessment through an online questionnaire. They were aware of the objectives of this assessment before they agreed to complete it.

To recruit participants for the AC group, several local authorities in Spain were contacted and asked for permission to present the study to their aftercare support agencies. Then, non-probabilistic convenience sampling was used. The care-leaving teams in each local authority contacted the youths to propose their participation in this study. They participated in a face-to-face interview (40–60 minutes) conducted by one of the research team members. The interviewer explained the objectives and voluntary nature of the study, as well as the confidentiality and anonymity guarantee of their participation before they signed an informed consent form. When the interview was finished, they were asked to complete the standardised instruments using paper and pencil. The interviews were conducted from March 2018 to September 2020.

Young people in the different groups received the same instructions for completing the instruments. Those who were not fluent enough in written Spanish were excluded from this part of the study, ranging from 22 to 32 per cent of exclusions depending on the test. The study received approval from the Research Ethical Committee of the University of Oviedo.

Data analysis

Descriptive statistics were used to describe participants' characteristics. Two-way multivariate analysis of variance (MANOVA) was carried out to measure the main and interaction effects of unaccompanied migrant status and care situation on a combination of three dependent variables, considered as a linear combination that measures an underlying construct of psychosocial adaptation. Two-way and one-way Welch analyses of variance (ANOVA) were conducted to study UMYP's differences in the studied quantitative variables across both groups, while the Chi-square test for independence was used for categorical variables. The Games-Howell test was used for post-hoc comparisons. Several one-way MANOVA were also carried out to assess the effect of multiple variables related to the situation of care-leavers on their psychosocial adaptation.

A value of $p < 0.05$ was established as the degree of significance in all analyses. Appropriate effect sizes were estimated, reported for each test and interpreted using Cohen's guidelines (1988). All analyses were performed using the Statistical Package for Social Sciences (SPSS) v26.

Results

Psychosocial adaptation

Means and standard deviations of participants' scores in PWI, RSES and PLANEA-ILS are displayed in Table 1.1, divided according to the care situation (CS: RC and AC groups), and to the unaccompanied migrant status (UMS: UMYP and comparison group, CG).

Table 1.1: Descriptive statistics of standardised questionnaires

Variables	UMYP		CG		TOTAL	
	M	SD	M	SD	M	SD
Residential care group (RC)						
RSES	30.95	4.28	31	5.98	30.97	4.91
PWI	73.77	16.98	73.91	18.98	73.81	17.59
PLANEA						
Total (ILS)	92.66	18.76	97.21	19.58	94.08	19.02
SCWB	47.35	8.45	49.82	8.09	48.12	8.37
DAOS	26.26	6.86	27.56	7.96	26.70	7.24
EA	18.53	5.57	18.38	6.09	18.48	5.72
Aftercare group (AC)						
RSES	31.44	3.94	33.26	4.59	32.69	4.46
PWI	79.81	13.06	77	13.43	77.93	13.30
PLANEA						
Total (ILS)	106.12	16.59	121.22	18.19	117.65	18.85
SCWB	51.25	6.90	56.42	5.86	55.11	6.50
DAOS	30.90	6.27	38.81	9.18	36.74	9.17
EA	23.48	5.02	25.15	5.22	24.63	5.19
Total sample						
RSES	31.10	4.17	32.44	5.21	31.78	4.76
PWI	75.65	16.04	75.89	15.61	75.77	15.79
PLANEA						
Total (ILS)	95.56	19.04	113.12	21.78	104.56	22.25
SCWB	48.30	8.23	54.30	7.30	51.39	8.31
DAOS	27.38	6.98	34.70	10.28	31.16	9.55
EA	19.97	5.84	22.68	6.42	21.32	6.27

Notes: UMYP = unaccompanied migrant young people; CG = control group; RSES = Rosenberg Self-Esteem Scale ($n = 190$); PWI = Personal Wellbeing Index ($n = 192$); ILS = Independent Living Skills ($n = 163$); SCWB = Self-Care and Well-Being; DAOS = Daily Arrangements and Organizational Skills; EA = Employment and Accommodation; M = mean; SD = standard deviation.

Figure 1.1: Mean scores of PWI items

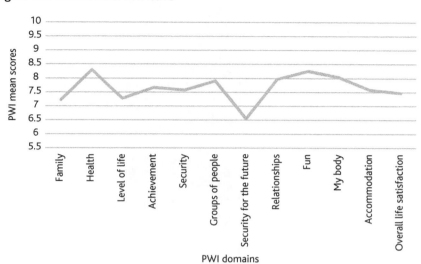

The mean scores of RSES were within the normal range for the entire sample, both for UMYP (M = 31.10; SD = 4.17) and CG (M = 32.44; SD = 5.21), as well as those of personal wellbeing (M_{UMYP} = 75.65; SD_{UMYP} = 16.04, and M_{CG} = 75.89; SD_{CG} = 15.61).

In both cases, the RSES scores of UMYP were slightly lower than those of the CG. However, the analysis of the different levels of RSES showed that 69.6 per cent of the sample obtained high levels, 19.4 per cent medium levels and 11 per cent low levels. Moreover, the mean scores obtained by the participants in each item of PWI showed that the area with which the participants were least satisfied was security for the future (Figure 1.1).

To verify whether the levels of RSES, PWI and PLANEA-ILS varied depending on the unaccompanied migrant status (UMS) and the care situation (CS), different types of analysis of variance were carried out. First, a two-way MANOVA was run, using UMS and CS as independent variables, and the total scores of RSES, PWI and PLANEA-ILS as combined dependent variables (Table 1.2), to assess the psychosocial adaptation of participants.

The analysis found a statistically significant interaction effect between UMS and CS on the combined dependent variables (p = 0.017). Follow-up univariate two-way ANOVAs were run to detect any statistically significant univariate interaction effects for each dependent variable separately (Table 1.2). These showed a statistically significant interaction effect between UMS and CS for PLANEA-ILS score (p = 0.037), but not for RSES's and PWI's scores. Therefore, a simple main effects analysis was conducted for PLANEA-ILS scores, which found significant differences between UMYP and CG for the AC group (F(1, 142) = 9.43, p = 0.003,

Table 1.2: Analyses of variance for psychosocial adaptation measures

Variables	Multivariate				Univariate								
					RSES			PWI			PLANEA Total (ILS)		
	F	p	*Wilk's* Λ	η^2	F	p	η^2	F	p	η^2	F	p	η^2
UMS	4.33	0.006	0.915	0.085	1.31	0.255	0.009	0.59	0.444	0.004	7.99	0.005	0.053
CS	7.11	0.000	0.868	0.132	0.88	0.350	0.006	2.03	0.156	0.014	21.55	0.000	0.132
UMS*CS	3.49	0.017	0.930	0.070	0.38	0.538	0.003	1.93	0.167	0.013	4.43	0.037	0.030

Notes: RSES = Rosenberg Self-Esteem Scale; PWI = Personal Wellbeing Index; ILS = Independent Living Skills; UMS = unaccompanied migrant status; CS = care situation; UMS*CS = interaction effect of UMS and CS on the combined dependent variables; F = F-Test; p = exact p value; *Wilk's* Λ= multivariate statistic test; η^2= effect size.

Figure 1.2: Interaction effect between unaccompanied migrant status and care situation in total score of PLANEA-ILS

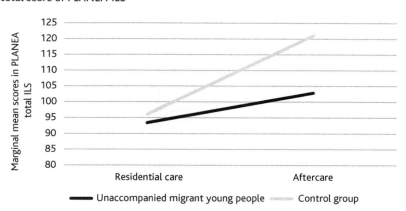

$\eta^2 = 0.062$) but not for the RC group ($p = 0.545$). Therefore, UMYP informed of lower levels of ILS than their peers in the CG but only for the AC group (Figure 1.2).

To further study ILS, multiple two-way between-groups ANOVAs were conducted to explore the influence of UMS on the differences between the CS groups regarding their levels of ILS in each subscale of PLANEA instrument. Means and standard deviations for each subscale, divided by UMS and CS groups, are displayed in Table 1.1, while the results of the ANOVAs are shown in Table 1.3.

Regarding the subscale Self-Care and Well-Being (SCWB), the interaction effect did not reach statistical significance. However, both the main effects for UMS and CS were significant (Table 1.3). This translates into young people in the AC group scoring higher than the RC group ($M_{AC} = 55.11$; $M_{RC} = 48.30$) with a moderate effect size ($\eta^2 = 0.093$). However, the main effect for UMS showed that UMYP tended to score lower than their peers in CG in both RC and AC groups ($M_{UMYP} = 48.30$; $M_{CG} = 54.30$) with a moderate effect size ($\eta^2 = 0.052$).

However, the interaction effect between UMYP and CS was statistically significant for the subscale Daily Arrangements and Organisational Skills (DAOS). While DAOS's scores were very similar for UMYP and CG in the RC group, clear differences are found between them in the AC group, as UMYP inform of less ability for performing this kind of tasks (Figure 1.3). However, the effect size of these differences was small.

Regarding the Employment and Accommodation subscale (EA), no significant interaction was found between the factors tested (Table 1.3). However, the main effect for CS reached statistical significance, as young people in the AC group showed higher levels of skill in this domain

Table 1.3: Two-way ANOVA for independent living skills

Variables	F	p	η^2
PLANEA-ILS			
SCWB			
UMS	8.99	0.003	0.052
CS	16.97	<0.001	0.093
UMS*CS	1.13	0.290	0.007
DAOS			
UMS	12.63	<0.001	0.067
CS	37.66	<0.001	0.176
UMS*CS	6.50	0.012	0.036
EA			
UMS	0.78	0.377	0.004
CS	46.32	<0.001	0.203
UMS*CS	1.12	0.292	0.006

Notes: UMS = unaccompanied migrant status; CS = care situation; UMS*CS = interaction effect of UMS and CS on the combined dependent variables; SCWB = Self-Care and Well-Being; DAOS = Daily Arrangements and Organizational Skills; EA = Employment and Accommodation; ILS = Independent Living Skills; F = F-Test; p = exact *p* value; η^2= effect size.

Figure 1.3: Interaction effect between unaccompanied migrant status and care situation in DAOS subscale of PLANEA-ILS

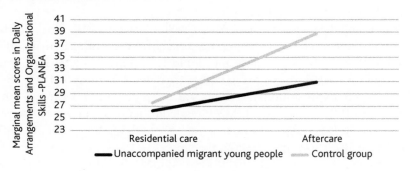

$(M_{AC} = 24.63)$ than their peers in care $(M_{RC}= 18.61)$, regardless of their UMYP status, although the size of the differences was small.

A one-way ANOVA was also conducted to determine if the satisfaction with the different areas of life assessed by the PWI was different for groups according to their UMS and CS. For this purpose, participants were classified into four groups: UMYP-RC, UMYP-AC, CG-RC and CG-AC. The PWI items were used as dependent variables and the generated group variable as independent variable. Homogeneity of variances was violated, as assessed by

Levene's Tests of Homogeneity of Variance. Therefore, the Welch ANOVA and Games–Howell post-hoc test results were interpreted. Satisfaction with their family, health, achievements in life, groups of people they belong to, ways to have fun, and their body was statistically different between groups (Table 1.4).

Games–Howell post-hoc analyses were conducted to study differences between the groups in these items. As Figure 1.4 shows, UMYP showed clearly higher satisfaction with their families than the CGs, especially for UMYP in the AC group, who also scored significantly higher than UMYP in the RC group. The effect size of this difference can be considered large (Table 1.4). Regarding satisfaction with their health and body, although UMYP in the AC group show the highest scores, they only show small-size significant differences with their CG peers in the AC group (Table 1.4).

On the other hand, young people in the AC group showed higher satisfaction with the things they had achieved in life than the RC group, regardless of their UMS. Finally, UMYP in RC scored significantly lower regarding their satisfaction with the groups of people they are part of and the way they have fun. In the first case, their scores were only significantly lower than those of the aftercare CG, while in the second case, their scores were significantly lower than the rest of the cases. The magnitude of these differences was medium (Table 1.4). A detailed description of the differences between the groups can be obtained from Figure 1.4, considering that means with different subscripts differ at least at $p < 0.05$ level of significance.

Table 1.4: One-way Welch ANOVA in PWI items

Variables	W	p	η^2
Satisfaction with:			
Your family	21.29	< 0.001	0.175
Your health	3.83	0.012	0.040
Your standard of living	0.69	0.560	0.012
What you have achieved	3.37	0.022	0.050
Feel safe	1.16	0.329	0.015
The groups you belong to	2.88	0.041	0.039
Safety for the future	2.13	0.102	0.027
Your relationships with other people	1.79	0.155	0.020
How do you have fun	5.22	0.002	0.090
Your body	4.69	0.004	0.051
Your accommodation	0.57	0.640	0.009
Your life considered globally (OLS)	2.07	0.110	0.029

Notes: OLS = Overall Life Satisfaction; W = Welch-Test; p = exact p value; η^2 = effect size.

Figure 1.4: Differences in PWI items, OLS and post-hoc comparisons

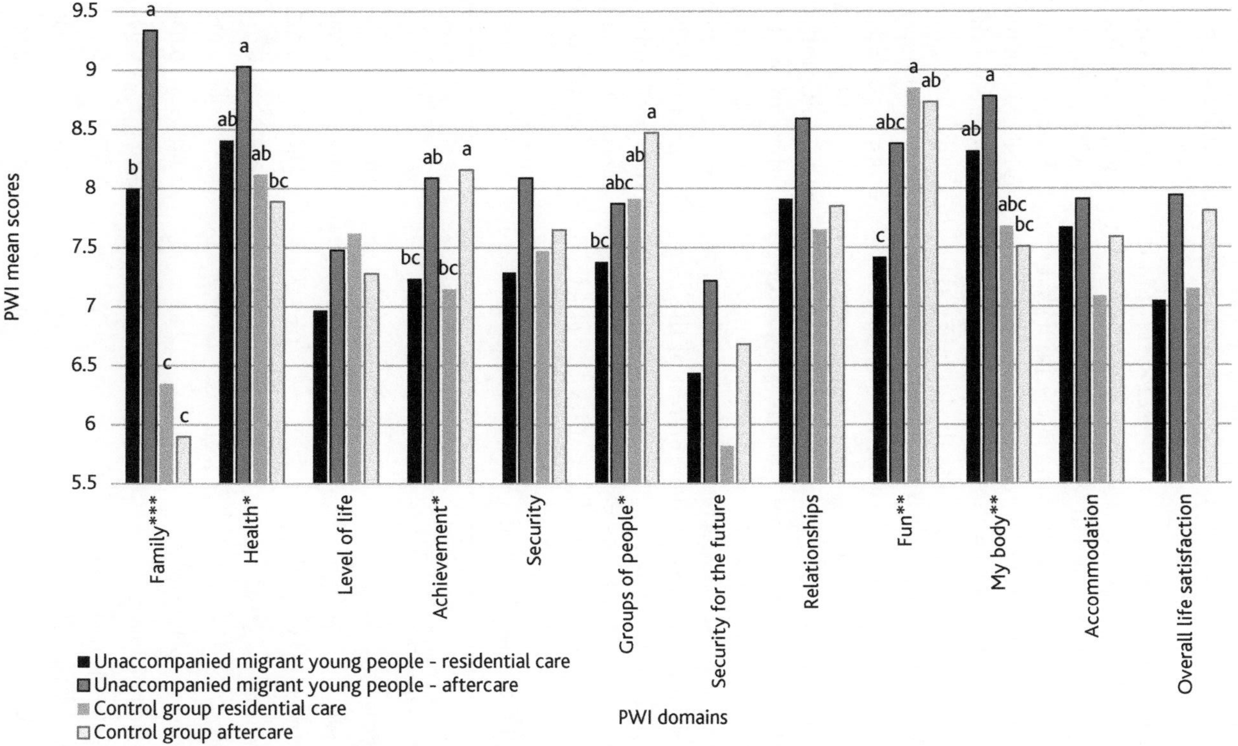

Notes: *$p < 0.05$; **$p < 0.01$; ***$p < 0.001$; Groups' means that do not share a subscript are significantly different between each other (e.g., in 'Fun' 'c' bar differs from 'a' and 'ab' bars, 'abc' bar does not differ from any, 'a' bar differs from 'c' bar, and 'ab' bar differs from 'c' bar).

Profiles and pathways into adulthood of care-leavers in aftercare services

Profile data on the current and past situations of participants from the AC group was collected through the semi-structured qualitative interview previously described. Results showed that the group of UMYP entered care on average at 16 years ($SD = 1.7$), later than the rest of the sample which entered at ten years old ($SD = 5.3$) (t (137) $= -8.74$, $p = 0.001$), and consequently spent less time under protection, with an average stay of two years ($SD = 1.7$), against an average stay of eight years for the CG ($SD = 5.3$) (t (137) $= 8.74$, $p = 0.001$).

Moreover, UMYP showed a lower percentage of maltreatment and neglect in their family context than the other young people in the sample (Table 1.5). There were differences in their types of studies, with UMYP attending more basic vocational training. Moreover, there were more young people with a job in the CG than among the UMYP. In terms of health, there were more young people in CG with some issues: mental health treatment, suicidal ideation, substances consumption and engagement in criminal behaviours.

As for their support network, UMYP were more likely to have contact with their family, but they did not always consider them a source of support. Moreover, they relied to a lesser extent on the support of friends and used to consider educators as reference figures. Regarding the aftercare services received, on the one hand, both groups benefited more from education, job and accommodation support. On the other hand, UMYP benefited less from financial and psychological support and more from legal support.

Several one-way MANOVA were run to determine the effect of these variables, related to the experiences of young people, on their self-esteem, wellbeing and readiness for independent living. Categorical variables were used as independent variables, while the RSES, PWI and PLANEA-ILS scores were used as dependent variables, as a measure of psychosocial adaptation. Significant differences were found in the combination of dependent variables depending on the presence of contact with parents and the number of years spent in out-of-home placement.

Results from the first one-way MANOVA showed that care-leavers who maintain contact with parents scored higher in RSES ($M = 33$ and $M = 30.54$, respectively) and PWI ($M = 79.61$ and $M = 71.43$, respectively) and lower in PLANEA ($M = 114.70$ and $M = 124$, respectively). The differences according to the presence or not of contact with parents on the combined dependent variables was statistically significant (F(4,53) $= 2.811$, $p = 0.048$; Wilks' $\Lambda = 0.863$; $\eta 2 = 0.137$). Nevertheless, follow-up univariate ANOVAs showed that only PWI score (F(1,55) $= 4.173$, $p = 0.046$; partial $\eta^2 = 0.071$) was statistically significantly different between care-leavers with or without contact.

The other one-way MANOVA showed that the differences according to the time spent in care were statistically significant (F(9,126) $= 2.132$, $p = 0.031$; Wilks' $\Lambda = 0.709$; $\eta^2 = 0.108$). Follow-up univariate ANOVAs

Table 1.5: Previous experiences and actual situation of aftercare group

Variables	Total n (%)	UMYP n (%)	CG n (%)	χ^2	p	Cramer's V
Maltreatment	68 (52.3)	11 (17.7)	57 (83.8)	56.768	<0.001	0.66
Neglect	80 (61.5)	19 (32.2)	61 (85.9)	39.277	<0.001	0.55
Time in out-of-home placement				58.08	<0.001	0.65
1–3 years	81 (58.3)	61 (91.0)	20 (27.8)	-	-	-
4–6 years	22 (15.8)	4 (6.0)	18 (25.0)	-	-	-
7–9 years	11 (7.9	1 (1.5)	10 (13.9)	-	-	-
10 or more years	25 (18.0)	1 (1.5)	24 (33.3)	-	-	-
Field of study				21.75	<0.001	0.47
High school	11 (11.1)	6 (12.2)	5 (9.8)	-	-	-
Intermediate vocational training	27 (27.3)	6 (12.5)	21 (41.2)	-	-	-
Basic vocational training	49 (49.5)	32 (65.3)	17 (33.3)	-	-	-
University	7 (7.1)	0 (0.0)	7 (13.7)	-	-	-
Language	5 (5.1)	4 (8.3)	1 (2.0)	-	-	-
Work	47 (33.3)	17 (25.0)	30 (41.1)	4.104	0.043	0.17
Health problems	21 (14.9)	1 (1.5)	20 (27.4)	18.67	<0.001	0.36
Mental health treatment	57 (40.4)	6 (8.8)	51 (69.9)	54.465	<0.001	0.62
Suicidal ideation	13 (9.8)	2 (3.0)	11 (16.9)	7.22	0.007	0.23
Substance consumption	30 (21.3)	6 (8.8)	24 (32.9)	12.16	<0.001	0.29
Delinquent activity	29 (20.7)	5 (7.5)	24 (32.9)	13.74	<0.001	0.31
Contact with parents	110 (81.5)	60 (95.2)	50 (69.4)	14.82	<0.001	0.33
Family support	76 (56.3)	32 (50.8)	44 (61.1)	1.45	0.228	0.10
Friends support	116 (84.7)	48 (75.90)	68 (93.2)	8.66	0.003	0.25
Reference adult educator	65 (46.1)	39 (57.4)	26 (35.6)	6.694	0.010	0.22
Social education support	115 (84.6)	55 (85.9)	60 (83.3)	0.18	0.675	0.04
Labour integration	83 (61.5)	39 (60.9)	44 (62.0)	0.02	0.902	0.01
Accommodation	81 (57.4)	43 (63.2)	38 (52.1)	1.80	0.180	0.11
Legal support	71 (52.2)	54 (85.7)	17 (23.3)	52.82	<0.001	0.62
Financial support	49 (34.8)	12 (17.6)	37 (50.7)	16.95	<0.001	0.35
Psychological support	13 (9.2)	3 (4.4)	10 (13.7)	3.63	0.057	0.16

Notes: UMYP = unaccompanied migrant young people; CG = control group; χ^2 = chi-square test; p = exact p value; Cramer's V = effect size.

showed that PWI scores (F(3,54) = 4.044, p = 0.011; η^2 = 0.183) were statistically significantly different between care-leavers. Tukey post-hoc tests showed that for PWI scores, care-leavers who spent between one and three years in care had statistically significantly higher mean scores (M = 82.99) than care-leavers who spent more than nine years in care (M = 69,78; p = 0.014).

Discussion

This study aimed to describe UMYP's backgrounds, profiles and levels of psychosocial adaptation through their transition from care to independent living by comparing them to those of their peers without this type of migratory background.

Self-esteem and wellbeing

Self-esteem and wellbeing scores were in a normal range for young people in our study, although below the average score found in the normative adolescent population for wellbeing, according to Casas et al (2013). It is important to note that safety for the future was the area with which the entire sample was least satisfied. This is especially relevant for care experienced young people, considering the impact of this dimension on their general wellbeing and on several spheres of their lives (Delgado et al, 2019).

No significant differences with respect to the total scores of both dimensions were found as a function of UMS across the groups, contrary to what was expected to be found in the light of previous research results about the greater vulnerability of this group (Bravo and Santos, 2017), the particular difficulties that the transition to adult life entails for them (Sirriyeh and Ní Raghallaigh, 2018) and the legal barriers that they usually encounter in the societies that receive them (López-Reillo, 2013). This result represents a significant advance in the knowledge of this population, given the lack of studies that apply standardised instruments for measuring these constructs.

Nevertheless, an exploration of the different areas of wellbeing evidenced that UMYP show higher levels of satisfaction with their families than their peers, to whom they were able to maintain contact through phone and online messaging. This is in line with the results of previous studies that captured the emotional support that families represent for UMYP, in contrast to the complicated relationships and lack of support that other care-leavers often suffer (Sulimani-Aidan, 2016). Moreover, UMYP showed higher scores in areas related to themselves. This could also be related to the lower incidence of negative experiences in the family context, which can have long-term effects on physical and emotional health (Mendes and Snow, 2016). However, they were also the ones with the lowest scores in areas related to social life, which points to their difficulties in adapting to a new context and creating new support networks (Keles et al, 2018).

On the other hand, the aftercare group showed higher satisfaction with their achievements in life than young people in care. This result agrees with Del Valle et al (2008), who found that care-leavers can achieve greater independence and integration over time, being more likely to experience difficulties for social integration during the first period after leaving care. However, positive assessments on this area might have been over-represented by the fact that only those UMYP with higher levels of written Spanish were able to answer the administered questionnaires. These young people may have gone further into their adaptation process and, therefore, be more likely to have successfully overcome main challenges.

Independent living skills

Regarding young people's perceived ILS, UMYP scored lower than their peers in all the domains studied except for the area of EA. This subscale measures the degree of skill in tasks related to searching and maintaining a job, being financially independent and looking for and keeping a home (García-Alba et al, 2021, 2022b). However, their scores were not significantly different in this area. These results agree with those of Alonso-Bello et al (2020), who found that UMYP in Spain usually have some previous work experience in informal economy areas but often struggle to succeed in the current job market.

The lower scores in SCWB, related to housekeeping, healthcare or healthy lifestyle, could also be explained by assumptions of traditional male gender roles present in patriarchal Arab cultures (Jamal et al, 2020), considering that most UMYP in Spain come from North Africa, mainly from Morocco (Ministerio de Justicia, 2020).

Interestingly, some of the differences between UMYP and the CG were dependent on their care situation, as scores in the DAOS area and Total ILS were substantially higher only for the CG in the aftercare group. This could point out a lower achievement over time in life skills development for UMYP, even for those engaged in aftercare services, for tasks as essential as making appointments or applications in the public offices.

These results might reflect some of the barriers that have already been highlighted by research regarding the delivery of preparation for leaving care and transitional support services for UMYP, such as the short duration of their itineraries prior to age of majority, the lack of adequate specialised services for them, or the low experience of staff with this group (Gimeno-Monterde et al, 2021). However, this lower ability to complete bureaucratic procedures, reflected in their higher rates of legal support as care-leavers, can be especially worrying for UMYP, as they will face complicated processes related to obtaining their residence and work permits (Bravo and Santos, 2017).

Their greater difficulties in obtaining these permits and starting to search for a job will also delay their opportunities of developing work-related skills in a natural workplace environment, which have proven to be essential for long-term success in the job market (Arnau-Sabatés and Gilligan, 2020) and have been related to higher perceived levels of ILS (García-Alba et al, 2022a).

Unaccompanied migrant young people's backgrounds and profiles

UMYP presented a totally different profile from that of the CG as care-leavers. Their stays in care were shorter and often free from risky behaviours, confirming the results of previous studies (González-García et al, 2017). They suffered fewer experiences of abuse and neglect in the family context compared to other youth, which confirms that unaccompanied youth in Spain are more likely to come from stable family situations with financial problems (Calzada, 2007). However, their support network was smaller in the new country, which can be due to the culture shock and the consequent complex adaptation they must face (Keles et al, 2018). Furthermore, the tendency to rely on educators is even more pronounced for them, which further demonstrates the need to expand the informal support networks of these young people to avoid becoming dependent on services and enhance their options for integration, since the help from professionals constitutes an essential source of both emotional and practical support (Sulimani-Aidan, 2016). In this sense, previous studies have highlighted that the combination of maintaining the transnational family and supporting the development of new support networks is especially beneficial for UMYP leaving care (Alarcón and Prieto-Flores, 2021).

Moreover, UMYP showed better health and less need for mental health treatment in our study, which is consistent with the results of other studies (González-García et al, 2017), and can be related to their reasons for undertaking the migratory journey, which are usually of an economic nature in Spain (Bravo and Santos, 2017). Such findings are in line with those of other authors about the resilience of these young people despite the difficulties related to their resettlement and possible traumas experienced before their arrival (Ní Raghallaigh and Gilligan, 2010; Hodes et al, 2018; Keles et al, 2018). While this topic has been extensively explored in other, it has not been sufficiently delved into in the Spanish context. Moreover, some studies have pointed out that Western mental health assessments can fail to recognise the needs of UMYP (von Werthern et al, 2019), since instrument translations may be available but without having been validated or culturally adapted for other specific group (Wells et al, 2015).

Predicting psychosocial adaptation

It is also interesting to note that, among the elements related to the participants' previous experiences, one that influenced their psychosocial adaptation, especially their wellbeing, was contact with parents. In line with our results, other researchers found that links with adult and caring figures, especially parents, contribute to better general wellbeing (Delgado et al, 2019). Another factor that seemed to influence their wellbeing was the time spent in childcare. Some authors pointed out that what is more important is not the time spent in care but the stability of the trajectory (Del Valle et al, 2008), which showed to be highly relevant for their subjective wellbeing (Llosada-Gistau et al, 2017), but longer trajectories might also be less stable, which would explain our results. However, these results must be taken with caution since, as we have seen, UMYP were those who spent less time in care.

In line with our results, international research points to the greater resilience of UMYP (Wade, 2011; Keles et al, 2018). However, we should not consider this group homogeneous since their individual characteristics, histories, origins, cultures and needs differ markedly and quickly evolve through time (Bravo and Del Valle, 2009). Our results have highlighted a series of characteristics of UMYP's profiles and trajectories in care that must be considered in the design of services to support their transition to adulthood. Services must consider the special role of the UMYP's family in their home country as a source of emotional support that they can maintain through virtual communication. They should also promote the creation of new relationships that can help them adapt more straightforwardly to a different culture and establish a strong support network. Also, it is necessary to develop adequate protocols and legal support services to help them navigate their settlement perspectives and consequent paperwork. Strategies must also be implemented so that UMYP do not fall behind their peers regarding their development of ILS. For these, as Gimeno-Monterde et al (2021) suggested, it is critical to design specialised services for UMYP, delivered by highly trained workers.

Limitations

Future research should address some of the limitations of this study, such as including female UMYP to explore their specific needs and trajectories. Furthermore, our sampling strategy might have over-represented care-leavers who have been receiving higher levels of support for a more extended period, as well as UMYP who had been able to better adapt to the new context. A different picture could be expected if we had reached care-leavers who dropped out or did not qualify for support services at 18 years old, who remain largely invisible to research in this field. Using sampling strategies that are not restricted to statutory services would also enhance free, unbiased participation from young people and avoid power imbalances, for example, being invited through informal networks rather than by a care-leaving worker (Chase et al, 2019). Therefore, it is necessary to develop culturally sensitive strategies to adapt instruments and research methods to this population. This would help avoid losing participants unable to answer to the instruments in a different language from their mother tongue. Finally, the use of longitudinal designs that allow the performance of repeated measures tests should provide higher quality evidence regarding the development of the psychosocial adaptation measures addressed in this study.

Conclusion

This chapter tried to highlight the specific characteristics that define young people preparing for or leaving care and the challenges they must face, comparing UMYP with other care-leavers. We evidenced their strengths and weaknesses and reflected on the necessary measures to support their journeys to entirely successful integration and transition to independent living. The use of quantitative research approaches, including the application of standardised questionnaires, has proven to be valuable enough to be considered in future studies. However, the absence of culturally adapted instruments leads to a substantial loss of participants, creating a potential bias in our results. This reflection calls for further development of best practice guidelines and approaches for research with this group of young people.

Note
[1]   The term 'migrant' is used instead of the common 'asylum-seeking', considering that underage migrant youths in Spain do not apply for asylum on a general basis.

References
Alarcón, X. and Prieto-Flores, O. (2021) 'Transnational family ties and networks of support for unaccompanied immigrant youths in Spain: The role of youth mentoring in Barcelona', *Children and Youth Services Review*, 128: Article 106140.
Alonso-Bello, E., Santana-Vega, L.E. and Feliciano-García, L. (2020) 'Employability skills of unaccompanied immigrant minors in Canary Islands', *Journal of New Approaches in Educational Research*, 9(1): 15–27.
Arnau-Sabatés, L. and Gilligan, R. (2020) 'Support in the workplace: How relationships with bosses and coworkers may benefit care leavers and young people in care', *Children and Youth Services Review*, 111: Article 104833.
Bravo, A. and Del Valle, J.F. (2009) 'Crisis y revisión del acogimiento residencial. Su papel en la protección infantil' [Crisis and review of residential care: Its role in child protection], *Papeles del Psicólogo*, 30(1): 42–52.

Bravo, A. and Santos, I. (2017) 'Asylum-seeking children in Spain: Needs and intervention models', *Psychosocial Intervention*, 26(1): 55–62.

Calzada, O. (2007) 'La protección de los menores extranjeros no acompañados en Cantabria' [The protection of unaccompanied foreign minors in Cantabria], Dirección General de Políticas Sociales.

Campbell, A., Converse, P.E. and Rogers, W.L. (1976) *The quality of American life: Perceptions, evaluations, and satisfactions*, New York: Russell Sage.

Casas, F., Sarriera, J., Alfaro, J., González, M., Malo, S., Bertran, I., Figuer, C., Abs, D., Bedín, L. and Paradiso, A. (2012) 'Testing the Personal Wellbeing Index on 12–16 years-old adolescents in 3 different countries with 2 new items', *Social Indicators Research*, 105(3): 461–482.

Casas, F., Fernández-Artamendi, S., Montserrat, C., Bravo, A., Bertrán, I. and Del Valle, J.F. (2013) 'El bienestar subjetivo en la adolescencia: Estudio comparativo de dos Comunidades Autónomas en España' [Subjective well-being in adolescence: Comparative study of two Autonomous Communities in Spain], *Anales de Psicología*, 29(1): 148–158.

Chase, E., Otto, L., Belloni, M., Lems, A. and Wernesjö, U. (2019) 'Methodological innovations, reflections and dilemmas: The hidden sides of research with migrant young people classified as unaccompanied minors', *Journal of Ethnic and Migration Studies*, 46(2): 457–473.

Cohen, J. (1988) *Statistical power analysis for the behavioral sciences*, Mahwah: Erlbaum.

Council of Europe (2019) 'Effective guardianship for unaccompanied and separated children in the context of migration', Recommendation CM/Rec(2019)11 of the Committee of Ministers. Available from: https://rm.coe.int/cm-rec-2019-11-guardianship-en/16809ccfe2

Cronbach, L.J. (1951) 'Coefficient alpha and the internal structure of tests', *Psychometrika*, 16: 297–334.

Cummins, R.A. and Lau, A.L.D. (2005) *Personal wellbeing index: School children*, 3rd edn, Victoria: Deakin University.

Cummins, R.A., Eckersley, R., Pallant, J., Van Vugt, J. and Misajon, R. (2003) 'Developing a national index of subjective wellbeing: The Australian unity wellbeing index', *Social Indicators Research*, 64: 159–190.

Del Valle, J.F. and García-Alba, L. (2021) *Manual del Programa Planea. Entrenamiento en habilidades para la vida independiente* [Manual of Planea Program: Training independent living skills], Consejería de Bienestar Social de la Junta de Comunidades de Castilla-La Mancha. Available from: https://infanciayfamilias.castillalamancha.es/sites/default/files/2021-07/Manual-Interactivo-Planea-CLM.pdf

Del Valle, J.F., Bravo, A., Álvarez, E. and Fernanz, A. (2008) 'Adult self-sufficiency and social adjustment in care leavers from children's homes: A long-term assessment', *Child and Family Social Work*, 13(1): 12–22.

Delgado, P., Carvalho, J.M.S., Montserrat, C. and Llosada-Gistau, J. (2019) 'The subjective wellbeing of Portuguese children in foster care, residential care and children living with their families: Challenges and implications for a childcare system still focused on institutionalisation', *Child Indicators Research*, 13(1): 67–84.

García-Alba, L., Postigo, Á., Gullo, F., Muñiz, J. and Del Valle, J.F. (2021) 'PLANEA Independent Life Skills Scale: Development and validation', *Psicothema*, 33(2): 268–278.

García-Alba, L., Gullo, F. and Del Valle, J.F. (2022a) 'Readiness for independent living of youth in residential child care: A comparative study', *Child and Family Social Work*, 28(1): 171–183.

García-Alba, L., Postigo, Á., Gullo, F., Muñiz, J. and Del Valle, J.F. (2022b) 'Assessing independent life skills of youth in child protection: A multiinformant approach', *European Journal of Psychology Applied to Legal Context*, 14(1): 1–10.

Gimeno-Monterde, C. and Gutiérrez-Sánchez, J.D. (2019) 'Fostering unaccompanied migrating minors: A cross-border comparison', *Children and Youth Services Review*, 99: 36–42.

Gimeno-Monterde, C., Gómez-Quintero, J.D. and Aguerri J.C. (2021) 'Unaccompanied young people and transition to adulthood: Challenges for childcare services', *Children and Youth Services Review*, 121: Article 105858.

Gonzales, R.G. (2011) 'Learning to be illegal: Undocumented youth and shifting legal contexts in the transition to adulthood', *American Sociological Review*, 76(4): 602–619.

González-García, C., Lázaro-Visa, S., Santos, I., Del Valle, J.F. and Bravo, A. (2017) 'School functioning of a particularly vulnerable group: Children and young people in residential childcare', *Frontiers in Psychology*, 8: Article 1116.

Hodes, M., Anagnostopoulos, D. and Skokauskas, N. (2018) 'Challenges and opportunities in refugee mental health: Clinical, service, and research considerations', *European Child & Adolescent Psychiatry*, 27(4): 385–388.

Jamal, A., Pagliani, P. and Hsu, E. (2020) *Arab Human Development Report. Research Paper*, United Nations Development Programme Regional Bureau for Arab States (RBAS). Available from: https://arab-hdr.org/wp-content/uploads/2021/03/Final-Citizenship-360-in-the-Arab-Region.pdf

Keles, S., Friborg, O., Idsøe, T., Sirin, S. and Oppedal, B. (2018) 'Resilience and acculturation among unaccompanied refugee minors', *International Journal of Behavioral Development*, 42(1): 52–63.

Llosada-Gistau, J., Casas, F. and Montserrat, C. (2017) 'What matters in for the subjective well-being of children in care?', *Child Indicators Research*, 10(3): 735–760.

López-Reillo, P. (2013) 'Young African migrants reinventing their lives in the Canary Islands', *The International Journal of Research into Island Cultures*, 7(2): 39–54.

Manzani, L. and Arnoso-Martínez, M. (2014) 'Psychosocial well-being in children and young immigrants without adult family referent: The risk and protective factors', *Norte de Salud Mental*, 12(49): 33–45.

Mendes, P. and Snow, P. (2016) *Young people transitioning from out-of-home care: International research, policy and practice*, London: Palgrave Macmillan.

Ministerio de Justicia (2020) 'Memoria anual de la Fiscalía General del Estado. Año 2019' [Attorney General annual report. Year 2019]. Available from: https://www.fiscal.es/memorias/memoria2020/FISCALIA_SITE/index.html

Ní Raghallaigh, M. and Gilligan, R. (2010) 'Active survival in the lives of unaccompanied minors: Coping strategies, resilience, and the relevance of religion', *Child & Family Social Work*, 15(2): 226–237.

Observatorio de la Infancia (2020) *Boletín de datos estadísticos de medidas de protección a la infancia* [Bulletin of childcare interventions], Ministerio de Derechos Sociales y Agenda 2030. Available from: https://observatoriod elainfancia.vpsocial.gob.es/productos/pdf/BOLETIN_22_final.pdf

Rosenberg, M. (1965) *Society and the adolescent self-image*, Princeton: Princeton University Press.

Salmerón-Manzano, E. and Manzano-Agugliaro, F. (2018) 'Unaccompanied minors: Worldwide research perspectives', *Publications*, 7: 2. https://doi.org/10.3390/ publications7010002

Sirriyeh, A. and Ní Raghallaigh, M. (2018) 'Foster care, recognition and transitions to adulthood for unaccompanied asylum-seeking young people in England and Ireland', *Children and Youth Services Review*, 92: 89–97.

Sulimani-Aidan, Y. (2016) 'In between formal and informal: Staff and youth relationships in care and after leaving care', *Children and Youth Services Review*, 67: 43–49.

UNHCR *(2020) Refugee and migrant children in Europe. Accompanied, Unaccompanied and Separated. Overview of trends, January to June 2020.* Available from: https://data2.unhcr.org/en/documents/details/85196

UNICEF (2019) *Los derechos de los niñosy niñas migrantes no acompañados en la frontera sur española* [The rights of unaccompanied migrant children at the southern Spanish border], UNICEF Comité Español.

von Werthern, M., Grigorakis, G. and Vizard, E. (2019) 'The mental health and wellbeing of unaccompanied refugee minors (URMs)', *Child Abuse and Neglect*, 98: Article 104146.

Wade, J. (2011) 'Preparation and transition planning for unaccompanied asylum-seeking and refugee young people: A review of evidence in England', *Children and Youth Services Review*, 33(12): 2424–2430.

Wells, R., Wells, D. and Lawsin, C. (2015) 'Understanding psychological responses to trauma among refugees: The importance of measurement validity in cross-cultural settings', *Journal and Proceedings of the Royal Society of New South Wales*, 148(455/456): 60–69.

2

'The question is: will the street leave us?' Care-leavers with a street-connected past

Marcela Losantos Velasco

Introduction

This study focuses on a significantly under-researched group: street-connected children who came into care and then aged out onto the street, rather than towards independent living as is normally hoped for among care-leavers. As such it draws together three important strands of vulnerability that contribute to this group living on the edges of society, namely street-connected children, care-leavers and street-connected youth.

This study uses the term 'street-connected' children and youth, which was coined by Thomas de Benitez and Hiddleston (2011). In previous research, the same author argued that, traditionally, two types of policy approaches were used to guide interventions aimed at street children and youth worldwide: reactive/repression-oriented and protective models (Thomas de Benitez, 2003). From a reactive/repression-oriented approach, street-connected children were described as antisocial, violent and even associated with criminal behaviour by their inappropriate use of public space. Therefore, the interventions based on this approach were repressive towards them (for example, forced removals and legal sanctions). On the other hand, from a protection-oriented perspective, they were perceived as immature, vulnerable and victims of family and street violence, assuming that they needed to be saved from the street by institutions until they reached adulthood. The focus of the protective approach was on the immediate causes of problems (for example, basic needs) rather than on their structural causes (for example, poverty and social exclusion) (Berckmans et al, 2012).

Nevertheless, a research review conducted by Thomas de Benitez and Hiddleston (2011) revealed a paradigm shift during the 2000s, from the aforementioned polarised conceptions to the recognition of their diverse and complex characteristics and circumstances. As a result, the review proposed 'street-connectedness' as a new term for street children, more consistent with a rights-based approach that perceives children and youth as social actors, growing up within interconnected environments, whose activities contribute to their identity construction. The focus thus moves away from children's physical presence on the street to their emotional belonging to public spaces, recognising the street not only as a source of problems and danger but also as a space of personal freedom, empowerment and independence. The term street-connectedness emphasises young people's different ways of connecting to and using the street.

Research on homelessness among care-leavers is quite well established. For example, a study in Uruguay reported an increased risk of physical and mental health problems, drug use and homelessness for care-leavers who left care abruptly, without finalising their preparation process (Bartora, 2016). Other studies from Australia (Chikwava et al, 2022), the US (Kelly, 2020) and Canada (Kovarikova, 2017) reported a relationship between leaving care and the risk of homelessness. A UK report concludes that 'one-third of care leavers (33 per cent) become homeless in the first two years after leaving care, and 25 per cent of all single homeless people have been in care at some point in their lives' (Stirling, 2018: 12). A study of youth ageing out of the foster care system in the US (Dworsky and Courtney, 2009) revealed that 14 per cent ended up living on the street or experiencing some form of homelessness during the first year after leaving care. In South Africa, Dickens and van Breda (2021) found that an average of 16 per cent of care-leavers reported experiences of homelessness each year (ranging from 0 per cent to 23 per cent) over their first seven years out of care. Moreover, a follow-up study in Australia showed that 50 per cent of care-leavers experienced a period of homelessness (Riggs and Coyle, 2002).

While there is substantial research on homelessness among care-leavers, there is scant research on care-leavers who lived on the street before entering a care programme and then returned to the street. Huang and Huang (2008) conducted research on street-connected children who came into care in La Paz, Bolivia. They found that around 97 per cent of these children left care prematurely and returned to the streets. Mokgopha (2019), in South Africa, examined the resilience of street-connected children who entered and later aged out of care. We have been unable to source any other research on this group.

Care-leavers with a street-connected past are an under-researched group whose voices should be heard because they have experiences both from the street and from care. Their street experiences and knowledge regarding care programmes could help provide information about what the street offers – in terms of supportive relationships, a sense of belonging, and a sense of freedom and autonomy – and what it is that care programmes are failing to provide.

The aim of this chapter, therefore, is to explore the journey of young people who came off the streets into residential care and, instead of ageing out into independent adult life, transitioned back onto the streets in the city of La Paz, Bolivia. To do so, I followed the stories of five street-connected young people who aged out of care onto the streets, despite having spent years away from it. Through a participatory methodology based on social constructionism, I studied this group of young adults to understand why they returned to the streets after many years of care. The participants themselves constructed the research questions of interest, analysed the data with me, and then endorsed their stories to be published as valuable lessons for care professionals.

The following section describes the research context of street-connected children and youth in Bolivia, followed by an explanation of the participatory and constructionist methodology of the research. Then, the findings section focuses on the factors that contribute to young people with a street-connected background returning to the street when they reach adulthood and must leave residential homes. Finally, the conclusion questions if residential care programmes, protection system practices, and society in general, offer real possibilities of social integration for street-connected youth after having lived for many years on the social margins or within institutional walls.

Research context: street-connected children and youth in Bolivia

The last census showed there are around 4,000 people of all ages living on the streets in Bolivia (Viceministerio de Defensa Social y Sustancias Controladas, 2015), although exact figures are practically impossible to calculate due to the high mobility of the groups from one city to another; the diverse situations, characteristics and distinctions between those who live on the street, those who work and sleep on the street and those who sleep in accommodations on a daily basis, but who spend the whole day on the streets; and poor monitoring of the life trajectory of street-connected youth once they become adults.

However, the scenario changed after the enacting of Law 548: New Code for Children and Adolescents (17 July 2014), which stressed the right of children to live with a family. Both private and public care programmes in Bolivia started to focus on promoting family and social reintegration of street children under 18 years old. Organisations are now working in a coordinated manner to encourage children to leave the street and temporarily enter a foster home while they search for sustainable family and social care alternatives.

Meanwhile, street-connected children who came into care before the New Code and subsequently aged out of care were in what could be termed a 'legal limbo', because they were too old to seek alternative forms of care – such as surrogate families or adoption – and too close to the age of 18 to receive permanent care or aftercare support. The Bolivian state offered no transitional measures of social protection for those who had to transition from care to independent adult life (Asociación Civil Doncel et al, 2016), and even less for care-leavers with different characteristics or conditions, such as leavers with a street background who have greater difficulties than other graduates in, for example, finding housing, connecting with birth families and securing stable jobs. As a result, many young people who left residential care centres in this period ended up back on the streets, despite having left street life for many years.

Methodology

The research reported in this chapter is based on a social constructionist epistemology. Social constructionist thinking developed through many influences, such as Goffman's (1959) dramaturgical approach and Berger and Luckmann's (1966) publication of *The social construction of reality*. Through this approach, research is seen as a collaborative process in which participants work with researchers in constructing new ways of knowing and understanding reality (Cisneros-Puebla, 2008; McNamee, 2012). It implies a shift in the roles of both the researcher, who now defines all steps of data collection and analysis together with the participants, and the participants themselves, who now are not just mere informants, but participate actively in all critical decisions regarding the research process. Thus, the findings are not presented independently and objectively, but rather through a joint construction between the researcher and the researched (Lock and Strong, 2010).

Social constructionist researchers conceive theories as products of a society in a particular time and context (Gergen, 2007). Thus, disciplinary discourses, which serve as a frame of reference for research, are understood as social products within cultural traditions that have the power to generate or degenerate the people they describe (Romaioli, 2011; Hamdan, 2012; McNamee, 2012; Tilley-Lubbs, 2014), which is particularly important when researching street-connected youth.

Participants

This chapter reports on one part of my doctoral research, in which I studied five purposively selected street-connected young adults, who I followed for four years in their process of leaving care when they turned 18 and returning to the streets where they lived before care. The five young adults – three males and two females – had previously lived on the street for around three to five years before being brought into care. While in care, they moved in and out of care several times until they decided to establish themselves in two residential programmes – one for women and one for men – until

Table 2.1: Participants of the research

Pseudonym	Gender	Age when they first entered care	Age when they left care	Age when returning to the street again
Carlota	Female	13	17	18
Paola	Female	12	18	18
Martin	Male	14	18	18
Eduardo	Male	13	19	20
Bernardo	Male	13	18	21

they reached adulthood. I met them in the street in these two critical moments, just before they entered care at ages 12 to 14 years, when I was working at a non-governmental organisation (NGO) that offered support to street-connected children and again, many years later, when they were back on the streets after leaving care at the age of 18, while I was finishing my PhD. I invited them to participate because my doctoral research aimed to understand why young people remained on the street, despite other care options available to them. Therefore, their experience was a key point in answering the research question comprehensively.

Table 2.1 shows two important features of the participants. First, most of them spent four to six years in residential care. Second, they did not go back immediately to the streets after leaving care at 18 years old; instead, they spent between six months and three years trying to live home-based and independently, before returning to the street.

Data collection and analysis

Data collection took place where I encountered the participants on the streets, while I was doing daily fieldwork during the last two years of my PhD. First, I had weekly 'small conversations' (that is, stories embedded in talk-in-interaction) (Georgakopoulou, 2007; Clifton, 2014) over 18 months, while I accompanied them during daily activities, such as doing laundry, going to the dentist or playing football. Second, I conducted ten formal interviews, two with each participant, at the completion of the study, to explore further the reasons why they returned to the street, after ageing out of care. Lastly, the participants produced a video, where they recorded separate individual testimonies and edited them together, to convey their own perspectives on social reintegration possibilities after leaving care.

A narrative analysis was used to fully understand the complexity of their life stories and daily accounts (Riessman, 2008). I decided to use a narrative analysis because, as Squire (2008: 5) describes, 'by doing so we are able to see different and sometimes contradictory layers of meaning, to bring them into useful dialogue with each other, and to understand more about individual and social interplay'.

The narrative analysis enabled the identification of the central plot in each of the young people's life stories, where participants shared their initial experiences and motivations to transition to adult life, look for a job and have stable housing. Furthermore, participants described how these plans started to fall apart because of difficulties associated with their street connection.

I then interviewed each participant for the second time. These interviews started with me sharing the findings of the first interview, followed by participants confirming and expanding their stories. Therefore, the themes presented in the findings section were constructed jointly with the participants and, given the in-depth insight they provide, they represent the challenges faced by the participants.

Ethical issues

The study's ethics was reviewed yearly by both Universidad Católica Boliviana 'San Pablo' and the Vrije Universiteit of Brussels, who supervised the joint PhD. The following ethical considerations were taken into account. First, to comply with the principle of participants' beneficence, the fieldwork was supervised by an NGO that worked with street-connected children and youth to guarantee their right to anonymity and their right for voluntary participation was respected. Second, to respect their own agency I requested written consent to participate in the study and for publication afterwards. And third, because the study was carried out under the supervision of an NGO, arrangements for referral for services (for example, medical care, food, shelter and trauma counselling) were jointly conducted if needed.

Finally, trustworthiness lies in three main characteristics of the study. First, the study involves prolonged engagement (Lincoln and Guba, 1985). The research on which this chapter reports is part of a study conducted over five years with 35 street-connected children and young people. This long-term relationship created a trustful relationship between me, as a researcher, and them as participants and co-creators of collective knowledge about the different challenges they faced to leave the street.

Second, the social constructionist epistemology, on which this study is based, allowed the participants' involvement in all stages of the research process. Participants were involved from the research question formulation to the joint analysis of the interviews. Findings were thus validated by the participants, which is a fundamental trustworthiness criterion when it comes to participatory research (Jordan et al, 2005).

Third, the transferability of at least aspects of the findings (Lincoln and Guba, 1985) is possible thanks to the provision of a detailed account of the context and methods of the study. Transfer to other contexts is made difficult by the lack of research on this group, but this study may help to generate initial hunches that can be further explored elsewhere.

The following section presents the main findings on the factors contributing to young people leaving the protection system and returning to the street. Each factor was identified with the participants and constructed from their own lived experiences.

Findings

The five main factors that contributed to care-leavers returning to the street upon leaving care are:

1. transfer rather than transition continues to be the most common practice for street-connected care-leavers;
2. there is no aftercare support;
3. the lack of family or social support;
4. their social network is still based on their street-connected peers; and
5. their street marks hinder their social reintegration.

Factor 1: Transfer rather than transition continues to be the most common practice for street-connected care-leavers

Being transferred to adult life, rather than accompanied in the transition, is at the heart of this first finding. The term transfer is generally used to refer to the user's transfer from one service to another (for example, from paediatric to adult healthcare). However, Liabo et al's (2017) research on care-leavers used the term to describe the sense of being moved from one place to another, rather than going through a process in which they feel accompanied. In the same vein, the narratives that follow relate to the experience of 'being moved' or transferred to adult life, without the necessary support or preparation. In-depth interviews and small conversations with street-connected youth showed they are pushed to leave care rather than guided in the process of doing so:

> '[Talking about when the institution gave him a final date to become independent] It is just as if your shift was over ... you have to move on, you have to leave. ... I became angry. I knew that the day will come, and to be honest I was happy to leave at the beginning, you know? I used to think, "No more rules, no more waking up and make my bed as a matchbox". ... Then I realised that I was going to be on my own, no support. I felt not ready, not ready at all.' (Eduardo, 19 September 2017)

Eduardo's testimony reflects how the independence process works for several young people who have to leave care. When the centre announces that their time in care is about to end, most of them feel happy, challenged and eager to be autonomous and unrestricted. However, when the departure date approaches, they begin to have reasonable doubts and fears about how to face life independently. These doubts often lead to erratic behaviour (for example, leaving their technical training hoping that their leaving date will be further extended, running away from the centre for a weekend, turning up at the centre after drinking alcohol).

All these behaviours are signs of insecurity about the prospect of independence. However, care professionals sometimes interpret these as signs of rebellion, so in response, they begin to pressure the young people by setting deadlines for leaving residential care. Martin's story is also evidence of this dynamic:

'I started to regret having enrolled in the training programme. At the beginning I felt very enthusiastic; really enthusiastic to learn about plumbing and stuff! Later I realised that this meant I had to leave [the institution] soon. The psychologist made me fill in something called "life project". A lot of sheets! And then we had to meet with her [the psychologist] to discuss the planning. ... I filled in whatever I could think of that time, so, pretty much whatever I wanted. But I didn't do it seriously, you know? ... So, as I was telling you, I started to fear that if I finished the plumbing course, I would have to leave, so I started missing classes. The director of the care centre eventually found out but she didn't care. She said I had misused the opportunity. ... At the end of that year, it was time for me to leave.' (Martin, 16 June 2015)

The participants' narratives reflect the sense of being transferred abruptly into adult life, instead of being led gradually towards it, despite professionals recognising the flaws in this transferring system. Clare et al (2017) describe it as a chronic *stuckness* of the welfare and protection system that prevents addressing the challenges related in the stories, although they were identified many years ago in Bolivia (for example, Universidad Católica Boliviana 'San Pablo' and Aldeas Infantiles SOS Bolivia, 2017).

Factor 2: There is no aftercare support

In addition to the abrupt end of care at the age of 18, another factor contributing to street-connected youth leaving care and returning to the street is the lack of aftercare support. The stories that follow demonstrate that there is a vacuum of aftercare support. Whether it is the lack of a social or family support network when leaving care or the non-existence of aftercare programmes, the fact remains that once they leave care, young people are left to face adult life virtually on their own.

'When you go to the fourth stage of [name of the programme from where they become independent], you then start to feel there is no way back. I mean … you know that when you become 18, you maybe have some more months. After that, you are by yourself. They say they will come to see us [after leaving care], but the truth is that no one else comes. We see our social workers probably once a year.' (Paola, 8 August 2015)

Paola's statement exposes one of the significant failures of the transition process, namely the experience of ceasing to be affiliated with what was her home for many years. Her experience shows that the relationship between her and the care centre she was affiliated to is far from resembling the parent–child relationship. Indeed, early independence that street-connected care-leavers face is very different from the gradual independence process of those raised in a family environment, in terms of both the abruptness of the separation and the rigidity with which it usually happens (Clare et al, 2017):

'[Did you have support?] To go out? One month. Yes, one month. Because it was not well organised, my departure was not well planned. Then, nobody supported me anymore, not even when I got sick. I was alone.' (Carlota, 19 December 2016)

Despite significant evidence that aftercare services are as important as care itself (Glynn and Mayock, 2019), there are no regulations in Bolivia that establish follow-up programmes as mandatory. Most of the care programmes claim it is not possible to provide housing upon reaching adulthood, even though the Bolivian Family Code establishes that:

Family assistance is granted until the beneficiary reaches the age of majority and may be extended until the beneficiary reaches twenty-five (25) years of age, in order to provide him/her with technical or professional training or to learn an art or craft, as long as the dedication to their training shows effective results. (Bolivian Family Code, Law N° 603: 30)

Instead, leaving-care programmes are entirely delegated by the state to two NGOs that do their best to accompany care-leavers in their transition to autonomous life. Still, none of them is focused or specialised on street-connected care-leavers although their needs require differentiated attention due to the absence or fragility of their family ties, previous history of drug use, and lack of academic preparation before entering the care system, which introduces unique challenges to their transition.

Factor 3: The lack of family or social support

The lack of social or family support to come back to in times of need when they live independently reveals another critical gap for street-connected youth. The fact that young people have a past life connected to the street is strong evidence of the fragility of their family relationships. Even though most of them have a family with whom they maintain sporadic contact, both when they live on the street and when they enter care centres, maintaining this bond is not the primary focus of care models, which in time results in the weakening of it (Universidad Católica Boliviana 'San Pablo' and Aldeas Infantiles SOS Bolivia, 2017).

One of the many risks for street-connected care-leavers with no family network is the tendency to jump very rapidly into a partner relationship without assessing the risk of early pregnancy and suffering intimate partner violence:

> 'After some time out of [the institution], I got to know [partner and father of her child] right after leaving care, and I thought he would be a good guy. When I met him, he was good; he took me out on trips, he took me out eating, he was loving, we went watching movies, like that. I thought he would always be like that, but he started hitting me once I was pregnant with my son. ... When there were new girls [in a meeting or a party], he would hit me and fight with me by harassing them in front of me.' (Carlota, 23 October 2016)

Experiencing this unsustainable situation, Carlota felt the need to move away from her partner and take care of the baby that was coming:

> 'I decided that if I were going to have my son, he would not be born in this situation; I had to have a room on my own [starts to cry]. I didn't steal anything or didn't do any of the things [she used to do on the street] anymore. I had a stable job that allowed me to provide a better future for my child and rent a room for him ... but then, [partner] appeared again. ... He claimed he would take my baby away if I did not return with him. He said everybody would know that [before care] I used to live on the street and that the social defence office [defensorías] would not allow that I would raise my child. ... I became terrified and concerned. We moved back together, and I realised I had no other place to be than with him. Then, he started to hit me again. I started to sniff glue again to cope with everything. Then everything evolved.

I ended up again on the street, and my child is in a care programme, like me when I was little. It is a shame. ... I sometimes think that if I had gone to a programme such as, you know, these programmes for women that suffer violence, or maybe I would have gone back to [name of the institution she lived in until she became adult], maybe all of this would not happen. Who knows, right?' (Carlota, 23 October 2016)

The lack of a family and social support network results in young people thinking that the street is their only alternative:

'I used to stay up during the nights saying: what do I do? I had a baby coming. I had no family to support me. I know I am a big girl, but I felt daunted. [I used to think] I have no place to go back if anything goes wrong. Well [laughing], I can always go back to the street. That is how it is *seño* [Spanish term for a street educator].' (Paola, 8 May 2015)

This lack of a social and emotional support network has been identified in other studies (Chase et al, 2006; Oshima et al, 2013) as a factor that leads young people in general, but especially women, to quickly look for a partner to settle down with and conceive a child with the idea of starting a family. The absence of a risk–need–responsivity model to support independent living and the lack of consideration of individual needs or risks, results in an accelerated journey (Stein, 2006) that drives these youth back to the street.

Factor 4: Their social network is still based on their street-connected peers

Care professionals tend to think that youth who have lived on the street should completely break their street bonds once they are admitted into care. However, empirical evidence shows that this is rarely the case (Velasco et al, 2020). The strongest bonds of street-connected youth are with their street peers. This fact has two significant consequences: on the one hand, as they do not have a social network outside of the street, it is more difficult for them to find work and access different social and learning opportunities. On the other, when they go through emotional hardships during their independent life, they turn to their street group, like other young people would turn to their family:

'I entered [the residential programme] to study, to become professional and to live a better life. But *seño*, it is not easy you know. ... When you leave the house [residential home], then real life hits you. Who do you turn to, to seek for support? Well, my street group.' (Bernardo, 8 September 2015)

The emotional bond between former and current street-connected youth is more than strong; it is essential in their lives. The strong experiences lived together on the street, where they had to protect each other to survive, form their street group into what Bowlby (1985), in attachment theory, calls their secure base:

> 'It all started when I spend hours walking downtown in the city. I was looking for a job – you know? – as most job opportunities are nearby where the street boys are. The more frustrated I got because I couldn't find a job, the more I visited the kids. Little by little, I decided to stay with them and now I live here again. It is cheaper and I have more company. I was very lonely.' (Carlota, 16 November 2016)

Research on independent living success factors (Cameron, 2007; Berckmans, 2014) points to having a social support network as crucial for a smooth transition to adult life, because it helps with practical daily issues and provides emotional support. However, in the case of street-connected care-leavers, their social network is based on their street relationships before care. Moreover, family contact is limited and adult contact is mediated by institutional relationships that end at 18. This entails a fundamental breach, compared to other care-leavers who do not have a street past.

Factor 5: Their street marks hinder their social reintegration

The last factor is related to the importance of the physical appearance of street-connected care-leavers as an obstacle to reintegrate into society. Their stories strongly emphasised that their facial deformities, caused by drug use and by scars from street fights, are evidence of their street background and hinder their social integration:

> 'The worst thing that can happen to you on the street is someone cutting your face. It is the worst punishment that one can receive because when you have that scar, it is impossible to hide that you are from the street or that you have a street past. So, who is going to want to hire you?' (Carlota, 13 May 2016)

Both Carlota's experience, and the one narrated by Eduardo that follows, express what Villanueva O'Driscoll and Loots (2014) call the embodied experience. Our bodies mediate all our experiences. The social relations that we build, how we perceive ourselves and how we are perceived are mediated by our bodies. In the case of street-connected youth, their bodies literally determine their permanent discrimination:

'When you already use a lot of drugs, it shows on your face. My nose has been deformed. Don't you see, *seño*? So, the question you ask is, if we can leave the street? But the question is not that. The question is: will the street leave us?' (Eduardo, 28 November 2017)

Carlota and Eduardo's testimonies clearly describe the interplay between street pull factors and society push factors. Care-leavers with a street-connected past are caught in the middle. The preparation process for leaving care does not consider the social barriers that they will have to face when transitioning to an independent life. Therefore, once out of the care system, and with little to no preparation, they have to deal with all the challenges described in this chapter, plus the social rejection due to their street connection, which is patently visible on their scarred faces.

Discussion and conclusion

This chapter has aimed to explain the factors contributing to care-leavers with a street-connected past returning to the street instead of starting independent life after ageing out care. Steens et al (2018) argue that the only way to improve interventions with street-connected groups is by looking critically at their successful and failed experiences.

These experiences were jointly collected and analysed through a highly participatory process with the young people, thus building valuable findings and lessons for practice and research. Findings show an interplay of factors, from failures in how their street past before entering residential care is considered, to how the care-leaving process of street-connected youth is planned, and the strong resistance from society to their reintegration as independent adults.

The first factor relates to how street-connected youth perceive their leaving process as being transferred to adult life instead of transitioning into it. The second factor brings to light that there are no formal aftercare programmes, which means they have to face an accelerated independence process on their own. Furthermore, the third factor reveals the lack of family and social networks, which results in the accelerated establishment of a new family to compensate for loneliness. This is especially hazardous for women who are caught in violent couple relationships and early pregnancy.

These first three findings taken together clearly show that there is a systemic failure in the process of street-connected youth's transition to adulthood. The care models of the institutions do contemplate issues like technical preparation, the transfer of skills necessary for independence, and the purchase of furniture for the house they will inhabit. But the most critical need is overlooked, which is arguably to provide continuous emotional support to face adult life.

Street-connected youth reach the street when the situation in their birth homes is untenable. Violence and precarity push them to make the most difficult decision a child can make, which is to move away from their parents and live on their own. Once on the street, their peer group becomes their emotional support. Finally, when they enter residential care, other needs are covered, but according to their own testimonies, not this emotional void.

How, then, should care and aftercare programmes formally include the emotional support component? Brown et al (2019: 358) sum it up brilliantly: through having caring professionals who 'really want to care'. Liabo et al (2017) emphasise that a determining success factor in independence is that care professionals are willing to go the extra mile to ensure that young people leaving care are supported and feel that there are people available to them, and even more so in the case of street-connected youth who have no one but their street network.

Indeed, this is precisely what the fourth finding shows: that in the absence of professional and family support, their primary social network is still based on the street. Street youth never really stop being connected to their street group. The personal relationships established within residential care programmes are neither as permanent nor as profound as those set on the street.

Finally, the findings show that care-leavers' facial scars disclose their past life on the street, hindering their social reintegration, because the scars are physical evidence of having lived on the margins of society. In this respect, researchers such as De Moura (2002), Conticini and Hulme (2007) and Gigengack (2008) reveal that there is a tendency to blame street youth for not being able to reintegrate into society because of their criminal past behaviour, their drug use and their 'untamed' attitude. However, the participants' stories debunk these arguments by revealing a relational dynamic with a society that does not allow street youth to integrate into adult life because they are rejected based on their appearance.

Kidd et al (2020) argue that because of their turbulent past, street-connected youth mistrust the welfare system, have difficulties in personal relationships and therefore tend to develop their social network around other marginalised young people. Nevertheless, the stories presented show a counterargument: street-connected care-leavers maintain their social network on the street not because they cannot establish a broader social support system, but because home-based social networks are out of reach. The findings question if there are real possibilities for the social integration of street-connected youth when they age out of care, especially when there are no specialised transition programmes or aftercare support.

Aftercare programmes are critical for helping street-connected care-leavers not to go back to the streets. Moreover, they need consistent emotional support: a worker who genuinely accompanies them and maintains the intensity and frequency of support through the early years of independence. Finally, sensitising communities to prepare them to receive and include aftercare street-connected youth is urgent. Without these social and structural changes, the possibilities for successful social integration will be significantly reduced and keep care-leavers at society's margins.

References

Asociación Civil Doncel, Hope and Homes for Children and UNICEF (2016) *Más autonomía, más derechos. Reporte para Bolivia* [More autonomy, more rights. Report for Bolivia]. Available from: http://redegresadoslatam. org/wp-content/uploads/2020/05/DONCEL_INV_regional_OKG-2.pdf

Bartora, C. (2016) *Desinstitucionalización: proceso de reintegro familiar de niños, niñas y adolescentes en Aldeas Infantiles SOS e intervención del/la Trabajador/a Social* [Deinstitutionalization: Process of family reintegration of children and adolescents in SOS Children's Villages and intervention of the social worker], Universidad de la República (Uruguay) Facultad de Ciencias Sociales. Available from: https://hdl.handle.net/20.500.12008/22968

Berckmans, I. (2014) *Sharing stories, reflecting and creating ideas about leaving the streets: Encounters with young persons in street situations, their family members and street educators through participatory action research projects in El Alto, Bolivia,* Brussels: VUB (unpublished doctoral dissertation).

Berckmans, I., Velasco, M.L., Tapia, B.P. and Loots, G. (2012) 'A systematic review: A quest for effective interventions for children and adolescents in street situation', *Children and Youth Services Review,* 34(7): 1259–1272.

Berger, P.L. and Luckmann, T. (1966) *The social construction of reality: A treatise in the sociology of knowledge,* New York Penguin Books.

Bowlby, J. (1985) *La separación afectiva* [Affective separation], Barcelona: Paidós.

Brown, R., Alderson, H., Kaner, E., McGovern, R. and Lingam, R. (2019) ' "There are carers, and then there are carers who actually care": Conceptualizations of care among looked after children and care leavers, social workers and carers', *Child Abuse & Neglect,* 92: 219–229.

Cameron, C. (2007) 'Education and self-reliance among care leavers', *Adoption and Fostering,* 31(1): 39–49.

Chase, E., Maxwell, C., Knight, A. and Aggleton, P. (2006) 'Pregnancy and parenthood among young people in and leaving care: What are the influencing factors, and what makes a difference in providing support?', *Journal of Adolescence,* 29(3): 437–451.

Chikwava, F., O'Donnell, M., Ferrante, A., Pakpahan, E. and Cordier, R. (2022) 'Patterns of homelessness and housing instability and the relationship with mental health disorders among young people transitioning from out-of-home care: Retrospective cohort study using linked administrative data', *PLoS ONE,* 17(9): e0274196.

Cisneros-Puebla, C.A. (2008) 'Los rostros deconstructivo y constructivo de la construcción social' [The deconstructive and constructive faces of social construction], *Forum: Qualitative Social Research*, 4(13): 63–75.

Clare, M., Anderson, B., Bodenham, M. and Clare, B. (2017) 'Leaving care and at risk of homelessness: The LIFT project', *Children Australia*, 42(1): 9–17.

Clifton, J. (2014) 'Small stories, positioning, and the discursive construction of leader identity in business meetings', *Leadership*, 10(1): 99–117.

Conticini, A. and Hulme, D. (2007) 'Escaping violence, seeking freedom: Why children in Bangladesh migrate to the street', *Development and Change*, 38(2): 201–227.

De Moura, S.L. (2002) 'The social construction of street children: Configuration and implications', *British Journal of Social Work*, 32(3): 353–367.

Dickens, L.F. and van Breda, A.D. (2021) *Resilience and outcomes of South African Girls and Boys Town care leavers seven years on*, Johannesburg: Girls and Boys Town South Africa and University of Johannesburg.

Dworsky, A. and Courtney, M.E. (2009) 'Homelessness and the transition from foster care to adulthood', *Child Welfare*, 88(4): 23–56.

Georgakopoulou, A. (2007) *Small stories, interaction and identities*, vol 8, Amsterdam: John Benjamins Publishing.

Gergen, K.J. (2007) 'Si las personas son textos', in G. Limón (ed) *Terapias Postmodernas: Aportaciones Construccionistas* [Postmodern therapies: Constructionist contributions], Ciudad de México: PAX, pp 111–140.

Gigengack, R. (2008) 'Critical omissions: How the street children studies could address self-destructive agency', in P. Christensen and A. James (eds) *Research with Children: Perspectives and Practices*, 2nd edn, London: Routledge, pp 205–219.

Glynn, N. and Mayock, P. (2019) '"I've changed so much within a year": Care leavers' perspectives on the aftercare planning process', *Child Care in Practice*, 25(1): 79–98.

Goffman, E. (1959) *The Presentation of Self in Everyday Life: Selections*, Garden City: Doubleday Anchor

Hamdan, A. (2012) 'Autoethnography as a genre of qualitative research: A journey inside out', *International Journal of Qualitative Methods*, 11(5): 585–606.

Huang, C.C. and Huang, K. (2008) 'Caring for abandoned street children in La Paz, Bolivia', *Archives of Disease in Childhood*, 93(7): 626–627.

Jordan, C., Gust, S. and Scheman, N. (2005) 'The trustworthiness of research: the paradigm of community-based research', in N. Scheman (ed) *Shifting ground: Knowledge and reality, transgression and trustworthiness*, Oxford: Oxford University Press, pp 39–58.

Kelly, P. (2020) 'Risk and protective factors contributing to homelessness among foster care youth: An analysis of the National Youth in Transition Database', *Children and Youth Services Review*, 108: 1–8.

Kidd, S.A., Vitopoulos, N., Frederick, T., Leon, S., Wang, W., Mushquash, C. and McKenzie, K. (2020) 'Trialing the feasibility of a critical time intervention for youth transitioning out of homelessness', *American Journal of Orthopsychiatry*, 90(5): 535–545.

Kovarikova, J. (2017) *Exploring youth outcomes after aging-out of care*, Toronto: Provincial Advocate for Children and Youth.

Ley 548. Código Niña, Niño y Adolescente. DS. 2377 [548 Law. Children and Adolescent Code. DS 2377], 17 July 2014 Available from: http://www. coordinadoradelamujer.org.bo/observatorio/archivos/marco/l548_389.pdf

Liabo, K., McKenna, C., Ingold, A. and Roberts, H. (2017) 'Leaving foster or residential care: A participatory study of care leavers' experiences of health and social care transitions', *Child: Care, Health and Development*, 43(2): 182–191.

Lincoln, Y.S. and Guba, E.G. (1985) *Naturalistic inquiry*, New York: SAGE.

Lock, A. and Strong, T. (2010) *Social constructionism: Sources and stirrings in theory and practice*, New York: Cambridge University Press.

McNamee, S. (2012) 'From social construction to relational construction: Practices from the edge', *Psychological Studies*, 57(2): 150–156.

Mokgopha, M.S. (2019) *Resilience development of former street children on the streets, in residential care and beyond care*, Johannesburg: University of Johannesburg (master's dissertation).

Oshima, K.M.M., Narendorf, S.C. and McMillen, J.C. (2013) 'Pregnancy risk among older youth transitioning out of foster care', *Children and Youth Services Review*, 35(10): 1760–1765.

Riessman, C.K. (2008) *Narrative methods for the human sciences*, Thousand Oaks: SAGE.

Riggs, E.H. and Coyle, A. (2002) 'Young people's accounts of homelessness: A case study analysis of psychological well-being and identity', *The Counselling Psychology Review*, 17: 5–15.

Romaioli, D. (2011) 'Opening scenarios: A relational perspective on how to deal with multiple therapeutic views', *Psychological Studies*, 57(2): 195–202.

Squire, C. (2008) *Approaches to narrative research*, London: National Centre for Research Methods.

Steens, R.J., Hermans, K. and Van Regenmortel, T. (2018) 'Construir una alianza de trabajo entre profesionales y usuarios de servicios en la preservación familiar Un estudio de caso múltiple' [Building a working partnership between professionals and service users in family preservation: A multiple case study], *Trabajo Social Infantil y Familiar* [Child and Family Social Work], 23(2): 230–238.

Stein, M. (2006) 'Young people aging out of care: The poverty of theory', *Children and Youth Services Review*, 28(4): 422–434.

Stirling, T. (2018) 'Youth homelessness and care leavers'. Available from: https://www.wcpp.org.uk/wp-content/uploads/2018/10/Youth-homelessness-and-care-leavers-Mapping-interventions-in-Wales.pdf

Thomas de Benitez, S.T. (2003) 'Reactive, protective and rights-based approaches in work with homeless street youth', *Children Youth and Environments*, 13(1): 134–149.

Thomas de Benitez, S. and Hiddleston, T. (2011) *Promotion and protection of the rights of children working and/or living on the street, OHCHR global study*, Geneva: The Office of the United Nations High Commissioner for Human Rights.

Tilley-Lubbs, G.A. (2014) 'Critical authoethnography and the vulnerable self as researcher', *Multidisciplinary Journal of Educational Research*, 4(3): 268–285.

Universidad Católica Boliviana 'San Pablo' and Aldeas Infantiles SOS Bolivia (2017) *Cada niño y niña cuenta: Situación de derechos de los niños y niñas que han perdido el cuidado familiar o están en riesgo de perderlo* [Every child counts: Rights situation of children who have lost or are at risk of losing family care], La Paz: Autores.

Velasco, M.L., Mostmans, L. and Peres-Cajías, G. (2020) 'Street children and social media: Identity construction in the digital age Bolivia', in L. Green, D. Holloway, K. Stevenson, T. Leaver and L. Haddon (eds) *The Routledge companion to digital media and children*, New York: Routledge, pp 449–459.

Viceministerio de Defensa Social y Sustancias Controladas (eds) (2015) *Censo de personas en situación de calle, 2014: Estudio realizado en niñas, niños, adolescentes y adultos de diez ciudades de Bolivia* [Census of people living on the streets, 2014: A study of children, adolescents and adults in ten Bolivian cities], La Paz: Autores.

Villanueva O'Driscoll, J. and Loots, G. (2014) 'Tracing subjective drives: A narrative approach to study youth's engagement with and disengagement from armed groups in Colombia', *Qualitative Research in Psychology*, 11(4): 365–383.

3

Care-leavers' reflections on resilience processes acquired while living on the street prior to coming into residential care in South Africa

Malose Samuel Mokgopha, Adrian D. van Breda and Sue Bond

Introduction

The transition from childhood to adulthood, termed youth transitions, is challenging for probably every young person (Furlong and Cartmel, 2006). It involves taking on new responsibilities, making choices about one's future, becoming financially self-sufficient, moving out of home and establishing one's own family. For those transitioning out of the child protection system (residential and foster care), this transition is arguably even harder, because of the frequently inadequate family support, the abruptness of the transition, often before young people are ready to launch into young adulthood, and because of the vulnerabilities that led the young person into care in the first place (Mann-Feder and Goyette, 2019). Research around the world has shown that among this population of care-leavers are some vulnerable sub-populations, such as care-leavers with disabilities (Kelly et al, 2016), unaccompanied asylum seekers (Barrie and Mendes, 2011) and care-leavers with mental health concerns (Butterworth et al, 2017).

One sub-group of care-leavers who have received almost no attention are care-leavers who came into care from the street, that is, street-involved children who entered care and have subsequently transitioned out of care. While all children come into care because of some kind of pre-care life challenge (such as child abuse or neglect, parental substance abuse or mental illness, or behavioural problems displayed by the child), children living on the street might be considered to be particularly at risk, due to their potential exposure to violence and exploitation, substance abuse and difficulties pursuing their education (Chettiar et al, 2010; Oppong Asante et al, 2014; Hills et al, 2016; Heerde and Hemphill, 2017; Dutta, 2018). Research also suggests that street-involved children experience substantial challenges in making the transition from the freedom of the street to the tight controls and regulation of the care context (Dziro and Rufurwokuda, 2013). Street-involved children are most certainly a group of children living on the edge.

Because of these accentuated pre-care and in-care challenges, one may deduce that former street-involved children are at heightened risk for negative post-care outcomes. Our experience of working with looked-after street-involved children, however, suggests that many former street-involved children who move through the care system developed resilience processes while living on the streets and utilised these processes after leaving care. It seems they may have built resilience processes to deal with life's challenges while on the streets, which they continue using in young adulthood.

This study, therefore, sets out to explore the resilience processes that care-leavers who formerly lived on the streets acquired while on the streets. Through this, we hope to shed light on the creative ways in which former street-involved children survived and even thrived on the streets, to propose how these resilience processes may facilitate their transition out of care into young adulthood. We believe this will expand the body of knowledge about care-leaving on the edges of society, namely, former street-involved children. We provide the context of street-involved children and a review of the literature on street-involved children in and leaving care, followed by a brief explanation of resilience as the theoretical framework for this study. After an account of the methods that we used, we present the three themes that emerged regarding resilience acquired on the street. We discuss these findings and formulate implications for care-leaving practice.

Context and review of literature

Research on care-leaving in South Africa has been burgeoning over the past several years (Van Breda, 2018b). Among others, there are publications on the contribution of social support to resilient outcomes using quantitative data (Van Breda, 2022), qualitative studies on the resilience processes of care-leavers (Van Breda, 2015; Van Breda and Hlungwani, 2019), qualitative studies on the contribution of possible selves to care-leaver resilience (Bond and Van Breda, 2018) and research on the contribution of both agency and structure to care-leaving outcomes (Van Breda, 2016). It is thus known that resilience processes – defined as the things young people do as they interact with their social environment to achieve better-than-expected outcomes (Van Breda, 2015) – are being used by care-leavers and do improve their outcomes after leaving care. None of these studies, however, focuses on street-involved children, and it is not known whether any of the study participants were formerly street-involved children.

The invisibility of street-involved children in care-leaving research appears to be the case globally as well. While there are a few studies that look at various aspects of street-involved children in and after care, none examines the experiences and views of care-leavers who were formerly street-involved children. Luwangula (2017: 312), for example, studied street-involved children's transition towards young adulthood in Uganda, but his participants were not care-experienced. He writes of them: 'Street children are typical of the category of children that remain outside family care and outside any prioritized alternative care arrangement. They represent the demise of the long-time cherished Ugandan family system, community and other child protection systems.' Premsingh and Ebenezer (2013) investigated children's homes' views of the challenges that street-involved children in India, who were now in residential care, faced while living on the street. These children were still in care and the focus was on challenges, not resilience, and data were collected from staff, not the street-involved children. One study looked at the resilience of South African street-involved children who were now living in a shelter (Malindi and Machenjedze, 2012), giving particular attention to how school engagement contributed positively to their development, for example, by promoting prosocial behaviour and cultivating a future orientation. The participants in this study were, however, still in care, and thus not care-leavers.

Most care-leaving studies that refer to living on the street speak about homelessness or street-dwelling *after* having left care (not before coming into care), thus as a 'negative' care-leaving outcome (Brien and Roumestan, 2010; Berzin et al, 2011; Fowler et al, 2011; Batsche and Reader, 2012; Dziro et al, 2013; Harwick et al, 2017; Purtell et al, 2017). Magnuson et al (2015), for example, studied youth living on the street in Canada and found that all had previously been in foster care. Takele and Kotecho (2020) provide a narrative account of a female care-leaver in Ethiopia living on the street. Pryce et al (2016) provide a narrative of a female care-leaver also in Ethiopia living and giving birth to two children on the street.

A few care-leaving studies mention that one of the reasons for children coming into care is that they were living on the street. For example, Oelofsen (2015: 23) notes that 5 per cent of her participants in South Africa had been working or living on the street. Adeboye et al (2019) refer to a case of a whole family living on the street in Portugal prior to the child coming into care. Dima and Bucuta (2015) refer to a similar case in Romania, and although they track this young person into adulthood, there are no links back to his previous experience of living on the street. Dutta (2017) indicates that 20 per cent of the girls in her study in India came into care from the street. Ucembe's (2013) study on care-leavers in Uganda includes several participants who came into care from the streets and who recounted harrowing experiences of life on the streets.

One study focused specifically on former street-involved children who were now in care in South Africa (Tanur, 2012). Tanur notes that these children's educational attainment was compromised by years of living on the street and not participating in education. Tanur's study focused on the Mamelani programme, which prepares young people for leaving care, and found that while before their programme many care-leavers returned to the street, after the implementation of their programme, this reduced to less than 10 per cent. Finally, Gwenzi (2018) reports that in Zimbabwe, children who come into care from the street struggle more than other young people to reintegrate into society. They are used to behaving in unruly ways and struggle to develop prosocial behaviours.

This review of the care-leaving literature suggests that while street-involved children may make up a significant proportion of children in care (particularly in countries in the Global South, such as India, Ethiopia, Zimbabwe, Uganda and South Africa), there is little research on this sub-population of children in care and even less attention given to their transition from care towards young adulthood.

Theoretical lens

This study makes use of resilience theory to understand the factors contributing towards more positive transitions from care towards young adulthood among former street-involved children. Resilience can be defined as 'the multilevel processes that [individuals] engage in to obtain better-than-expected outcomes in the face or wake of adversity' (Van Breda, 2018a: 4). Resilience theory recognises that while adversities impact negatively on human wellbeing and psychosocial functioning, some people, perhaps even many people, manage to navigate through the adversities and achieve a positive degree of wellbeing and functioning. This capacity to navigate adversity is referred to as 'resilience'. Thus, resilience is a process mediating between adverse life experiences and 'positive' outcomes. Many prefer the term 'better-than-expected' outcomes because these are less normative and allow the determination of what constitutes a 'positive' outcome to be based both on what the individual sees as positive and on an individual's outcome in relation to the outcomes of others in similar circumstances.

Resilience theory has been criticised for individualising the responsibility for overcoming adversity and ignoring or even subtly endorsing adversity (Garrett, 2016). In this way, resilience theory can, and often has been, co-opted by a neoliberal agenda, which obviates the state's responsibility to address macro, structural and systematic social ills that compromise the wellbeing and psychosocial functioning of individuals, families and communities.

While these critiques are valid, there are significant efforts among many resilience scholars to avoid a neoliberal and individualised approach to resilience research (Ungar, 2011; Theron, 2019; Van Breda, 2019). This is particularly expressed through the recognition that resilience is not an intrapsychic function, but rather located in the social ecology. Some scholars emphasise the social environment as the most important source of resilience resources, exceeding the usefulness of individual resources (Ungar, 2012). Other scholars emphasise the interaction between people and their environment (that is, the person-in-environment) as the nexus of resilience (Van Breda, 2018c), as illustrated in the earlier definition of 'resilience processes'.

This study is informed by these ecological approaches to resilience, in that the emphasis is not on the internal resilience capacities of individual care-leavers who were formerly street-involved children, but rather on the interface between care-leavers and their social environments, and the ways in which these interfaces work collaboratively to create supportive and caring contexts that facilitate better-than-expected outcomes.

Methodology

This study adopted a qualitative research approach (Corbin and Strauss, 2015) to allow us to dig more deeply into the life experiences and reflections of participants. Specifically, we drew on aspects of constructivist grounded theory (Charmaz, 2014), such as coding data using gerunds, to emphasise the social interactions between care-leavers and their social environment. Similar approaches have been used in previous studies on care-leaving in South Africa (Van Breda, 2015).

This study was conducted with care-leavers from Kids Haven, a children's home in Johannesburg. Kids Haven was established in 1992 to provide residential care to street-involved children, in contrast to most children's homes which accepted any child found to be in need of care and protection. It accommodates up to 180 children and disengages about 40 young people per year.

Participants were purposively sampled from the population of Kids Haven care-leavers who had come into care from the street. Sampling criteria were that they had to have lived on the street for at least six months, have lived in Kids Haven for at least 12 months, have left Kids Haven at least 12 months previously and be at least 18 years of age. Given that the first author is an employee of Kids Haven, responsible for the aftercare programme, considerable effort was invested in carefully recruiting participants, to allow them the freedom to decline to participate and to avoid subtle or overt coercion. Those who expressed interest in participating in the study came in for an interview about a week after the initial contact, when further discussions were held about their participation, and only then was the consent form signed. Data saturation was reached at nine participants.

The sample comprised six males and three females, aged 19–29 years (mean 24.3). Participants had lived on the street prior to coming into care for 6–36 months (mean 20.7) and were in care for 1–10 years (mean 4.6). Five had not completed secondary school. They had been out of care for 1–6 years (mean 4.8) and six were renting their accommodation and three living with their family of origin. Six were employed and three were unemployed and not in education or training. Three had a child.

Data collection took place prior to the COVID-19 pandemic. In line with grounded theory methods (Charmaz, 2014), data were collected and analysed iteratively. Data were collected in three rounds of three participants, followed by analysis of those interviews. Subsequent rounds of data collection were informed by previous rounds. Each participant was interviewed twice using semi-structured interview schedules. The first interview focused on participants' experiences on the street, in care and since leaving care, while the second focused on their reflections on the resilience processes that they acquired during these stages. After all data collection and analysis had been completed, participants were invited back to participate in a focus group interview using similar questions to those in the individual interviews. Five of the nine participants attended the focus group.

Data were analysed using Charmaz's (2014) procedures. First, line-by-line initial coding was done using gerunds (verbs ending with -ing, such as negotiating, exploring and mobilising). Second, focused coding involved searching for commonalities among the initial codes and formulating tentative focused codes to cluster these. In addition, focused coding involved identifying initial codes that were most salient to the research aim and that appeared most prominently (for example, frequently or with strong feelings). Constant comparison was conducted throughout, in which the focused codes emerging in a transcript were compared constantly with all previously analysed transcripts, so that over the course of coding the 18 transcripts, coding became increasingly confirmatory, leading to the refining of the emerging codes.

The trustworthiness and rigour of the study were promoted through several mechanisms (Lincoln and Guba, 1985; Shenton, 2004). The first author was responsible for data analysis, and his coding was checked and verified by the second and third authors. This verification led at times to revisions to the first author's original coding. The first author had long contact with Kids Haven as an employee and knew the participants previously, which together with the two substantial interviews per participant, constituted prolonged engagement, contributing to credibility. However, because of his insider perspective, the first author also kept a reflexivity journal and worked closely with the other authors to monitor his personal views (Probst and Berenson, 2014). The grounded theory methods of data analysis, through constant comparison and the iteration of data collection and analysis, contribute to the dependability of the findings. A detailed audit trail has been maintained so that the findings reported can be traced back to the original texts of participants in context, promoting confirmability.

The researchers, as practitioners and academics working with care-leavers, were committed to ensuring the ethical protection of participants. The processes of recruitment and informed consent were conducted about a week apart to allow opportunity for recruits to decline to participate in the study, as some did. Confidentiality was assured and pseudonyms are used in this and all other reports. Counselling services were available to participants who needed support. This study was approved by the Faculty of Humanity's Research Ethics Committee at the University of Johannesburg (#01-063-2016) and the Kids Haven director gave written permission for the study.

Findings

The findings from this study indicate that the participants developed helpful resilience processes in their life on the streets. These processes, which helped them survive on the streets, remain clear in their memory, even after leaving care years later, and participants were frequently able to show how these resilience processes continue to benefit them today. The young people in our study acquired resilience in three domains: building a safe, collaborative family; networking people for resources; and reflective learning and life lessons.

Building a safe, collaborative family

Participants reported how, as street-involved children, they established groups that are safe and collaborative, sometimes described as 'family'. Group living offers protection and belonging and assists in acquiring resources. In a group, they get back-up, motivation and support from each other in times of need when under threat, or when they need emotional or physical support. Once they had networked for protection and resources, the participants took their resilience one step further when they organised their activities to maximise their survival efforts. They used social processes such as teamwork and shared decision making, to plan and strategise about accessing and distributing the resources they needed, demonstrating a further acquisition of resilience.

Lindokhuhle recognised his vulnerability and the importance of being with people he knew for safety. He teamed up with a group of bigger boys for protection, saying:

'As long as I had enough food, as long as I had enough smoke with me and as long as I had a place to sleep and people who I knew, if ever there was some other street kid who takes others and who is bigger than me who would hit me at any time or use me in a very bad way, like abusing me in the worst way when I am there in the street; I knew that those guys will not let anyone take me. So, by then all I had in my mind is that they were taking care of me. So, they were like my brothers.'

Fistos said that he kept to a group of street-involved children for "protection because I was alone. I was away from my family, so I needed a sense of belonging err ... protection". Similarly, Sloya said, "it is tough out there so if you do not have a backup. ... So, street children do walk in groups, because they protect them. That is how they protect themselves: like the wolves".

Fistos pointed out the benefit of being in a group in an emergency:

'If anything happens to you in the street, at least there is someone who can go and get help for you, they don't know where your family is, but they will run and get help. They are the ones who will run and go to a public phone and dial numbers for an ambulance if I am sick and dying there in the street. But if I am alone, alone, alone then I wouldn't cope, more especially in the street; it is very tough.'

Within the context of a safe group, participants also reported how the group collaborated to the mutual benefit of all group members. Berth gave an example of this:

'We started saying: no, this thing of fighting does not work, so let us divide ourselves. One group will be called food group and the other group will be called the money group, because if we all go for food there is no money and if we all go for money there is no food, so we have to divide and share and see how a day goes. Maybe we can get food, maybe we can get money, maybe we can get more food, maybe we can get more money. Days are not the same.'

Similarly, Sloya confirmed this collective response to challenge and the sharing of risk and responsibility, saying:

'We split ourselves into two groups of three and four. Three goes door to door knocking on doors asking for food, four asking for money from people in car parking lots. At night we combine all the moneys we made and we buy glue and food then we sleep and wake up in the morning.'

Sloya's narrative illustrates how participants used close relationships to share risk and responsibility. They responded collectively to a challenge and distributed tasks equally. The resources of food and money they acquired through this collaborative effort were distributed equitably, even when someone had not been successful and returned to the shelter empty-handed. Fistos frames this safe collaboration as being 'family': "My tricks [to obtain resources] did not work for me. Someone will just come with bread and someone will just come with food. ... Guys let's eat, yah, let us eat! We are a family here."

These experiences of building a safe, collaborative family on the street spill into life after care. Fistos explains how this taught him the importance of his own family:

'As I experience love in the street, I have learned that there is no place like home. Each and every child needs to be with their family, no matter what. Even today I carried that: I am a father to a two-year-old daughter. I will always be there no matter what. No matter my daughter can grow up and get to some stages, I will always be there and give her love and protect her.'

Networking people for resources

Participants reported networking other people, outside of their group, for their physical needs. The young people expressed knowledge of the areas they beg and live in. They knew some individuals and organisations, such as churches and welfare organisations, that would help them with basic needs, like food, clothes and blankets. They also familiarised themselves with times and days that food, clothes, blankets and other resources were distributed. The participants established strong networks to share information about their environment and the services that could be of help to them. Former street-involved children used these resilience processes to find places to sleep at night, and find individuals, churches, non-governmental organisations and other organisations to help them.

Lindo mentioned a church organisation that was known to the young people: "Well we would ask for blankets at the Salvation Army. It is a church organisation. There were other churches that had feeding schemes where we would get food and then we would go back to the robots [traffic lights] and ask for money."

Similarly, Albert commented that young people know where to go for food, saying, "Some places we used to go there in town where we used to get like free food because at this corner there is breakfast. You go to that corner and you can get lunch. Just going around." In addition to networking for material goods and food, young people networked for personal hygiene. Berth said, "So you have to know what to do, where to go, where to sleep and bath."

The participants had to move around to access resources for survival, and in this they showed considerable creativity and resilience, making use of public transport, primarily trains which are an inexpensive mode of transport, and, if there are no ticket inspectors, the young people could ride for free. Although this caused them some anxiety, they still opted to try for a free train ride. Fistos said, "So, we used a free train to come here in Kids Haven and it was my first time and I was scared because we did not have a train ticket." Fistos also travelled by train to other areas of Johannesburg without a ticket, although he did say "we were scared of ticket examiners there".

These networking activities taught the participants how to interact with others, developing lessons for life after care. Berth, for example, explained that 'communication' is one of the main networking skills he learned on the streets and uses today:

'Communication helped me very well because I can communicate with people right now and survive, I cannot survive on my own unless I have got help from a friend. … I had to communicate with people in different languages, so it was hard for me to cope with what they are saying. So, I had to be patient and listen to them and communicate nice, so I can figure out what is happening, yes.'

Reflective learning and life lessons

Another resilience process developed on the street was the process of reflecting on adverse life situations and drawing positive learning from them. In this regard, the participants showed considerable resilience as they discussed their experiences of living on the streets and the life lessons they had learned as a result. They engaged in a social process of reflective learning that they used to transform their lives positively. This learning translated into street smarts, where they understand and can navigate challenging environments. Sloya was able to find good lessons from his time on the streets:

'Some of the good lessons that I have learned on the street, they are helping me even now. I learned to stand on my own. … I learned to stand on my feet. I learned to be myself. I learned not to be afraid. … So, even today I am using that thing. I do not care who says what, as long as I am doing the right thing.'

Pertunia said, "My life on the streets was not nice," but went on to say, "but I went through it and then I survived." She was using her previous experiences of life on the streets as a way of measuring her current difficulties. She said, "I empower myself every day by judging similar situations." Pertunia was taking the learning from living on the streets and applying it to her current situation to improve: "There are similar situations that I face now, like in the past, so I look at myself and check how I responded then and what I can do better now." Similarly, Lindo commented, "Even today, I can still notice someone who is not coming with a positive mind. ... I can notice when someone is taking advantage of me."

Fistos reflected on his overall gains from having lived on the streets:

'If I didn't live on the streets, or I never happened to be a street kid, I would not be able to be a diesel mechanic today. I would not be able to be in Kids Haven, I was not going to be the man I am today ... and I was not going to have all these experiences from Kids Haven that I will teach my brothers and sister.'

Discussion

Living on the street is recognised as a significant social issue for children in South Africa (Polk, 2017). Street-involved children are among the most marginalised and deprived groups in the country (Hills et al, 2016). However, although street-involved children are recognised as vulnerable and facing multiple challenges, there is evidence in this study of how the participants engaged in resilience processes while on the streets and in some instance of how they brought these processes into their life after care. In reflecting on the findings from this study, we noticed many unanticipated similarities with a model of care-leaving among non-street-involved young people, developed in South Africa by Van Breda (2015) and confirmed with a different sample by Van Breda and Hlungwani (2019).

One of the resilience processes centres on building relational networks that facilitate survival and experiences of belonging. While living on the streets, children build co-operative, collective and family-like networks among themselves. While these networks facilitate safety and resources, participants also emphasise the quality of the relationships themselves. Participants use terms like brothers, a pack (of wolves) and family to describe this safe, collaborative group/family experience on the streets. Fistos explicitly links these street-involved processes with his aftercare life.

This relational process resonates with previous studies of non-street-involved care-leavers in South Africa (Van Breda, 2015; Van Breda and Hlungwani, 2019), particularly with their resilience process of 'striving for authentic belonging', which refers to young people's efforts to build deep, meaningful and enduring relationships. Young people in care frequently have poor early attachment experiences and an insecure base, which can manifest in difficult behaviour in adolescence (Smith, 2011). Their need for attachment can, however, be expressed as a striving for meaningful and authentic relationships, even when they are not well equipped for such relationships. Brendtro and Larson (2006) place 'belonging' as the foundation of the circle of courage, and essential for healthy child and youth development.

A second resilience process centres on the participants' capacity to mobilise other people into helpful roles, notably providing resources. This capacity has been termed 'networking people for goal attainment' in previous studies (Van Breda, 2015; Van Breda and Hlungwani, 2019). This involves the mobilisation of other people, outside of their group, often acquaintances or strangers, to take on helpful roles that help the young person achieve their goals. This contrasts with the previous theme, which had a relational focus; here the focus is instrumental.

The primary goal for our participants living on the streets was survival, thus they regard people as sources of food, clothing, bedding and transport. Participants report mobilising people at charities, shops and restaurants to obtain the resources they needed. In other cases, they mobilise an actual resource, such as trains, by avoiding conductors who check for tickets. They also share information about resourceful people and places with each other, as a collective survival effort. Berth emphasised how useful these processes are to him now, after leaving care.

The third resilience process concerned our participants' capacity for reflection on their life situations and experiences and the construction of a meaningful narrative. Three participants (Sloya, Pertunia and Lindo) made direct links here between life on the streets and life after leaving care. While living on the street, participants report learning about their strengths to stand alone, not be afraid and avoid exploitation. They also begin to self-define as a survivor or as powerful. These ways of constructing themselves suggest 'grit', which refers to working persistently and even under difficult circumstances to achieve one's goals (Duckworth et al, 2007). They also point to 'building hopeful and tenacious self-confidence', which emerged in previous studies of care-leavers (Van Breda, 2015, Van Breda and Hlungwani, 2019), in which young people cognitively shape their life experiences into affirming self-definitions of capacity and positive future expectations.

The young people in our study, who had prior experience of living on the streets, show similar resilience processes to care-leavers in previous studies without street experience. This suggests that Van Breda's (2015) model of care-leaving has credibility with street-involved care-leavers also. However, the details of resilience processes among our sample differ substantially from those reported by Van Breda (2015), giving particular attention to the capacities developed while living on the streets, rather than only after leaving care. This suggests an accumulation of resilience processes over a long period, that for our study extends back to when participants were living on the streets. Given this long continuity, we suggest that these resilience processes should be nurtured in young people while in care, to strengthen their utility after leaving care.

Practice implications

These findings suggest that residential care facilities and practitioners should recognise the distinctive profile of this sub-group of care-leavers who were living on the streets prior to coming into care. Street-involved children are at greater risk than other categories of looked-after children, because of their exposure to multiple harsh circumstances. They may therefore be more vulnerable and in need of specialised services. However, practitioners should also recognise and celebrate the kinds of resilience processes that these children learned while living on the streets. Not only is there evidence of care-leavers drawing these processes from the streets into life after care, but there is also considerable synergy between their on-the-street resilience processes and the resilience of care-leavers in previous studies.

These findings suggest that street-involved children in care may have already experienced and mastered some of the resilience processes that may be useful for them after they age out of care. Given that these processes are shown to have significant potential to enable successful transitioning back into the world after leaving care (Van Breda, 2015; Van Breda and Hlungwani, 2019), identifying, naming, celebrating and advancing these resilience process among children with a street-involved history may contribute significantly to their later transition out of care into young adulthood.

Particular attention should be given to helping these children recognise the care setting (both children and staff) as a safe and collaborative family, in which they can build relationships of belonging and protection, similar to what they formed on the streets. This would build on and expand the close relationships that young people often form with one or two caregivers. This capacity to constitute a 'family' of supportive relationships can continue to pay dividends after leaving care, facilitating improved care-leaving outcomes (Van Breda, 2022).

Practitioners should assist former street-involved children in care to see the care setting as a resource to be 'exploited'. This capacity to network people for resources may be better developed among these children than those who come from families. Given that this networking capacity is useful in life after care (Van Breda, 2015), assisting them to apply this process within the care setting, as well as settings outside, such as at school, may tap into their *street smarts* and help them adjust and flourish.

Practitioners can also engage children who came into care off the streets to reflect – individually and/or in groups – on what they learned on the streets about life, and how they think these lessons could assist them now and in the future. Such reflective conversations could stimulate the capacity for internal conversations or self-talk, which can contribute to cognitively reappraising current situations and making stronger links between earlier and current life experiences (Appleton et al, 2021).

Limitations

The interpretation and generalisation of the findings in this study are subject to some limitations. The findings in this study cannot be generalised to all former street-involved children who went through care, as this was a small study using participants from one organisation. Therefore, the perspectives and experiences of the participants do not necessarily represent the larger population from which they were drawn. Also, there were more male participants than female. As a result, women's reflections of their resilience processes are under-represented.

Conclusion

Street-involved children can be considered a vulnerable group living on the edges of society. Former South African street-involved children who were taken up into residential care and later aged out of care into young adulthood, however, report engaging in a range of resilience processes while living on the streets, many of which they continue to mobilise as young adults. These resilience processes centre on their capacity to build networks of meaningful and supportive relationships, to mobilise other people into helpful roles of resource provision, and to reflect on their struggles and opportunities, and locate them within a meaningful narrative. We suggest that identifying, celebrating and encouraging these resilience processes will assist in reframing the adverse experience of leaving home and living on the streets and bolstering the resilience processes that emerged out of these experiences, equipping young people for a better life after care.

References

Adeboye, T.K., Guerreiro, M.d.D. and Höjer, I. (2019) 'Unveiling the experiences of young people in foster care: Perspectives from Portugal and Nigeria', *International Social Work*, 62(1): 433–446.

Appleton, P., Hung, I. and Barratt, C. (2021) 'Internal conversations, self-reliance and social support in emerging adults transitioning from out-of-home care: An interpretative phenomenological study', *Clinical Child Psychology and Psychiatry*, 26(3): 882–893.

Barrie, L. and Mendes, P. (2011) 'The experiences of unaccompanied asylum-seeking children in and leaving the out-of-home care system in the UK and Australia: A critical review of the literature', *International Social Work*, 54(4): 485–503.

Batsche, C.J. and Reader, S. (2012) 'Using GIS to enhance programs serving emancipated youth leaving foster care', *Evaluation and Program Planning*, 35(1): 25–33.

Berzin, S.C., Rhodes, A.M. and Curtis, M.A. (2011) 'Housing experiences of former foster youth: How do they fare in comparison to other youth?', *Children and Youth Services Review*, 33(11): 2119–2126.

Bond, S. and Van Breda, A.D. (2018) 'Interaction between possible selves and the resilience of care-leavers in South Africa', *Children and Youth Services Review*, 94: 88–95.

Brendtro, L.K. and Larson, S.J. (2006) *The resilience revolution: Discovering strengths in challenging kids*, Bloomington: Solution Tree Press.

Brien, T. and Roumestan, L. (2010) 'Agents of change', *The Big Issue*, 9–30 April.

Butterworth, S., Singh, S.P., Birchwood, M., Islam, Z., Munro, E.R., Vostanis, P., Paul, M., Khan, A. and Simkiss, D. (2017) 'Transitioning care-leavers with mental health needs: "They set you up to fail!"', *Journal of Child Adolescent Mental Health*, 22(3): 138–147.

Charmaz, K. (2014) *Constructing grounded theory*, London: SAGE.

Chettiar, J., Shannon, K., Wood, E., Zhang, R. and Kerr, T. (2010) 'Survival sex work involvement among street-involved youth who use drugs in a Canadian setting', *Journal of Public Health*, 32(3): 322–327.

Corbin, J. and Strauss, A.L. (2015) *Basics of qualitative research: Techniques and procedures for developing grounded theory*, Thousand Oaks: SAGE.

Dima, G. and Bucuta, M.D. (2015) 'The process of transition from public care to independent living: A resilience-based approach', *Revista de Cercetare si Interventie Sociala*, 50: 53–65.

Duckworth, A.L., Peterson, C., Matthews, M.D. and Kelly, D.R. (2007) 'Grit: Perseverance and passion for long-term goals', *Journal of Personality and Social Psychology*, 92(6): 1087–1101.

Dutta, N. (2018) 'Street children in India: A study on their access to health and education', *International Journal of Child, Youth and Family Studies*, 9(1): 69–82.

Dutta, S. (2017) 'Life after leaving care: Experiences of young Indian girls', *Children and Youth Services Review*, 73: 266–273.

Dziro, C. and Rufurwokuda, A. (2013) 'Post-institutional integration challenges faced by children who were raised in children's homes in Zimbabwe: The case of "Ex-girl" Programme for one children's home in Harare, Zimbabwe', *Greener Journal of Social Sciences*, 3(5): 268–277.

Dziro, C., Mtetwa, E., Mukamuri, B. and Chikwaiwa, B.K. (2013) 'Challenges faced by western-modelled residential care institutions in preparing the residents for meaningful re-integration into society: A case study of a Harare-based children's home', *Journal of Social Development in Africa*, 28(2): 113–130.

Fowler, P.J., Toro, P.A. and Miles, B.W. (2011) 'Emerging adulthood and leaving foster care: Settings associated with mental health', *American Journal of Community Psychology*, 47(3/4): 335–348.

Furlong, A. and Cartmel, F. (2006) *Young people and social change*, Maidenhead: McGraw Hill.

Garrett, P.M. (2016) 'Questioning tales of "ordinary magic": "Resilience" and neo-liberal reasoning', *British Journal of Social Work*, 46(7): 1909–1925.

Gwenzi, G.D. (2018) 'The transition from institutional care to adulthood and independence: A social services professional and institutional caregiver perspective in Harare, Zimbabwe', *Child Care in Practice*, 25(3): 248–262.

Harwick, R.M., Lindstrom, L. and Unruh, D. (2017) 'In their own words: Overcoming barriers during the transition to adulthood for youth with disabilities who experienced foster care', *Children and Youth Services Review*, 73: 338–346.

Heerde, J.A. and Hemphill, S.A. (2017) 'The role of risk and protective factors in the modification of risk for sexual victimization, sexual risk behaviors, and survival sex among homeless youth: A meta-analysis', *Journal of Investigative Psychology and Offender Profiling*, 14(2): 150–174.

Hills, F., Meyer-Weitz, A. and Oppong Asante, K. (2016) 'The lived experiences of street children in Durban, South Africa: Violence, substance use, and resilience', *International Journal of Qualitative Studies on Health & Well-Being*, 11: 1–12.

Kelly, B., McShane, T., Davidson, G., Pinkerton, J., Gilligan, E. and Webb, P. (2016) *Transitions and outcomes for care leavers with mental health and/or intellectual disabilities: Final report*, Belfast: Queen's University Belfast.

Lincoln, Y.S. and Guba, E.G. (1985) *Naturalistic inquiry*, Newbury Park: SAGE.

Luwangula, R. (2017) 'Preparing older street children for successful transition to productive adult life: The need to prioritize tailor-made skills training in Uganda', in D. Kaawa-Mafigiri and E.J. Walakira (eds) *Child abuse and neglect in Uganda*, Cham: Springer, pp 311–334.

Magnuson, D., Jansson, M., Benoit, C. and Kennedy, M.C. (2015) 'Instability and caregiving in the lives of street-involved youth from foster care', *Child & Family Social Work*, 22: 440–450.

Malindi, M.J. and Machenjedze, N. (2012) 'The role of school engagement in strengthening resilience among male street children', *South African Journal of Psychology*, 42(1): 71–81.

Mann-Feder, V.R. and Goyette, M. (2019) *Leaving care and the transition to adulthood: International contributions to theory, research, and practice*, Oxford: Oxford University Press.

Oelofsen, M. (2015) *Young adults' experiences of their transition from residential care to independent living*, Potchefstroom: North-West University.

Oppong Asante, K., Meyer-Weitz, A. and Petersen, I. (2014) 'Substance use and risky sexual behaviours among street connected children and youth in Accra, Ghana', *Substance Abuse Treatment, Prevention, and Policy*, 9(1): 1–9.

Polk, D.M. (2017) 'Building community one child at a time: A grassroots approach to taking young South Africans off the streets', *Education, Citizenship and Social Justice*, 12(3): 227–243.

Premsingh, J.G. and Ebenezer, W.D. (2013) 'Homelessness and residential care', *Journal of Humanities and Social Science*, 9(1): 46–52.

Probst, B. and Berenson, L. (2014) 'The double arrow: How qualitative social work researchers use reflexivity', *Qualitative Social Work*, 13(6): 813–827.

Pryce, J.M., Jones, S.L., Wildman, A., Thomas, A., Okrzesik, K. and Kaufka-Walts, K. (2016) 'Aging out of care in Ethiopia: Challenges and implications facing orphans and vulnerable youth', *Emerging Adulthood*, 4(2): 119–130.

Purtell, J., Mendes, P. and Baidaw, S. (2017) *Evaluation of the Berry Street Stand by Me Program: Wraparound support during the transition from out-of-home care*, Melbourne: Monash University.

Shenton, A.K. (2004) 'Strategies for ensuring trustworthiness in qualitative research projects', *Education for Information*, 22(2): 63–75.

Smith, W.B. (2011) *Youth leaving foster care: A developmental, relationship-based approach to practice*, Oxford: Oxford University Press.

Takele, A.M. and Kotecho, M.G. (2020) 'Female care-leavers' experiences of aftercare in Ethiopia', *Emerging Adulthood*, 8(1): 73–81.

Tanur, C. (2012) 'Project Lungisela: Supporting young people leaving state care in South Africa', *Child Care in Practice*, 18(4): 325–340.

Theron, L.C. (2019) 'Championing the resilience of sub-Saharan adolescents: Pointers for psychologists', *South African Journal of Psychology*, 49(3): 325–336.

Ucembe, S. (2013) *Exploring the nexus between social capital and individual biographies of 'care leavers' in Nairobi, Kenya: A life course perspective*, The Hague: Institute of Social Studies.

Ungar, M. (2011) 'Community resilience for youth and families: Facilitative physical and social capital in contexts of adversity', *Children and Youth Services Review*, 33(9): 1742–1748.

Ungar, M. (2012) 'Social ecologies and their contribution to resilience', in M. Ungar (ed) *The social ecology of resilience: A handbook of theory and practice*, New York: Springer, pp 13–31.

Van Breda, A.D. (2015) 'Journey towards independent living: A grounded theory investigation of leaving the care of Girls & Boys Town South Africa', *Journal of Youth Studies*, 18(3): 322–337.

Van Breda, A.D. (2016) 'The roles of agency and structure in facilitating the successful transition out of care and into independent living', *Social Work Practitioner-Researcher*, 28(1): 36–52.

Van Breda, A.D. (2018a) 'A critical review of resilience theory and its relevance for social work', *Social Work/Maatskaplike Werk*, 54(1): 1–18.

Van Breda, A.D. (2018b) 'Research review: Aging out of residential care in South Africa', *Child & Family Social Work*, 23(3): 513–521.

Van Breda, A.D. (2018c) '"We are who we are through other people": The interactional foundation of the resilience of youth leaving care in South Africa', Professorial Inaugural Lecture, University of Johannesburg, South Africa.

Van Breda, A.D. (2019) 'Reclaiming resilience for social work: A reply to Garrett', *British Journal of Social Work*, 49(1): 272–276.

Van Breda, A.D. (2022) 'The contribution of supportive relationships to care-leaving outcomes: A longitudinal resilience study in South Africa', *Child Care in Practice*, ahead of print.

Van Breda, A.D. and Hlungwani, J. (2019) 'Journey towards independent living: Resilience processes of women leaving residential care in South Africa', *Journal of Youth Studies*, 22(5): 604–622.

4

LGBTQIA+ foster-care-leavers: creating equitable and affirming systems of care

June Paul

LGBTQIA+ youth in foster care

Examination of the risks and challenges experienced by LGBTQIA+ (lesbian, gay, bisexual transgender, queer and questioning) foster youth is an important area of focus for researchers. In addition to being disproportionally represented in foster care (Wilson and Kastanis, 2015; Fish et al, 2019), LGBTQIA+ youth face discrimination, mistreatment and rejection in relation to their sexual orientation and/or gender identity and expression (SOGIE) both within and outside of the child welfare system. Although studies on LGBTQIA+ care leavers are scarce, it is reasonable to assume that disparities in health and wellbeing may be exacerbated for these youth when compared to their non-LGBTQIA+ peers. For instance, difficulties that are commonly experienced by youth in the general population of foster-care-leavers such as lower levels of educational attainment, unemployment, economic instability and poor health may be compounded for LGBTQIA+ youth during their transition to young adulthood (Courtney et al, 2011).

Despite the paucity of research, there is some evidence to suggest that LGBTQIA+ former foster youth are at substantially higher risk than heterosexual and cisgender youth for experiencing problems such as homelessness and diminished mental, physical and sexual health after leaving care. Indeed, evidence finds that LGBTQIA+ care leavers are over-represented in populations of homeless youth, and as a result, often engage in survival crimes (for example, sex work, theft, drugs sales) to pay for basic necessities (Freeman and Hamilton, 2008; Wilson and Kastanis, 2015; Irvine and Canfield, 2016; Forge et al, 2018). Capous-Desyllas and Mountz (2019) also noted a high prevalence of substance use and mental health issues in their study exploring the experiences of LGBTQIA+ former foster youth of colour.

LGBTQIA+ foster-care-leavers may also experience greater levels of disconnection from systems of support. For instance, youth exiting the foster care system often face the transition to adulthood at an earlier time period and with fewer support persons in their lives than their peers in the general population (Collins et al, 2010). Again, although research on this population is limited, qualitative studies exploring the experiences of LGBTQIA+ foster-care-leavers mirror these results. Two studies revealed that in addition to having difficulty accessing safe, knowledgeable and affirming caregivers, LGBTQIA+ youth may not receive the types of support they need for healthy development and functioning (for example, gender-affirming medical care, connection to the LGBTQIA+ community) (Capous-Desyllas and Mountz, 2019; Paul, 2020).

Overall, more research is needed to gain a better understanding of the needs, experiences and outcomes of LGBTQIA+ care leavers. Specifically, the majority of existing studies have been conducted in the United States, resulting in gaps in understanding about how these youth are faring in other countries (Kaasbøll et al, 2022). Additionally, there is a significant need for research that investigates the demographics of these youth, as well as the factors that may increase or decrease their exposure to various risks and challenges. For example, little is known about the health and wellbeing of LGBTQIA+ youth after exiting care, or if/how these outcomes may differ among specific sub-populations of these youth (for example, youth of colour, trans and nonbinary youth) (Burwick et al, 2014). There is also a need for research that examines the extent to which policies and practices have been implemented to protect and support LGBTQIA+ care leavers, and if so, how effective they are at addressing these youths' needs. Advances in research in these areas would greatly improve the knowledge base for working with LGBTQIA+ foster-care-leavers, and in turn, offer insights that may help to mitigate risks and provide more inclusive systems of care.

Shifting from risk to resilience

While research highlighting adversities is integral to understanding the experiences of LGBTQIA+ care leavers, it is also important to identify and promote the ways in which this population may be resilient to these risks and challenges. Broadly, resilience is defined as the capacity of individuals, families and communities to successfully find the resources they need to overcome adverse conditions and help them achieve health and wellbeing (Fleming and Ledogar, 2008; Ungar, 2008). It should also be noted that the meanings and manifestations (that is, processes) of resilience are reflexive, such that patterns in the development of resilience vary across political, social, economic, and environmental cultures and contexts (Masten, 2018). In other words, resilience patterns among LGBTQIA+ youth leaving foster care are likely to be different than those of youth in the general population. Therefore, interventions designed to promote resilience among these youth must be culturally and contextually relevant to them.

Resilience research is an emerging area of study among scholars focused on improving adolescent health and the development of LGBTQIA+ youth in foster care. Only a few studies have sought to identify how LGBTQIA+ foster youth engage in resilience processes or how this might impact their transition from care. One particularly salient study in the Netherlands highlighted several ways in which LGBTQIA+ foster youth displayed resilience (González-Álvarez et al, 2022). Specifically, youth relied on themselves as well as their relationships with others (peers, family, friends) to help them navigate and prevail over the challenges they faced. Additionally, these youth were able to locate resources that offered them pathways for exploring, developing and affirming their identities. Youth also talked about how their involvement in activism and civic engagement offered meaning and purpose and provided them with opportunities to give back to others. Some youth even found positive adaptations within themselves to overcome harmful attitudes and behaviours in situations where support from social workers, caregivers and others were lacking.

In another study, Paul (2018) documented that LGBTQIA+ youth who were in the process of leaving foster care managed safety and exposure to risk by relying on a variety of different strategies for evaluating the supportiveness of practitioners and caregivers in their lives. Most youth were open to having relationships with adults that were directly affirming of, responsive to, or knowledgeable about people that identify as LGBTQIA+. Less explicitly, some youth reported that they were more willing to trust adults that were persistent and patient ("She just didn't give up on me"), open to learning ("They was very new to everything, but they was respectful at the same time"), and seemed genuine or had a good 'vibe' ("It was just how she presented herself. I could tell she was a nice lady. You know how you can see a good spirit?"). Others expressed that being confident and open about their LGBTQIA+ identities made it easier for them to establish connections with adults, because they were not ashamed or afraid of how adults might treat them (*Participant*: "I have to tell them what they need to know [referring to sexuality and gender identity] because pretty much, if I don't, how they gonna know what to do?" *Interviewer*: "Did you have any concerns about any of them knowing?" *Participant*: "No, I didn't care. I'm confident in who I am").

Studies examining house and ballroom communities in the United States also highlight the strength and resourcefulness of LGBTQIA+ youth – many of whom have foster care histories – when supportive resources are absent in formal systems of care. These communities consist of adults and youth, primarily Black and Latinx individuals of various sexual and gender identities, that function much like families. Houses are led by adults that take on parental roles and provide resources, guidance and affirmation to youth that have experienced identity-based rejection and discrimination (Arnold and Bailey, 2009; Kubicek et al, 2013). Former foster youths' ability to find their way into these communities, which are often hidden from the general public, exemplifies their capacity to be creative and successful in seeking out resources that are uniquely supportive of their intersecting SOGIE, racial and ethnic identities.

Other studies exploring the resilience of LGBTQIA+ youth, albeit not in foster care, have documented their use of social media as a catalyst for resilience. In the absence of support from family, peers and society at-large, many LGBTQIA+ youth have turned to social media to explore their identities, access information about dating and other LGBTQIA+-related issues (for example, sexual health, gender transition), find role models and connect to others that have similar identities/experiences (Fox and Ralston, 2016). Researchers have also documented how LGBTQIA+ youth have used online networks to share their knowledge with others such as participating in debates or providing education and insight about their identities or experiences (Asakura, 2016; Robinson and Schmitz, 2021).

In sum, although risk-based research has been instrumental in helping to create policies and practices that seek to prevent and minimise harm towards LGBTQIA+ care leavers, solely focusing on risk limits our ability to understand the ways in which these youth develop adaptive strategies and achieve positive outcomes. Alternatively, studies examining the strengths and resourcefulness of LGBTQIA+ care leavers can help to highlight their many successes in navigating the transition from foster care to young adulthood and may be used to develop programming that promotes and contributes to these strengths. A focus on resiliency may also help to create a positive sense of identity, encourage adaptive coping skills and lead to furthering supportive connections, relationships and community involvement among these youth (González-Álvarez et al, 2022). To this end, this chapter examines how we can continue to reduce exposure to the challenges faced by LGBTQIA+ foster-care-leavers, while also engaging in efforts to recognise and facilitate their strengths and resilience.

Theoretical frameworks and perspectives

Four theoretical frameworks are central to exploring this question and for improving the lives of LGBTQIA+ youth leaving foster care: minority stress, life course and resilience theories, and anti-oppressive practice.

Minority stress theory

Minority stress theory has heavily influenced how we think about the impact of oppressive social environments on LGBTQIA+ populations over the last few decades. The theory suggests that LGBTQIA+ individuals experience increased psychological distress as a result of both direct and indirect forms of discrimination and victimisation associated with their sexual and/or gender minority statuses (Meyer, 2003; Hendricks and Testa, 2012). Direct stressors are external to the individual and include experiences such as targeted violence, harassment and microaggressions. Indirect stressors, such as guilt, isolation, shame and fear, are internalised forms of stress and are often connected to the individual's direct experiences of sexual orientation and/or anti-transgender-based discrimination. Expressly, this theory proposes that ongoing exposure to direct forms of psychological distress may lead LGBTQIA+ individuals to conceal their identities, function in a state of hypervigilance, and experience negative feelings in connection to being LGBTQIA+, which can result in longer-term deficits in health and wellbeing.

Life course theory

The life course model considers how historical, geographic, political, community and family contexts shape the development and functioning of individuals over time (Elder, 1998). Within these contexts, scholars of life course theory focus attention on the impact of transitions and/or events that may produce serious and long-lasting effects over the life span. Each transition or event has the potential to serve as a 'turning point', or a major change that alters the life trajectory of the individual, whether positively or negatively (Elder, 1998; White and Wu, 2014; Hutchison, 2019). This approach is central to how we think about LGBTQIA+ care leavers in that it allows for consideration about the connection between LGBTQIA+ young people's experiences within the foster care system, and the structural, social and cultural contexts in which their lives unfold over time.

Resilience theory

Resilience models help to conceptualise the ways in which LGBTQIA+ foster-care-leavers are able to successfully navigate the challenges they face. Although operational definitions and measures of resilience have varied over time, many resilience science scholars have shifted towards an integrative, systems-based perspective (Masten, 2018). Specifically, this framework suggests that human development is impacted by multiple levels of dynamic, interacting and interdependent systems (inter-individual, intra-individual, socio-ecological) and that adaptive functioning occurs in response to factors that exist within and among these systems (for example, socioeconomic status, health behaviours, biology, laws/policies, family, education, social connections) (Liu et al, 2017). Positive or negative adaptations to adversity can impact how well LGBTQIA+ care leavers are able to communicate, access emotional support, establish and maintain relationships, and engage in other life skills as young adults. Further, as LGBTQIA+ care leavers continue to face challenges throughout the lifecycle, so do their capacities for resilience.

Anti-oppressive practice perspective

The anti-oppressive practice (AOP) perspective focuses on decreasing the harmful effects of structural and systemic inequality on people's lives by centering the needs of marginalised groups and capitalising on their strengths and resilience to reduce the negative effects of their environments (Dominelli, 1996; Strier and Binyamin, 2014). An AOP perspective shifts the focus from deficit-based approaches to those that focus on how marginalised communities engage in unique and creative ways to overcome a variety of adverse experiences. For example, social work practitioners that use an AOP approach seek to engage clients in their own liberation and that of others through individual and collective empowerment practices such as participatory action – which includes a range of activities that enable individual to play an active and influential role in shaping the decisions that affect their lives (Christian and Jhala, 2015). Incorporating the knowledge and experiences of LGBTQIA+ foster-care-leavers increases our ability to solve problems and develop interventions that make positive differences in the lives of these youth (Jones, 2004).

When considered together, these theoretical lenses offer an overall framework for understanding how experiences of discrimination may impact the health and wellbeing of LGBTQIA+ foster youth over time, as well as to inform efforts to provide safe, supportive and appropriate care and services that build upon their strengths and resilience. Specifically, inclusion of the minority stress theory is important for recognising that normative criteria for health may not be appropriate for conceptualising the positive adaptations of LGBTQIA+ foster youth. In considering this, minority stress helps to highlight how resilience manifests in the ways that LGBTQIA+ youth navigate discrimination and oppression in their daily lives to achieve greater wellbeing (Asakura, 2019).

Likewise, AOP and resilience theories exemplify the ways in which social workers should recognise the capacity of LGBTQIA+ foster youth to learn and grow. These perspectives not only reinforce the inherent dignity and worth of LGBTQIA+ foster youth, a key value of the social work profession (NASW, 2021), but also creates awareness among youth about their current situations and the need to take action that is necessary in making the successful transition from foster care to young adulthood. Finally, life course theory reminds us how LGBTQIA+ youths' experiences in adolescence are linked to their developmental processes and outcomes, both now and in the future. Thus, prevention and intervention efforts used to understand

and support LGBTQIA+ youth leaving care have lifelong implications for their health and wellbeing.

Structural approaches to protecting and supporting LGBTQIA+ youth

Failure among child welfare systems to cultivate and implement methods that identify, understand and address the needs and experiences of LGBTQIA+ youth contributes to the challenges these youth face both during and after they leave care. In response, several child welfare professionals, advocacy organisations and researchers have developed recommendations for improving systems of care for LGBTQIA+ youth (Marksamer et al, 2011; Burwick et al, 2014; Martin et al, 2016; U.S. Department of Health and Human Services, 2016a, 2016b; McCormick, 2018; Ashley et al, 2020; Paul, 2020; Mallon, 2021; Shelton and Mallon, 2021). As outlined in what follows, these endorsements include legal and institutional strategies (for example, improvements to research, policy and data collection), as well as individual- and agency-level strategies (for example, training and coaching) to protect LGBTQIA+ foster youth and improve their levels of health, safety and wellbeing.

Research and evaluation

Research is critical for helping us to develop knowledge-building tools and resources, and informs our approaches to policy, programme and practice (Burwick et al, 2014; Mallon, 2018). Despite these benefits, research regarding LGBTQIA+ youth in foster care, and those leaving care as young adults, is still relatively limited, particularly among sub-populations such as trans and nonbinary youth and youth of colour. Although scholars are making some important advancements, more studies are needed to fully understand the specific needs and experiences of this population and how other characteristics (for example, race, class) may be linked to short- and longer-term life outcomes (Tilbury and Thoburn, 2009; Grooms, 2020). Ongoing measurement of the effectiveness of services provided to LGBTQIA+ foster-care-leavers is also needed to help inform our decisions about whether care and services are reaching their intended goals, and what, if any, alterations need to be made (Burwick et al, 2014). Such information is necessary for holding government organisations, public and private funding agencies accountable to making measurable, positive differences in the lives of these youth.

Policies and guidelines

At the most basic level, policies and guidelines that prevent anti-LGBTQIA+ harassment/victimisation and address existing disparities are essential for providing LGBTQIA+ care leavers with equitable care and services. Indeed, LGBTQIA+ foster youth should receive fair and appropriate treatment and be protected from harassment and abuse at the same level as heterosexual and cisgender youth in care (Weeks et al, 2018). This includes making sure that they have access to safe and supportive placements, programmes and services, and that mistreatment directed at LGBTQIA+ youth is appropriately addressed (Paul et al, 2023). Public systems should also ensure that LGBTQIA+ foster youth experience freedom from religious indoctrination and the right to freely express themselves (McCormick, 2018). Additionally, guidance is needed to help child welfare agencies and social work professionals carry out regulatory protections, develop high-quality policy and practice models, and ultimately, leverage national and local funding.

Sexual orientation, gender identity and expression data collection

The need for national and regional governments to include SOGIE information as a part of administrative data collection is critical. Without this data, it is difficult to identify the actual number of LGBTQIA+ youth involved in foster care, or to adequately meet their safety, permanency and wellbeing needs. Conversely, having access to SOGIE data could greatly improve our capacity to conduct needed research on LGBTQIA+ youth leaving care, and potentially, various diverse sub-groups within this population. Agencies would also benefit from express guidelines about how to properly collect and safeguard SOGIE data, as well as how to use this data to assess and serve LGBTQIA+ youth and their families (Martin et al, 2016). Although some governments include SOGIE measures as part of their administrative data collection, many public child welfare agencies do not collect this information from youth (Martin et al, 2016).

Mandated training

Despite increases in societal awareness and acceptance of LGBTQIA+ individuals, requiring specialised education and training about the needs, experiences and development of LGBTQIA+ foster youth may help to ensure that practitioners have access to the knowledge, skills and resources necessary to care for this population (McCormick, 2018; Weeks et al, 2018; Paul, 2020). Although more research is needed regarding recommendations for content and format, a few studies suggest the importance of using a bilateral curriculum (U.S. Department of Health and Human Services, 2016a, 2016b; Weeks et al, 2018). Bilateral curriculum includes:

1. instruction on inclusive language, recognising anti-LGBTQIA+ bias and behaviors, LGBTQIA+ identity development, increasing safety and

permanency, managing information related to SOGIE status, and the legal framework for LGBTQIA+ youth in care; and

2. workshops and coaching to assist practitioners in the practical application of knowledge and skills.

Evidence regarding the effectiveness of this curriculum suggests that both components must be implemented to reduce bias attitudes and behaviours and increase practitioners' capacity to engage in supportive and affirming practices (Weeks et al, 2018).

Universally safe, inclusive and affirming resources and environments

One of the most significant challenges LGBTQIA+ care leavers face is having access to care and services that are safe, appropriate and affirming of who they are. As mentioned in the beginning of this chapter, numerous studies have shown that LGBTQIA+ youth may experience rejection and mistreatment by the very individuals whose job it is to provide them with care, including child welfare case managers, foster parents and caregivers (Mallon, 1998; Woronoff et al, 2006; Gallegos et al, 2011; Wilson et al, 2015; Mountz et al, 2018; Paul, 2020). As a result, LGBTQIA+ youth may experience added traumas and suffer from a lack of access to resources that are needed to support their healthy development and functioning.

Alternatively, having access to culturally responsive caregivers and services provides LGBTQIA+ care leavers with a greater chance of achieving positive outcomes in adulthood (Higa et al, 2014; Russell and Fish, 2016). Examples of such care include ensuring that:

1. practitioners and caregivers actively demonstrate a sense of respect and understanding towards LGBTQIA+ youth;
2. youth are placed into safe, permanent homes with stable, nurturing families; and
3. resource and service provisions are universally appropriate and affirming of youth with diverse sexual orientations and gender identities, including those that are in the process of exploring this aspect of themselves, or are not out to others (McCormick et al, 2018; Paul, 2018, 2020; Mallon, 2021; Shelton and Mallon, 2021).

Critical approaches for working with LGBTQIA+ care leavers

The development and implementation of the aforementioned strategies almost certainly improve our capacity to service LGBTQIA+ foster-care-leavers. However, it is essential that social service organisations and caregivers also concentrate on practice approaches that recognise the unique needs of these youth, accept them unconditionally, and place youth at the centre of every process (Baines, 2011; Christian and Jhala, 2015). Informed by the minority stress, life course, resilience and anti-oppressive practice frameworks, this section highlights critically based, mindful practice approaches that public child welfare systems and caregivers should consider in order to fully support LGBTQIA+ youth leaving care. It should be also noted these strategies draw heavily on US/Global North experiences and are not offered in a peremptory manner, but rather, to promote critical attention – that has long been absent – towards the experiences and needs of LGBTQIA+ foster-care-leavers wherever they are located globally. Notably, the strategies documented within this section, while critical for promoting equitable and affirming care to LGBTQIA+ care leavers, may also be useful in supporting a variety of marginalised populations of youth leaving care.

Strengths and empowerment-based practices

Focusing on practices that recognise strengths and highlight the resilience of LGBTQIA+ care leavers helps build their capacity to adapt to conflict-laden life experiences and avoids working with them from a deficit-based lens. Strengths-based practice also compels practitioners to work closely with LGBTQIA+ care leavers to collectively solve problems and meet co-created goals (Singh et al, 2014). To this end, practitioners should seek to involve youth in the process of developing their own care plans, identifying and accessing supports and services, and managing their lives. Such an approach empowers youth to have a say in decisions that affect their lives and provides them with opportunities to build stronger and more trusting relationships with the individuals and organisations that are entrusted with their care (Asakura, 2016). Moreover, working alongside youth as partners can lead to increased levels of confidence and self-esteem, positive changes in beliefs and attitudes about the future, improvements in development and functioning, and ultimately, better life outcomes (Blank et al, 2009).

Building and enhancing supportive networks

One way to build the empowerment of LGBTQIA+ youth is to provide them with opportunities to bolster their formal and informal support networks, both in and outside the child welfare system. Social support is tied to resilience for LGBTQIA+-identified youth through its ability to lower reactivity to prejudice and contribute to identity development and emotional wellbeing (Kwon, 2013; Poteat et al, 2016). Specifically, studies document that support distinct to sexual orientation and gender identity reduces levels of emotional distress, acts as a protective factor against the harmful effects of stigma and discrimination-related stress on psychological wellbeing, and is closely connected to outcomes related to positive adjustment (for example, life situation, LGBTQIA+ self-esteem) (Doty et al, 2010; Snapp et al, 2015).

A potential tool for partnering with LGBTQIA+ care leavers to enhance their access to supportive resources is the 'Support Systems Ecomap for LGBTQIA+ Youth' (Paul, 2021). The tool helps youth and practitioners in engage in focused knowledge-building for the purpose of identifying and enhancing LGBTQIA+ youths' access to different types of support. Co-constructing the ecomap also encourages youth to critically reflect on the strength and structure of their support systems by teaching them to actively explore, identify and address any resource and relational challenges that arise in their lives (Correa et al, 2011). Additionally, the tool may help to facilitate productive dialogue by increasing practitioners' levels of competence and comfort in discussing identity-related issues with LGBTQIA+ youth and fostering further trust between the youth and the practitioner.

Trauma-informed care

Given LGBTQIA+ foster youths' increased exposure to bias and mistreatment, some scholars have suggested that it is necessary for practitioners to engage in a trauma-informed approach when working with this population (McCormick, 2018; Mallon, 2020). Although there are numerous definitions, existing literature consistently refers to trauma as an event or a series of events that is/are experienced as psychologically damaging, threatening or overwhelming to the individual (Goodman, 2017). Trauma-informed care is a service-delivery approach in which practitioners engage in emotionally supportive practices that focus on safety, empowerment and restoring a sense of control – a method that has shown success in working with adolescents that have been exposed to high rates of victimisation and violence (Ko et al, 2008). This includes creating an atmosphere that is respectful to LGBTQIA+ youths' need for security, respect and acceptance, and understanding the need to minimise the potential for traumatisation (Elliott et al, 2005; Mallon, 2020). Responses that fail to understand the context of LGBTQIA+ youths' lives and experiences can inadvertently elicit a trauma response such as psychological reactivity, engagement in risky behaviours, suicidal ideation and self-harm (Butler et al, 2011).

Trauma-informed care should focus on working with families to increase their levels of acceptance around the youth's SOGIE, furthering one's understanding the interrelationship between trauma and symptoms of trauma, and integrating knowledge about and responses to trauma into policies, procedures and practices (Butler et al, 2011; McCormick, 2018). Caregivers and practitioners should also actively engage in the processes of critical self-awareness and reflection to ensure that their practices with LGBTQIA+ care leavers are appropriate and affirming. Such practices include, but are not limited to, using youths' chosen name and pronouns, responding immediately to instances of harassment and victimisation, and helping youth gain access to safe and affirming resources and services.

Positive youth development

In relation to a trauma-informed approach, it is essential for social work professionals to focus on positive youth development (PYD) as a means for supporting and affirming LGBTQIA+ youth leaving foster care. PYD approaches help to ensure that programmes and practices are relevant and accessible to LGBTQIA+ youth, promote their strengths, and provide for the continuity of services in an environment of limited resources. Practitioners can also engage in PYD practices by developing a working knowledge of the LGBTQIA+ community's needs and resources and by initiating the involvement of community members in programme development and the delivery of services (Mancini and Marek, 2004). Creating a shared vision and working with key stakeholders within the LGBTQIA+ community helps us to better understand the experiences of LGBTQIA+ foster-care-leavers and identify the best approaches for meeting their needs. Moreover, engagement with the LGBTQIA+ community can lead to improved youth outcomes, increase the chance of programmatic success, and broaden participation and investment in the lives of these youth beyond the child welfare system.

Efforts should also include collaboration with LGBTQIA+ youth-serving organisations that seek to engage LGBTQIA+ youth in healthy and productive ways and use methods that recognise and enhance their strengths. These agencies are also uniquely positioned to foster resilience among LGBTQIA+ foster-care-leavers by connecting them to others with similar backgrounds and experiences (Gamarel et al, 2014). In addition, PYD efforts can be promoted by connecting youth to student-led, school-based initiatives, such as Gender and Sexuality Alliances and community-service organisations that support LGBTQIA+-based social justice initiatives such as queer youth theatres. Such programmes aim to build a sense of empowerment among LGBTQIA+ youth through reflection and consciousness-raising activities and by providing safe spaces where they can feel supported and freely express themselves (Wernick et al, 2014). They may also improve youth outcomes (for example, psychosocial wellbeing, educational attainment), and in some cases, reduce the negative effects of anti-LGBTQIA+ victimisation on youth wellbeing (Toomey et al, 2011).

Perhaps most importantly, programming for LGBTQIA+ foster-care-leavers should include strategies that facilitate partnerships between youth and the professionals that provide them with care and services. Such strategies focus on prioritising the perspectives of LGBTQIA+ youth as the primary method for constructing knowledge and developing solutions to assist the foster care system in providing respectful and responsive care (Capous-Desyllas et al, 2019). Initiatives that focus on 'youth as experts' can provide LGBTQIA+ care leavers with the opportunity to develop a sense of empowerment and leadership, while simultaneously advancing programme sustainability (Forenza and Happonen, 2016).

Conclusion

Historically and contemporaneously, child welfare systems across the globe have yet to fully acknowledge or support LGBTQIA+ foster-care-leavers. With this goal in mind, this chapter explored how the minority stress, life course, resilience and anti-oppressive frameworks may be used to help conceptualise how experiences of discrimination impact the health and development of these youth over time, and develop research, policy and practice approaches that are theoretically grounded in strengths-based perspectives. In particular, this chapter discussed the need to integrate critically based practice with structural approaches in order to provide a more culturally responsive and effective platform for increasing the health and wellbeing of these youth. A combination of both general and critical approaches not only ensures that LGBTQIA+ foster-care-leavers have access to effective and affirming care and services, it also helps empower them to challenge, resist and redesign oppressive structures that exist within the foster care system.

In addition to this two-tiered approach, researchers must continue to shift from focusing almost exclusively on the risks and challenges faced by LGBTQIA+ foster-care-leavers to studies that recognise and build upon youths' strength and resilience. While risk-related research has provided crucial information for promoting changes to policy and practice, the lack of research on resilience processes has resulted in a predominantly deficit-based approach for working with LGBTQIA+ youth in foster care. Alternatively, resilience research helps us to understand the ways in which these youth cope and thrive, despite the adversities they face. Together, these paradigm shifts offer the chance to move beyond traditional methods of research and practice to more progressive and effective strategies for assisting LGBTQIA+ foster-care-leavers in achieving positive outcomes in young adulthood.

References

Arnold, E.A. and Bailey, M.M. (2009) 'Constructing home and family: How the ballroom community supports African American GLBTQ youth in the face of HIV/AIDS', *Journal of Gay & Lesbian Social Services*, 21(2–3): 171–188.

Asakura, K. (2016) 'It takes a village: Applying a social ecological framework of resilience in working with LGBTQ youth', *Families in Society*, 97(1): 15–22.

Asakura, K. (2019) 'Extraordinary acts to "show up": Conceptualizing resilience of LGBTQ youth', *Youth & Society*, 51(2): 268–285.

Ashley, W., Lipscomb, A. and Mountz, S. (2020) 'A toolkit for collaborative safety and treatment planning with transgender youth of color', in J.S. Whitman and C.J. Boyd (eds) *Homework assignments and handouts for LGBTQ+ clients: A mental health and counseling handbook*, New York: Routledge, pp 140–148.

Baines, D. (2011) 'An overview of anti-oppressive practice: Roots, theory, tensions', *Doing Anti-Oppressive Practice: Social Justice Social Work*, 2: 1–24.

Blank, M., Jacobson, R. and Pearson, S. (2009) 'Well-conducted partnerships meet students' academic, health, and social service needs', *American Educator*, 33(2): 30–36.

Burwick, A., Gates, G., Baumgartner, S. and Friend, D. (2014) *Human services for low-income and at-risk LGBT populations: An assessment of the knowledge base and research needs* [OPRE Report no. 2014–79], Office of Planning Research and Evaluation. Available from: https://www.acf.hhs.gov/opre/report/human-services-low-income-and-risk-lgbt-populations-assessment-knowledge-base-and

Butler, L.D., Critelli, F.M. and Rinfrette, E.S. (2011) 'Trauma-informed care and mental health', *Directions in Psychiatry*, 31(3): 197–212.

Capous-Desyllas, M. and Mountz, S. (2019) 'Using photovoice methodology to illuminate the experiences of LGBTQ former foster youth', *Child & Youth Services*, 40(3): 267–307.

Capous-Desyllas, M., Mountz, S. and Pestine-Stevens, A. (2019) Critically examining participation, power, ethics and the co-construction of knowledge in a community-based photovoice research project with LGBTQ former foster youth, in *Complexities of researching with young people*, New York: Routledge, pp 158–169.

Christian, M.A. and Jhala, N. (2015) 'Social work needs Paulo Freire', *International Journal of Humanities & Social Science Invention*, 4(6): 36–39.

Collins, M.E., Spencer, R. and Ward, R. (2010) 'Supporting youth in the transition from foster care: Formal and informal connections', *Child Welfare*, 89(1): 125–143.

Correa, V.I., Bonilla, Z.E. and Reyes-MacPherson, M.E. (2011) 'Support networks of single Puerto Rican mothers of children with disabilities', *Journal of Child and Family Studies*, 20(1): 66–77.

Courtney, M.E., Dworsky, A., Brown, A., Cary, C., Love, K. and Vorhies, V. (2011) *Midwest evaluation of the adult functioning of former foster youth: Outcomes at age 26*, Chicago: University of Chicago, Chapin Hall.

Dominelli, L. (1996) 'Deprofessionalizing social work: Anti-oppressive practice, competencies and postmodernism', *The British Journal of Social Work*, 26(2): 153–175.

Doty, N.D., Willoughby, B.L.B., Lindahl, K.M. and Malik, N.M. (2010) 'Sexuality related social support among lesbian, gay, and bisexual youth', *Journal of Youth and Adolescence*, 39(10): 1134–1147. https://doi.org/10.1007/s10964-010-9566-x

Elder, G.H. (1998) 'The life course as a developmental theory', *Child Development*, 96(1): 1–12. https://doi.org/10.1111/j.1467-8624.1998.tb06128.x

Elliott, D.E., Bjelajac, P., Fallot, R.D., Markoff, L.S. and Reed, B.G. (2005) 'Trauma informed or trauma denied: Principle and implementation of trauma informed services for women', *Journal of Community Psychology*, 33(4): 461–477.

Fish, J.N., Baams, L., Wojciak, A.S. and Russell, S.T. (2019) 'Are sexual minority youth overrepresented in foster care, child welfare, and out-of-home placement? Findings from nationally representative data', *Child Abuse and Neglect*, 89: 203–211.

Fleming, J. and Ledogar, R.J. (2008) 'Resilience, an evolving concept: A review of literature relevant to Aboriginal research', *Pimatisiwin*, 6(2): 7–23.

Forenza, B. and Happonen, R.G. (2016) 'A critical analysis of foster youth advisory boards in the United States', *Child & Youth Care Forum*, 45(1): 107–121.

Forge, N., Hartinger-Saunders, R., Wright, E. and Ruel, E. (2018) 'Out of the system and onto the streets: LGBTQ-identified youth experiencing homelessness with past child welfare system involvement', *Child Welfare*, 96(2): 47–74.

Fox, J. and Ralston, R. (2016) 'Queer identity online: Informal learning and teaching experiences of LGBTQ individuals on social media', *Computers in Human Behavior*, 65: 635–642.

Freeman, L. and Hamilton, D. (2008) *A count of homeless youth in New York City*, New York: Empire State Coalition of Youth and Family Services,.

Gallegos, A., Roller White, C., Ryan, C., O'Brien, K., Pecora, P. and Thomas, P. (2011) 'Exploring the experiences of lesbian, gay, bisexual, and questioning adolescents in foster care', *Journal of Family Social Work*, 14(3): 226–236.

Gamarel, K.E., Walker, J.N.J., Rivera, L. and Golub, S.A. (2014) 'Identity safety and relational health in youth spaces: A needs assessment with LGBTQ youth of color', *Journal of LGBT Youth*, 11(3): 289–315.

González-Álvarez, R., Parra, L.A., Ten Brummelaar, M., Avraamidou, L. and López, M.L. (2022) 'Resilience among LGBTQIA+ youth in out-of-home care: a scoping review', *Child Abuse & Neglect*, 129: 105660.

Goodman, R. (2017) 'Contemporary trauma theory and trauma-informed care in substance use disorders: A conceptual model for integrating coping and resilience', *Advances in Social Work*, 18(1): 186–201.

Grooms, J. (2020) 'No home and no acceptance: Exploring the intersectionality of sexual/gender identities (LGBTQ) and race in the foster care system', *The Review of Black Political Economy*, 47(2): 177–193.

Hendricks, M.L. and Testa, R.J. (2012) 'A conceptual framework for clinical work with transgender and gender nonconforming clients: An adaptation of the minority stress model', *Professional Psychology: Research and Practice*, 43(5): 460–467. https://doi.org/10.1037/a0029597

Higa, D., Hoppe, M.J., Lindhorst, T., Mincer, S., Beadnell, B., Morrison, D.M., Wells, E.A., Todd, A. and Mountz, S. (2014) 'Negative and positive factors associated with the well-being of lesbian, gay, bisexual, transgender, queer, and questioning (LGBTQ) youth', *Youth & Society*, 46(5): 663–687.

Hutchison, E.D. (2019) 'An update on the relevance of the life course perspective for social work', *Families in Society*, 100(4): 351–366.

Irvine, A. and Canfield, A. (2016) 'The overrepresentation of lesbian, gay, bisexual, questioning, gender nonconforming and transgender youth within the child welfare to juvenile justice crossover population', *American University Journal of Gender, Social Policy & the Law*, 24: 243–261.

Jones, J. (2004) *Report of an action research project to improve the quality of family placement assessments*, United Kingdom: Mindful Practice Ltd.

Kaasbøll, J., Pedersen, S.A. and Paulsen, V. (2022) 'What is known about the LGBTQ perspective in child welfare services: A scoping review', *Child & Family Social Work*, 27(2): 358–369.

Ko, S.J., Ford, J.D., Kassam-Adams, N., Berkowitz, S.J., Wilson, C., Wong, M. et al (2008) 'Creating trauma-informed systems: Child welfare, education, first responders, health care, juvenile justice', *Professional Psychology: Research and Practice*, 39(4): 396–404. https://doi.org/10.1037/0735-7028.39.4.396

Kubicek, K., McNeeley, M., Holloway, I.W., Weiss, G. and Kipke, M.D. (2013) '"It's like our own little world": Resilience as a factor in participating in the ballroom community subculture', *AIDS and Behavior*, 17(4): 1524–1539.

Kwon, P. (2013) 'Resilience in lesbian, gay, and bisexual individuals', *Personality and Social Psychology Review*, 17(4): 371–383. https://doi.org/10.1177/1088868313490248

Liu, J.J., Reed, M. and Girard, T.A. (2017) 'Advancing resilience: An integrative, multi-system model of resilience', *Personality and Individual Differences*, 111: 111–118.

Mallon, G.P. (1998) *We don't exactly get the Welcome Wagon: The experiences of gay and lesbian adolescents in child welfare systems*, New York: Columbia University Press.

Mallon, G.P. (2018) 'Knowledge for practice with LGBT people', in G.P. Mallon (ed) *Social work practice with lesbian, gay, bisexual, and transgender people*, 3rd edn, New York: Routledge, pp 1–18.

Mallon, G.P. (2020) 'Trauma informed approaches to competent practice with lesbian, gay, bisexual, transgender and questioning (LGBTQ) youth and their families in child welfare systems', in M.D Hanna, R. Fong, N. Rolock and R. McRoy (eds) *Introduction to child welfare: A culturally responsive, multi-systemic, evidenced-based approach*, Solana Beach, CA: Cognella, pp 252–276.

Mallon, G.P. (2021) *Strategies for child welfare professionals working with transgender and gender expansive youth*, London: Jessica Kingsley.

Mancini, J.A. and Marek, L.I. (2004) 'Sustaining community-based programs for families: Conceptualization and measurement', *Family Relations*, 53(4): 339–347. https://doi.org/10.1111/j.0197-6664.2004.00040.x

Marksamer, Spade and Arkels (2011) *A place of respect: A guide for group care facilities serving transgender and gender non-conforming youth*, San Francisco: National Center for Lesbian Rights. Available from: https://www. nclrights.org/wp-content/uploads/2013/07/A_Place_Of_Respect.pdf

Martin, M., Down, L. and Erney, R. (2016) *Out of the shadows: Supporting LGBTQ youth in child welfare through cross-system collaboration*. Available from: https://cssp.org/wp-content/uploads/2018/08/Out-of-the-Shad ows-Supporting-LGBTQ-youth-in-child-welfare-through-cross-system- collaboration-web.pdf

Masten, A.S. (2018) 'Resilience theory and research on children and families: Past, present, and promise', *Journal of Family Theory & Review*, 10(1): 12–31.

McCormick, A. (2018) *LGBTQ youth in foster care: Empowering approaches for an inclusive system of care*, New York: Routledge.

McCormick, A., Schmidt, K. and Terrazas, S. (2018) 'Foster family acceptance: Understanding the role of foster family acceptance in the lives of LGBTQ youth', *Children and Youth Services Review*, 61: 69–74. https:// doi.org/10.1016/j.childyouth.2015.12.005

Meyer, I.H. (2003) 'Prejudice, social stress, and mental health in lesbian, gay, and bisexual populations: Conceptual issues and research evidence', *Psychological Bulletin*, 129(5): 674–697. https://doi.org/10.1037/ 0033-2909.129.5.674

Mountz, S., Capous-Desyllas, M. and Pourciau, E. (2018) ' "Because we're fighting to be ourselves": Voices from former foster youth who are transgender and gender expansive', *Child Welfare*, 96(1): 103–125.

NASW (National Association of Social Workers) (2021) *Code of ethics of the National Association of Social Workers*. Available from: https://www.social workers.org/About/Ethics/Code-of-Ethics/Code-of-Ethics-English

Paul, J.C. (2018) *Under the radar: Exploring support for lesbian, gay, bisexual, transgender, queer and questioning (LGBTQ) youth transitioning from foster care to emerging adulthood* (doctoral dissertation). ProQuest (10931481). https:// search-proquestcom.libproxy01.s

Paul, J.C. (2020) 'Exploring support for LGBTQ youth transitioning from foster care to emerging adulthood', *Children and Youth Services Review*, 119: 105481. https://doi.org/10.1016/j.childyouth.2020.105481

Paul, J.C. (2021) 'Commentary: Utilization of a modified ecomap as a practice approach for identifying and enhancing support networks for LGBTQ youth', *Journal of Clinical Pediatrics and Neonatalogy*, 1(3): 45–48.

Paul, J.C., Mountz, S., Dyette, J. and MacDonald, A. (2023) 'LGBTQ youth in child welfare: An intersectional, multitheoretical approach', in R.W. Denby and C. Ingram (eds) *Child and family-serving systems: A compendium of policy and practice. Approaches to child & family protections, core opportunities and challenges in child and family serving systems*, Washington, DC: Child Welfare League of America Press, pp 219–251.

Poteat, V.P., Calzo, J.P. and Yoshikawa, H. (2016) 'Promoting youth agency through dimensions of gay–straight alliance involvement and conditions that maximize associations', *Journal of Youth and Adolescence*, 45(7): 1438–1451. https://doi.org/10.1007/s10964-016-0421-6

Robinson, B.A. and Schmitz, R.M. (2021) 'Beyond resilience: Resistance in the lives of LGBTQ youth', *Sociology Compass*, 15(12): e12947.

Russell, S.T. and Fish, J.N. (2016) 'Mental health in lesbian, gay, bisexual, and transgender (LGBT) youth', *Annual Review of Clinical Psychology*, 12: 465–487.

Shelton, J. and Mallon, G.P. (eds) (2021) *Social work practice with transgender and gender variant youth*, 3rd edn, New York: Routledge.

Singh, J.P., Desmarais, S.L., Sellers, B.G., Hylton, T., Tirotti, M. and Van Dorn, R.A. (2014) 'From risk assessment to risk management: Matching interventions to adolescent offenders' strengths and vulnerabilities', *Children and Youth Services Review*, 47: 1–9.

Snapp, S.D., Watson, R.J., Russell, S.T., Diaz, R.M. and Ryan, C. (2015) 'Social support networks for LGBT young adults: Low cost strategies for positive adjustment', *Family Relations*, 64(3): 420–430. https://doi.org/10.1111/fare.12124

Strier, R. and Binyamin, S. (2014) 'Introducing anti-oppressive social work practices in public services: Rhetoric to practice', *The British Journal of Social Work*, 44(8): 2095–2112.

Tilbury, C. and Thoburn, J. (2009) 'Using racial disproportionality and disparity indicators to measure child welfare outcomes', *Children and Youth Services Review*, 31(10): 1101–1106.

Toomey, R.B., Ryan, C., Diaz, R.M. and Russell, S.T. (2011) 'High school gay–straight alliances (GSAs) and young adult well-being: An examination of GSA presence, participation, and perceived effectiveness', *Applied Developmental Science*, 15(4): 175–185. https://doi.org/10.1080/10888691.2011.607378

Ungar, M. (2008) 'Putting resilience theory into action: Five principles for intervention', in L. Liebenberg and M. Ungar (eds) *Resilience in action*, Toronto: University of Toronto Press, pp 17–38.

U.S. Department of Health and Human Services (DHHS) (2016a) *Findings from the RISE youth qualitative interviews*, Office of the Administration of Children and Families. Available from: https://www.acf.hhs.gov/opre/resource/findings-from-the-rise-youth-qualitative-interviews

U.S. Department of Health and Human Services (DHHS) (2016b) *RISE summary, current status, lessons learned, findings and results*, Office of the Administration of Children and Families. Available from: https://www.acf.hhs.gov/sites/default/files/documents/cb/pii_rise_summary.pdf

Weeks, A., Altman, D., Stevens, A. and Lorthridge, J. (2018) 'Strengthening the workforce to support youth in foster care who identify as LGBTQ+ through increasing LGBTQ+ competency: Trainers' experience with bias', *Child Welfare*, 96(2): 125–150.

Wernick, L.J., Woodford, M.R. and Kulick, A. (2014) 'LGBTQQ youth using participatory action research and theater to effect change: Moving adult decision-makers to create youth-centered change', *Journal of Community Practice*, 22(1–2): 47–66. https://doi.org/10.1080/10705422.2014.901996

White, K.R. and Wu, Q. (2014) 'Application of the life course perspective in child welfare research', *Children and Youth Services Review*, 46: 146–154.

Wilson, B.D. and Kastanis, A.A. (2015) 'Sexual and gender minority disproportionality and disparities in child welfare: A population-based study', *Children and Youth Services Review*, 58: 11–17.

Woronoff, R., Estrada, R. and Sommer, S. (2006) *Out of the margins: A report on regional listening forums highlighting the experiences of lesbian, gay, bisexual, transgender, and questioning youth in care*, New York: Lambada Legal. Available from: https://www.lambdalegal.org/publications/out-of-the-margins.

PART II

Methods of care-leaving research

5

Institutional ethnography: linking the individual and the institutional in care-leaving research

Ingri-Hanne Brænne Bennwik and Inger Oterholm

Introduction

Much research on leaving care focuses on two areas of inquiry: the individual experiences of care-leaving (by care-leavers, social workers and families) and organisational factors, including policy analysis or programme evaluations. Both are important. Individual experiences can help us better understand the challenges young people face and how to develop appropriate support (for example, Paulsen and Berg, 2016; Rutman and Hubberstey, 2016). Research into organisation, policy and programmes can provide evidence of what works and how best to organise support (Mendes et al, 2014; Woodgate et al, 2017). However, focusing on *either* individual *or* organisational matters creates dichotomised perceptions of the leaving care process. Looking only to individuals' experiences risks ignoring the powerful structural mechanisms that shape them. Similarly, research limited to the organisation of services may fail to recognise the everyday experiences of service recipients. Moreover, an analysis only of power structures can ignore the agency of people within these structures.

Some may argue that if taken in combination, the existing body of research on leaving care provides a holistic picture of both organisational matters and the experiences of care-leavers. However, attempting to aggregate such bifurcated research can provide only limited insight into the interactions between the two dimensions. What is needed is an approach that has as its focus the edge – the meeting place – between individual experiences and the institutional practices that shape them. Institutional ethnography is one such method of inquiry with potential to develop research on leaving care that integrates institutional perspectives.

In this chapter, the core concepts of institutional ethnography are presented, showing how this research approach combines people's everyday experiences with institutional perspectives. Thereafter two examples from research in Norway during the past decade are presented and institutional ethnography is used to analyse these data. The studies are related, first, to social workers' considerations about aftercare and, second, to disabled care-leavers' experiences about their aftercare support. The emergent themes from these analyses point to the importance of comprehending how support for care-leavers is organised within different services and how institutional complexes differ among them.

About institutional ethnography

Institutional ethnography was developed as an 'alternative sociology' by Dorothy Smith (2005), a Canadian sociologist committed to doing research *with* and *for* people rather than *about* them. Institutional ethnography is both a methodology and a theory that has gradually spread across the world and is recognised as an important contribution to the social sciences in several countries (Lund and Nilsen, 2020). Fundamental to institutional ethnography is an epistemological and ontological understanding of the social, emphasising that all activity in the contemporary world is coordinated from the outside by larger social and institutional arrangements (Kim, 2018). Institutional ethnography takes an interest in how such social coordination takes place and how things happen as they do (Campbell and Gregor, 2004). The term 'institution' does not refer to a certain type of organisation, but rather to a complex of relationships organised around a distinctive function, such as education, healthcare, law or, as in this chapter, care-leaving. Therefore, an 'institution' occurs both at the immediate, local site of our embodied practice (for example, the act of writing, sitting in a meeting, making phone calls) and through translocal social relations (for example, rules, regulations, discourses) that impact the local activity across space and time (Lund and Nilsen, 2020: 5).

Since institutional ethnography privileges inquiry over theory, scholars interpret the methodology differently, which aligns with Smith's idea that there is no one way of conducting institutional ethnography (Smith, 2005). However, some guiding concepts and ideas apply. As a framework, the two studies described in this chapter draw upon DeVault and McCoy's (2006: 20) description of the research sequence in institutional ethnography: '(a) identify an experience; (b) identify some of the institutional processes that are shaping that experience; and (c) investigate those processes in order to describe analytically how they operate as the grounds of the experience'. Importantly, institutional ethnography is an iterative approach, and the analysis moved between these three steps continuously.

'The data-collection process in institutional ethnography calls for a process of tracking back or following clues forward from the local site and the data collected there' (Campbell and Gregor, 2004: 81). Analytically, there are two sites of interest: the 'local' setting where people live their daily lives and the 'translocal', which cross the boundaries of a particular place (Campbell and Gregor, 2004: 29). The first step is to identify a standpoint, which refers to a local 'site' or a subject position from which institutional ethnographers may begin an inquiry into the social, as it extends from people's everyday lives (Smith, 2005: 10). From the standpoint of individuals – from the local actualities of their lives – institutional ethnography enlarges the scope of what is visible from that site and maps the relationships that connect one local site to others (Smith, 2005: 29). The individual with the experience of the local is the expert on what is occurring locally, and therefore guides the researcher into the institutional context. In the context of care-leaving research, institutional ethnography emphasises what youths, families and social workers know, experience or believe about care-leaving, and thus, that is the standpoint of an investigation into the institutional system they face.

After identifying the standpoint, inquiry continues with an investigation of the institutional processes that impact the standpoint experience (DeVault and McCoy, 2006). The concept of 'ruling relations' helps to understand how this impact is achieved and maintained (Kim, 2018). This concept is used by Smith to name the socially organised exercise of power that shapes people's actions and their lives (Campbell and Gregor, 2004: 32). Ruling relations do not point simply to 'structure' or 'power', but instead refer to an apparatus of management and control (Kim, 2018). Ruling relations are embedded in and created through practices in which people are both objects and producers of ruling, and not something that is necessarily forced upon individuals by an external source. Consequently, an institutional ethnography links people's experiences and the institutional context in which they occur by analysing how ruling relations shape people's actions and how people's agency activates certain institutional elements (Campbell and Gregor, 2004: 60).

Often there is a disjuncture between how institutional conditions are presented in authoritative translocal texts and how people in the standpoint position experience them, which points to the *problematic* in an institutional ethnography. Rather than referring to people's problems or a research question, the problematic here describes a project of exploration developed when the researcher engages with people about what is happening to them and their own doings and how this relates to what is beyond their experience. The researcher, then, must move beyond the local to discover the institutional process and its organisation that impacts the local setting (Smith, 2005: 41).

When practising institutional ethnography, the researcher needs two levels of data: entry-level data about the local setting, including the individuals that interact there and their experiences; and translocal data that helps explicate individuals' experience (Campbell and Gregor, 2004: 60). Throughout the research, institutional ethnography requires analytical work to trace the institutional presence and to focus on how *ruling relations* shape people's experiences.

Finally, the coordinating *force*, or the bridge between individual experience and social institutions, is the *text* (Talbot, 2018), or a kind of document or representation that can be copied, distributed widely and stored, and therefore plays a standardising and mediating role (DeVault and McCoy, 2006: 34). Texts induce people to act in particular ways (Campbell and Gregor, 2004). For example, when social workers fill out a form, the questions guide their answers and shape the participants' experience. Some texts, such as care plans or application forms, are directly activated in a local context while others, such as laws, circulars or guidelines, often impact local actions from a distance.

Introduction to the studies

The Norwegian care and care-leaving context is briefly described in the following section, followed by an overview of the two studies conducted by the authors that are used in this chapter to illustrate the use of institutional ethnography.

The Norwegian context

In 2021, approximately 50,500 children and youth in Norway received support from child welfare services, of which approximately 16 per cent were age 18 and older. About 8,700 were placed in out-of-home care, and approximately 41,800 received in-home services, which represents a small decline from previous years (Statistics Norway, 2022). According to the Child Welfare Act (1992), assistance initiated before a child reaches age 18 may be maintained or replaced by other assistance until the age of 25. Child welfare workers must inform these young people about their right to such 'aftercare' before they reach the age of majority (18 years), and subsequently complete an overall needs assessment as they cooperate with the youths to consider their wishes and obtain their consent for aftercare (Child Welfare Act, 1992).

Aftercare in Norway is part of the regular public child welfare services in the municipalities and most commonly includes extended foster care, supported housing and financial assistance (Statistics Norway, 2022). Unlike several other countries, Norway does not utilise independent living or other aftercare programmes. Among the 356 Norwegian municipalities in 2021, most had their own child welfare services (local authorities), although some had inter-municipal collaborations. As municipalities differ in area and population size, so do local child welfare services, and aftercare support is organised in the way that local authorities deem best. Social workers have the discretion to decide the content of specific aftercare support measures, but the support must be considered in the young person's best interests. If a care-leaver has a disability, child welfare services have a special responsibility to assist them to contact adult services and coordinate services with aftercare, if both serve the young person's best interests (Ministry of Children, Equality and Social Inclusion, 2011).

The two studies

Neither of the two studies began as an institutional ethnography inquiry. However, during analysis both researchers became aware of how the institutional context seemed to impact on the social workers' considerations and on the youths' experiences of aftercare. Hence, it became important to understand more of this dimension. The theoretical and methodological framework of institutional ethnography was found useful when the data turned out to have many references to texts such as laws, circulars and care plans – or general ideas about rules and regulations. Both projects were approved by the Norwegian Centre for Research Data (NSD) and carried out according to ethical guidelines for research in the social sciences and guidelines for inclusion of children in social science research (Ethics approval numbers 701529 and 22271).

Study 1: The first study explored social workers' considerations as they sought to support young people who were leaving care and transitioning to adulthood (Oterholm, 2015). Young people between 18 and 25 can be supported by both child welfare services and adult social services, each of which has different target groups and mandates. The former aids and protects vulnerable children and youth while the latter provides welfare services for adults. The study started out by questioning whether it mattered which service provided support to the youths in their transition to adulthood, an important question because the way local authorities organise support for care-leavers varies. In some municipalities, child welfare services almost always offer aftercare support, including financial assistance, while other municipalities set guidelines for transferring to adult services, especially for financial matters. Nevertheless, support provided by these services is discretionary with no clear-cut eligibility criteria. Therefore, social workers' considerations are significant.

The study was based on qualitative interviews with 27 social workers: 15 from child welfare services and 12 from adult social services. The interviewees represented services with different numbers of employees and degrees of specialisation and were located in various parts of Norway. In the interviews, social workers considered a series of vignettes or short stories about youths leaving care, which were intended to resemble actual situations in practice. The use of vignettes can be especially helpful for obtaining knowledge about the considerations behind professionals' practice (Monrad and Ejrnæs, 2012).

Study 2: The second study sought to examine disabled care-leavers' experiences of the support they received from child welfare services in their transition to adulthood. The study involved qualitative interviews with eight young people aged 19 to 27 years who had been in out-of-home care during their childhood and identified as having experienced one or more impairments, including poor mental health (for example, post-traumatic stress disorder, depression, anxiety, bipolar disorder, suicidal behaviour), learning difficulties, intellectual disability, autism spectrum disorder, physical impairment (for example, paralysis, rheumatic diseases) and behavioural disorders. Many youths in the study, who lived in various parts of Norway, had more than one diagnosis. The interviews focused on three stages of the transition out of out-of-home care: planning, the transition itself and the current situation at least six months after child welfare measures were terminated.

DeVault and McCoy's (2006: 20) three steps approach to analysing interviews, which was used in both studies, is used to structure the illustration of the institutional ethnography from the two studies, namely, (a) the experience, (b) identifying institutional processes and (c) investigating institutional processes.

Study 1: Analysing social workers' discretionary judgement about aftercare

Study 1 compared and contrasted the experiences of social workers in two agencies: child welfare services and adult social services.

The experience

The starting point for an institutional ethnography inquiry is the experiences of specific individuals whose everyday activities are hooked into, shaped by and constituent of the ruling relations under exploration (DeVault and McCoy, 2006: 18). The interviews focused on the social workers' considerations as they sought to support youth with a child welfare background to transition to adulthood. During the interviews, it was striking how differently the social workers from the two different services described the conditions for support and the assistance provided to the youths by each service organisation. Thus, the problematic and starting point of this analysis was the different experiences of the social workers' judgements. These judgements were important when identifying institutional processes, as described in the next section.

In the interviews, the following vignette about Anna was presented to social workers from child welfare services and those from adult social services: 'Anna is 18 years old. She has been in care since she was 10 years old and lives in foster care. She has quit upper secondary school and wants to move and live on her own now that she has turned 18.' For social workers from adult social services, this was added: 'She is therefore applying for financial assistance benefits' (Oterholm, 2015: 141, all translations by authors). The social workers commented on how they would evaluate Anna's situation and meet her needs. Julie, from child welfare services, made a typical comment: 'I would have tried to motivate her to remain. ... I try to persuade the youths to maintain support from child welfare. ... I often say to them that other young people stay home longer now' (Oterholm, 2015: 181).

The child welfare social workers underlined Anna's need for further support and said they would try to persuade her to continue receiving it from child welfare. This view was often related to statements about the extra support youths in child welfare need. For example, Frida said: 'The conditions for youth with a child welfare background are often worse than for other youths. I do not always think the youths understand what they say yes or no to. And how can they know?' (Oterholm, 2015: 182). The child welfare social workers also underlined that they had a special responsibility for youth in care. Henriette explained: 'When it comes to the youth in care, we have a rule that we always follow them as far as through upper secondary school. We mainly continue the placement in foster care' (Oterholm, 2015: 171).

All the child welfare social workers emphasised this special responsibility; however, they also said that the youths had to meet certain conditions. Susann noted this about Anna's case:

Susann:	We would give support, but we have a criterion that they attend school. Then we would have given her support for housing and living costs.
Interviewer:	The fact that she has quit school, would that be a reason for not getting support?
Susann:	Yes, I think so. (Oterholm, 2015: 229)

In other words, there were limits to the responsibility Susann expressed. Because Anna had quit school, she no longer met the requirements they had set.

By contrast, the social workers in adult social services responded to Anna's story with quite different considerations. Laila's comment was typical:

Yes, she would get a social worker regarding her need for financial assistance benefits ... then she would have to apply for housing support, but also get into activity. If there is no illness, they must take part in some activities. There will be conditions for getting financial assistance benefits. It is about not being passive for too long. And if they do not follow the requirements, we will stop benefits. (Oterholm, 2015: 242)

Laila and other adult services social workers emphasised that the same procedures are followed for all new clients, and a care background is no exception. Illness is the only circumstance that could justify a client not engaging in education, training or employment (activation measures) or supporting themselves financially.

When commenting about Anna, the social workers in adult social services also pointed out differences between the amount of support child and adult services provide. For example, Hanne commented: 'I think about the differences in legal basis. In child welfare they will take care of her. She is in their care. But then there is a change when they turn 18. We would expect things of that person because they are 18 and an adult' (Oterholm, 2015: 179). Similarly, Trine also noted the differences in support between the services:

> There is a big difference. When you are receiving support from child welfare, you are a child and have more rights. However, you do not have the same duties as an adult; but when you turn 18, you reach the age of majority and are defined as an adult without necessarily being so. That is the law. Suddenly they must follow the Social Services Act, and the rights are clear, but you also have obligations. (Oterholm, 2015: 189)

Despite acknowledging the clients' young age, social workers in adult social services treated the youths as adults who must meet adult requirements and focus on activation. By contrast, the social workers in child welfare services focused more on the youths' need for support.

Identifying institutional processes

Following the methodology of institutional ethnography, the next step of inquiry was to look for information from the translocal level (so-called level-two data) that might explain the experiences described (Campbell and Gregor, 2004: 60). Institutional presence was traced through the kind of texts that the social workers mentioned. Texts, which are usually a document or representation that can be replicated, such as a law, are the bridge between individual experience and social institutions (Talbot, 2018).

Child welfare social workers often referred to a rule that explained their responsibility for youth in care. Henriette said, "We have a rule that we always follow", which may be a law or certain guidelines. When Susann talked about the requirement to attend school, she called it a criterion for getting support. Such a criterion is most likely rooted in a text such as the Child Welfare Act, circulars about aftercare work or other documents.

Social workers in adult services also mentioned examples of texts being activated. When describing the level and kind of support given, they referred explicitly to the Social Services Act. As Trine pointed out, the act provides certain rights and requires related obligations. Hanne referred to the difference in legal basis to explain the distinction between child and adult services. Although Laila did not explicitly refer to the Social Services Act or specific guidelines, she used concepts like need for activation and distinguished between sick and healthy when determining eligibility. These statements resonated with other social workers' comments and could be rooted in texts such as the Norwegian Public Report (NOU 2004: 13, 2004).

Investigating institutional processes

The next step in our institutional ethnography inquiry was to investigate these texts as institutional traces to understand their content and how they might shape considerations at the local level. The inquiry began with child welfare services: Do they have a special responsibility for youth in care? Is there a rule about that, as Henriette said? The first Norwegian Child Welfare Act from 1896 detailed aftercare provisions for youths placed in residential school homes (Oterholm, 2015). Hence, there appears to be a long, legislated tradition of aftercare responsibility for youths placed in care by child welfare. According to the law at the time of the interviews, child welfare services must consider whether a young person's placement should continue after age 18 or other support measures should be given (Child Welfare Act, 1992: § 4-15, 4th paragraph). Youths who live with their parents and receive support from child welfare services may also receive aftercare support; however, considerations regarding aftercare for these young people are not stated in the same way in the Child Welfare Act, even though the government stipulates that having been in care is not a requirement for receiving aftercare (Ot.prp. nr. 69, 2008–2009: 39). Nevertheless, the act makes a distinction that could impact practitioners to understand they have a special responsibility towards youth in care.

However, the Child Welfare Act does not mention any *conditions* for accessing aftercare support, and in fact, the Norwegian Board of Health Supervision notes that such conditions are a serious misinterpretation of the Act (Statens Helsetilsyn, 2020). Yet, Susann and others referred to conditions like 'attending school' for receiving aftercare support, and if such criteria are not in the Child Welfare Act, where can they be found? Other sources were investigated, which uncovered criteria in local guidelines, both written texts and oral transmission of practices, of 'how we do it' (Oterholm, 2015). Earlier research into local guidelines also uncovered these kinds of criteria (Oterholm, 2008). The reasons why such criteria are set are complex and outside the scope of this chapter, but we point out that social workers were following local guidelines that were more detailed and stricter than national law.

In adult social services, social workers explicitly referred to the Social Services Act (2009: § 20) when describing how they would support Anna. As Susann said, this legislation establishes both rights and duties. According to the Act, financial assistance benefits are subsidiary and may be conditional, but they are an entitlement for those with no other means of income. There are also green papers that emphasise work requirements and participation in job training or education to get people off welfare benefits (NOU 2004: 13, 2004). Thus, the social workers' understanding mirrored the conditions outlined in the law, which they cited and applied to all younger or older adults. The Social Services Act does not stipulate any special responsibility towards young people leaving care, and thus they are treated just like any other service user.

From a viewpoint of institutional ethnography, activities in local human services are shaped by and give expression to institutional ruling relations. Therefore, the differences between child and adult services may stem from their different mandates and legal frameworks, which make them part of different institutional ruling relations. In some municipalities, the practice is to refer care-leavers to adult services for financial assistance, even though child welfare services also can provide this aid (Oterholm, 2008, 2015; Paulsen et al, 2020). Getting this support from adult services implies other duties and adult responsibilities, which some youths may find difficult to fulfil. Such differences are, perhaps, not unexpected but clearly make a difference in the experience of care-leavers at a local level, enabled by the translocal level. Accordingly, it is important to uncover and examine how these differences, with their advantages and disadvantages to care-leavers, emerge as processes that unfold, giving expression to both individual agency and institutional structure.

Study 2: Analysing the experience of disabled care-leavers

In the second study, which focused on disabled care-leavers, the interviews were analysed through a thematic analysis (Braun and Clarke, 2006), which provided understanding of individual experiences of leaving care. However, this was not sufficient to understand the institutional context of aftercare that appeared in the data. Hence, data was re-analysed by tracing institutional influence (Rankin, 2017). In this process, institutional ethnography was utilised.

The experience

The inquiry started from the standpoint of disabled care-leavers in Norway and their experiences of support from child welfare services in their transition to adulthood. All the youths who participated in the study described widespread lack of support from child welfare services related to their disability, despite the impact these factors had on their transition to adulthood:

Interviewer: So, what about child welfare services, did they talk about your [impairments]?
Fanny: No, they stayed away from all of that. (Bennwik, 2022)

Similar statements were repeated in most of the interviews and none of the youths said the issue of their disability was on the child welfare services' agenda. Often, they had different understandings of why this happened, such as: "It is not the mandate of child welfare services"; "The social workers in child welfare services do not care about me"; "They did not know about my disability." However, the fact that their disability was not addressed did not necessarily imply that all support from child welfare services was terminated, only that the assistance did not relate to their disability. For example, some youths said they received assistance to find housing, but disability was not addressed during this process.

Even for youths with severe disabilities and a clear medical diagnosis, disability was not addressed in the dialogue between the youths and child welfare services. For instance, after having an accident, Greg received extensive support from a variety of health services and care facilities, but noted:

'I was supposed to be within child welfare services till I turned 20, or something like that. But I do not know. ... Because everything related to child welfare just stopped [at the time of the accident]. I do not really know what happened. They disappeared. I do not know why. Honestly.' (Bennwik, 2022)

Greg did not receive any information about why this happened and had no say in the decision.

Other youths without clear medical diagnoses also gave accounts of disabling experiences. Ida was a young woman with several mental health challenges, but she did not have a diagnosis that qualified her for the disability benefits or support measures she needed. Ida felt that practitioners in child welfare services treated her disability as an individual 'flaw' or problem, rather than addressing the deficiencies in the healthcare system:

'They [child welfare services] talked a lot about how difficult I was. And that they did not think I would manage well in my adulthood. ... And I had this idea, that it was my fault. Everything that happened. That something was wrong with me. Since everybody treated me like that. ... And I did not want to show them how hard I struggled, because I felt that I needed them too much. And they did not have to help me, because I had turned 18.' (Bennwik, 2022)

Finally, the youths reported how they ended up 'managing' their own disability work, as they tried to compensate for disabling mechanisms and lack of support. Many of the youths used rather bureaucratic language when describing this experience, such as 'referring myself to the psychologist'. Bea described how much work is involved in managing one's own support:

'They [child welfare services] told me that if I moved to that city, I would get no more support from them. They said it was voluntary and then it was just bye-bye! … And right now, nobody helps me. I am trying to get adult social services to take the reins, but they just recently rejected my application. And well, tomorrow I am going back there—I have fought my way to a new meeting. Because I must tell them that … now you HAVE to help me.' (Bennwik, 2022)

These encounters between care-leavers and child welfare services became the 'problematic' in Study 2. The continued investigation aimed at exploring how the institutional processes could create conditions that made it possible for child welfare services to not address disability as part of transition planning and how this impacted care-leavers' everyday lives.

Identifying institutional processes

With an aim to identify institutional forces at play in the everyday experiences described by the youths, the interview transcripts were searched for information about which role the 'aftercare system' played each youth's life. Unlike the social workers in Study 1, the youths in Study 2 often did not refer directly to legislation, circulars or other institutional texts, but rather to care plans, decisions on support, letters they had received, descriptions of legal frameworks and organisational structures present during their transition from child welfare services. Sometimes such institutional traces were clearly defined, but mostly they took the form of underlying understandings or truths about the 'system'.

After identifying a wide range of 'institutional traces', these were analysed through core organising concepts that could be linked to the institution of aftercare. The analysis identified that three ruling relations – mandate, organisation and understandings of disability – were activated in the lives of the youths who participated in the study:

1. Disability was not included in the dialogue with child welfare services, as if it were not part of the institutional understanding of the *mandate* of child welfare services (for example, Fanny).

2. In alignment with the *organisation* of disability and child welfare services in Norway, disabled care-leavers with clear and severe medical diagnoses were transferred rapidly to adult disability services and received no aftercare support from child welfare services (for example, Greg).

3. Many of the challenges faced by youths without a medical diagnosis were not categorised as disability but as individual problems or norm-breaking behaviour (for example, Ida), which could imply that the *medical model* of disability informs child welfare services when planning the transition to adulthood for disabled care-leavers.

Institutional ethnography encourages a continued inquiry into how these locally occurring institutional processes may be linked to processes in the translocal. This study investigated high-order texts like legislation, policy, national guidelines and circulars to gain a deeper understanding of the three ruling relations – mandate, organisation and understandings of disability – with an overall aim to understand how the youths' experiences came about as they did.

Investigating institutional processes

The next step of inquiry involves a change of 'stage' in which people's experiences are still in focus, but the investigation moves from the everyday lives of individuals to professional or organisational work sites (DeVault and McCoy, 2006). As few youths mentioned explicit texts, the scope of the search was enlarged by including both descriptions of organisational structures and legal frameworks/policy. A previous study that analysed governmental white papers about aftercare and disability in Norway identified several high-order texts that were largely unknown to the youths who participated in the study. These texts provided insight into the child welfare services' mandate related to aftercare (Bennwik and Oterholm, 2021). The following examples illustrate the relationship between the translocal and locally occurring institutional processes in this study.

The mandate: policy on aftercare support

A previous analysis of governmental white papers related to adult disability services, reported no notions of aftercare support, nor any descriptions of forms of support for adults in papers about aftercare support from child welfare services (Bennwik and Oterholm, 2021). 'The purpose of aftercare is to facilitate a good transition towards an independent adulthood. Young adults shall gradually become more self-reliant and be able to take responsibility for their own adulthood' (Ministry of Children, Equality and Social Inclusion, 2013: 167, authors' translation). The underlying assumption seems to be that when a young person reaches adulthood, support – at least public support – is no longer needed (Bennwik and Oterholm, 2021).

The fact that these high-order texts describe aftercare as only a transient concept in the transition towards independent adulthood, implies that child welfare services does not consider their mandate to include planning a transition to adult support – understood as dependence. Hence, it is logical that disability is not on the agenda when planning the transition to adulthood, as the interview with Fanny exemplified.

Organisation of services

In Norway, there is an organisational split between disability services and social services/child welfare services, which may explain the youths' experiences of their disabilities going unrecognised by child welfare services. According to the national guidelines for cooperation between child welfare and disability services, the municipality of origin is responsible for aftercare measures and the municipality of residence for disability services (Norwegian Directorate for Children, Youth and Families, 2018). The funding of services by different municipalities, depending on a person's master identity as either a care-leaver or a disabled young adult, creates a schism in the support system for these young people and confusion regarding responsibility for the delivery and coordination of services. As such, the complex inter-relationship of mental health, disability, childhood trauma and post-care challenges is artificially separated by a structural division of funding and service provision that can be used to justify discontinuation of child welfare services. An example is Greg's story of his rapid transition to adult disability services and termination from child welfare services.

Models of disability

While several Norwegian high-order texts, like white papers and circulars, propose a social-relational model of disability, much service provision is granted upon medical diagnosis (Bennwik and Oterholm, 2021). Our analysis suggests that disability is considered the responsibility of adult health or disability services rather than child welfare services, thus implying a medical understanding of disability. For example, young people with a clear medical diagnosis were rapidly transferred to adult disability services and did not receive any further aftercare support (Greg); however, those without a diagnosis received aftercare from child welfare services, and their disability was often framed as norm-breaking behaviour or a problematic individual feature (Ida). This individualisation of disability does not recognise the social oppression that disabled youths encounter in their daily lives. As care-leavers were prepared for a transition to independent adulthood, their ongoing needs and challenges became their own responsibility, as Bea's interview showed; an approach that strongly aligns with the medical model understanding of disability.

How institutional ethnography benefits the two studies

Although these two studies did not begin as institutional ethnographies, this method of inquiry was a beneficial means to explore institutional traces and thus gain a deeper, more complex understanding of the data. In hindsight, it would have been helpful to have woven institutional ethnography more deliberately into our study designs, which could have yielded a more systematic search for texts.

Nevertheless, this approach provided a useful way to understand ruling relations in care-leaving. First, institutional ethnography expanded the analytical gaze from solely local observations to include the translocal, by providing a theoretical framework and methodology to guide the inquiry into the institutional, while retaining sight of the social workers' and youths' initial experiences. This approach afforded an opportunity to challenge some of the conceptual borders, or edges, in the institutional complex of care-leaving. As an example, institutional ethnography illuminated how aftercare texts that emphasised adult independence impacted local aftercare support to ignore disability as a dimension of leaving care.

Second, institutional ethnography can nuance the concept of power, because it shows how people are embedded in institutions, not passively, but rather as active knowers and people with agency. Therefore, people may be both subjected to power and empowered at the same time. This was evident in the study with disabled care-leavers, who expressed a high degree of vulnerability to many decisions made about them, while at the same time showing strong agency in managing their lives.

Likewise, the concept of ruling relations was very helpful in revealing how both care-leavers and social workers were embedded in the same institutional complex and exposed to many of the same institutional forces. This provided understanding of how things were happening, and thus avoided blaming individuals for the challenges that occurred. For example, the analysis showed that the social workers' decisions were impacted by both institutional forces and individual judgement.

Finally, using people's knowledge about their everyday lives as a starting point for inquiry challenged objectified forms of knowledge and rejected the subordinate external knower. What people know matters and constitutes their everyday lives. However, people often may not recognise ruling relations and how these shape their experiences. Therein lies the empowering potential of institutional ethnography. Institutional ethnography makes ruling relations visible for people, and thus, provides grounds for understanding differently and acting differently. The provision of good quality aftercare for care-leavers is not merely in the hands of an individual social worker, but rather is impacted by a much wider network of social connections. Likewise, 'poor transition outcomes' for disabled care-leavers is not the 'individual mistakes' of problematic youths, but rather an intricate interaction between the young person and the way they are seen, supported and understood within the institutional complex of child welfare.

In conclusion, institutional ethnography allowed a strong emphasis on the individual experiences of the study participants (both social workers and care-leavers) combined with the recognition that these experiences are embedded in institutional complexes. An important contribution of this research is a rejection of simplified understandings of the leaving care process. This outline of key concepts of institutional ethnography and the way they can be used may inform and inspire other researchers in the field of care-leaving to employ institutional perspectives in their studies.

References

Bennwik, I.H.B. (2022) *Bridges and barriers. Support in the transition to adulthood for disabled young people leaving care*, Oslo: VID Specialized University (unpublished PhD dissertation).

Bennwik, I.H.B. and Oterholm, I. (2021) 'Policy values related to support for care leavers with disabilities', *European Journal of Social Work*, 24(5): 884–895. https://doi.org/10.1080/13691457.2020.1751589

Braun, V. and Clarke, V. (2006) 'Using thematic analysis in psychology', *Qualitative Research in Psychology*, 3(2): 77–101. https://doi.org/10.1191/1478088706qp063oa

Campbell, M. and Gregor, F. (2004) *Mapping social relations: A primer in doing institutional ethnography*, Lanham: Alta Mira.

DeVault, M.L. and McCoy, L. (2006) 'Institutional ethnography: Using interviews to investigate ruling relations', in D. Smith (ed) *Institutional ethnography as practice*, Oxford: Rowman & Littlefield, pp 15–44.

Kim, E. (2018) 'Explicating translocal organization of everyday life: Stories from rural Uzbekistan', in P. Schröder and M. Stephan-Emmrich (eds) *Mobilities, boundaries, and travelling ideas: Rethinking translocality beyond Central Asia and the Caucasus*, Cambridge: Open Book Publishers, pp 151–176.

Lund, R.W.B. and Nilsen, A.C.E. (2020) 'Introduction', in R.W.B. Lund and A.C.E. Nilsen (eds) *Insitutional ethnography in the Nordic region*, London: Routledge, pp 1–20.

Mendes, P., Baidawi, S. and Snow, P. (2014) 'Young people transitioning from out-of-home care: A critical analysis of leaving care policy, legislation and housing support in the Australian state of Victoria', *Child Abuse Review*, 23(6): 402–414. https://doi.org/10.1002/car.2302

Ministry of Children, Equality and Social Inclusion (2011) *Rundskriv om tiltak etter barnevernloven for ungdom over 18 år* (Q-2011-13 av 22.6.2011) [Circular about support measures for youths over 18 years, after the Child Welfare Act], Oslo: Ministry.

Ministry of Children, Equality and Social Inclusion (2013) *Endringer i barnevernlove.* (Prop. 106 L. 2012–2013) [Prop. 106 L Changes in the Child Welfare Act], Oslo: Ministry.

Monrad, M. and Ejrnæs. M. (2012) 'Undersøgelsesresultaternes troværdighed' [The reliability of reserach], in M. Ejrnæs and M. Monrad (eds) *Vignetmetoden: sociologisk metode og redskab til faglig udvikling* [The vignette method: A sociological method and tool for professional development], København: Akademisk Forlag, pp 141–161.

Norwegian Directorate for Children, Youth and Families (2018) *Barn med nedsatt funksjonsevne – Veileder barnevern og helse- og omsorgstjenester* [Children with disabilities – Handbook for child welfare services and health- and care-services], Oslo: Directorate.

NOU 2004: 13 (2004) En ny arbeids- og velferdsforvaltning. Om samordning av Aetats, trygdeetatens og sosialtjenestens oppgaver [A new work and welfare administration. About coordinating public employment system, social security and social services], Oslo: Sosialdepartementet.

Oterholm, I. (2008). 'Barneverntjenestens arbeid med ettervern' [Child welfare and aftercare], in E. Bakketeig and E. Backe-Hansen (eds) *Forskningskunnskap om ettervern* [Scientific knowledge about aftercare], Oslo: NOVA, pp 161–208.

Oterholm, I. (2015) *Organisasjonens betydning for sosialarbeiders vurderinger* [How organization matters to social workers discretionary judgment about aftercare], Oslo: Høgskolen i Oslo og Akershus.

Ot.prp. nr. 69 (2008–2009) 'Om lov om endringer i barnevernloven' [Ot.prp 69 Concerning the Act on Changes in the Child Welfare Act], Oslo: Barne-, likestillings- og inkluderingsdepartementet.

Paulsen, V. and Berg, B. (2016) 'Social support and interdependency in transition to adulthood from child welfare services', *Children and Youth Services Review*, 68: 125–131. https://doi.org/10.1016/j.childyouth.2016.07.006

Paulsen, V., Wendelborg, C., Riise, A., Berg, B., Tøssebro, J. and Caspersen, J. (2020) *Ettervern – en god overgang til voksenlivet? Helhetlig oppfølging av ungdom med barnevernerfaring* [Aftercare – a good transition to adulthood? Holistic support for youth with experiences from child welfare], Trondheim: NTNU Samfunnsforskning.

Rankin, J. (2017) 'Conducting analysis in institutional ethnography: Guidance and cautions', *International Journal of Qualitative Methods*, 16(1): Article 1609-4069. https://doi.org/10.1177/1609406917734472

Rutman, D. and Hubberstey, C. (2016) 'Is anybody there? Informal supports accessed and sought by youth from foster care', *Children and Youth Services Review*, 60: 21–27. https://doi.org/10.1016/j.childyouth.2016.02.007

Smith, D.E. (2005) *Institutional ethnography: A sociology for people*, Lanham: AltaMira.

Statens Helsetilsyn (2020) *Oppsummering av landsomfattende tilsyn 2019 med ettervern og samarbeid mellom barnevernet og Nav 'En dag – så står du der helt aleine'* ['One day, you're just standing there all alone' Summary of the 2019 nationwide audit of aftercare and cooperation between Child Welfare Service and Norwegian Labour and Welfare Administration (NAV)], Oslo: Helsetilsynet.

Statistics Norway (2022) *10661: Barnevernstiltak i løpet av året* [Child welfare support measures on an annual basis]. Available from: https://www.ssb.no/statbank/table/10661

Talbot, D. (2018) 'The dialogic production of informant specific maps', in J. Reid and L. Russel (eds) *Perspectives on and from institutional ethnography*, Bingley: Emerald Publishing Limited, pp 1–28.

Woodgate, R.L., Morakinyo, O. and Martin, K.M. (2017) 'Interventions for youth aging out of care: A scoping review', *Children & Youth Services Review*, 82: 280–300. https://doi.org/10.1016/j.childyouth.2017.09.031

6

Methodological issues when interviewing disabled care-leavers: lessons learned from South Africa, Norway and Northern Ireland

Wendy Mupaku, Ingri-Hanne Brænne Bennwik and Berni Kelly

Introduction

Research on care-leaving is growing globally. However, for disabled young people,[1] this is still an emerging field of study (Cheatham et al, 2020). Disability prevalence within the care-leaving population varies from 11 per cent (Gundersen et al, 2011) to 50 per cent (Slayter, 2016) depending on inclusion criteria and national context. Existing research indicates that the most common impairment types within the care-leaving population are intellectual disability and autistic spectrum disorder, often co-existing with mental health needs (Lee et al, 2018; Kelly et al, 2022) with varying outcomes reported across disability types (Cheatham et al, 2020). Care-leavers may also experience others forms of impairment including physical, sensory or speech impairments.

As disabled care-leavers reach the age of 18, they often have a dual experience of ageing out of both child welfare services and children's disability services. A small body of research has begun to highlight the complexity of these transitions and the range of challenges facing disabled care-leavers including lack of appropriate housing, restricted post-care education or employment opportunities, limited informal support networks, high risk of mental ill health and vulnerability to exploitation (Mendes and Snow, 2014; MacDonald et al, 2016; Crous et al, 2020; Kelly et al, 2022). However, the evidence base on the transitional experiences of disabled care-leavers is limited with calls for further research to advance knowledge of the experiences of disabled young people leaving care and, in particular, studies that seek to ascertain the views of disabled young people (Harwick et al, 2017).

Given the limited focus of research on disability and care-leaving, little is known about how to design studies to recruit and involve disabled care-leavers or how to negotiate the complexities of interviewing care-leavers who use alternative communication styles or who may need support to participate in research (MacDonald et al, 2016). There is a strong body of work on participatory disability research more generally (Curran et al, 2021; McNeilly et al, 2021) and also a range of care-leaver studies that have employed participatory methods (Dadswell and O'Brien, 2022). However, the inclusive approaches adopted in these separate bodies of participatory research have not been widely integrated to support the development of inclusive research with disabled young people leaving care. Indeed, much of the research on care-leaving has ignored disability issues or excluded disabled care-leavers (Kelly et al, 2016; Dadswell and O'Brien, 2022). There is an onus, therefore, on academics who have conducted research with disabled care-leavers to share their experiences and offer guidance and encouragement to other scholars interested in researching the transitions of disabled care-leavers.

This chapter, therefore, aims to highlight the methodological issues encountered by the authors as they engaged disabled care-leavers in qualitative research in Norway, South Africa and Northern Ireland (NI). Rather than providing a descriptive comparison of each study (details of each study have been published elsewhere: Kelly et al, 2016; Bennwik and Oterholm, 2021; Mupaku et al, 2021), the chapter will present a thematic discussion of the common challenges and methodological issues identified across all three studies and offer guidance to inform future care-leaving research that is more inclusive of disabled youth. While the primary focus is on research with disabled care-leavers, the discussion will also have relevance to the ongoing advancement of leaving-care research more widely to ensure it is inclusive of the heterogeneous experiences of youth leaving care. Before we consider the methodological challenges and issues, it is important to consider the positioning of disability and the country context for each study as these both have implications for research with disabled care-leavers.

Positioning disability

Many disability policies globally are now informed by the social model of disability which, since the 1970s, has challenged the dominant medical model's main focus on individual incapacity. The social model highlights how people with impairments are disabled by societal barriers that hinder the fulfilment of their rights and their full inclusion in society and seeks to eradicate these disabling barriers (Oliver, 2013). The social relational model expanded on the social model's focus on disabling structural barriers to further consider the bodily experience of impairment and the impact of oppressive social relations on the psycho-emotional wellbeing of people with impairments (Thomas, 2007). Contemporary critical disability studies, however, has further advanced thinking about disability. Although still grounded in a commitment to human rights, critical disability studies shifts away from the dichotomous view of disabled and non-disabled people upheld by both the social model and the social relational model to place greater emphasis on fluid interpretations of disability, exposing and resisting normative ideas that stigmatise and produce disability (Campbell, 2009). From this perspective, disability is not a fixed biological condition and traditional dichotomous positions of disabled or non-disabled are challenged and disrupted (Goodley et al, 2018). This perspective bears particular relevance to this chapter on research with disabled care-leavers given the complex identities of disabled youth leaving care and the struggle for care-leavers as they seek a sense of belonging in a society where they experience much stigma and social exclusion (van Breda, 2018). In alignment with contemporary disability theory, advancing the field of leaving-care research requires more proactive efforts to develop participatory methods that engage disabled care-leavers and greater attention to addressing intersectional, disabling barriers and discourses that limit their participation in research and hinder their full inclusion in society.

Methodological approach: bringing three studies together

This chapter draws on the authors' experiences of conducting qualitative interviews with disabled care-leavers across three studies conducted in South Africa, Norway and NI. Each study had a qualitative design and sought to recruit a small sample for in-depth exploration of transitions from care. Table 6.1 summarises the approach taken in each study, including the aims, sample and interview methods used. Across each study, purposive sampling was used to recruit participants with a range of experiences across both leaving care and disability. In all studies, parents/guardians and/or social workers were also interviewed.

The authors have collaborated in different ways over the past few years, and have all participated in the International Research Network on Transitions to Adulthood from Care's Disability and Leaving Care Interest Group. In addition, one author (Kelly) had an overview of the issues relating to all three studies as lead for the NI study and co-supervisor for the doctoral studies in Norway and South Africa. Through this collaboration, the authors have reflected upon methodological issues in their research which led to an interest in synthesising their experiences of carrying out qualitative interviews with disabled care-leavers. The authors began this process by holding a series of meetings focused on the methodological issues relevant to each study to identify common issues and challenges. This process began with each author presenting the key issues for their study followed by a discussion with the co-authors in relation to how these challenges related

Table 6.1: Overview of studies

Country	Norway	South Africa	Northern Ireland (NI)
Study aim	To explore how ruling understandings of aftercare and disability shaped support for care-leavers with disabilities in Norway	To investigate the transition from alternative care for youth with intellectual disabilities in South Africa	To investigate the transitions of care-leavers with mental health and/or intellectual disabilities in NI
Timeframe	2019–2020	2019–2021	2012–2016
Number of care-leaver participants	Eight young people aged 19–27 years old (two males and six females) leaving a range of care settings including residential care and foster care	Six young people aged 17–21 years old (two females and four males) leaving residential Child and Youth Care Centres (CYCC)	31 young people aged 16–23 years old (14 males and 17 females) leaving a range of alternative care settings including family-based foster care and residential care
Recruitment	Recruited via aftercare service providers and social media groups for child welfare professionals or forums for care-experienced youths and/or their biological parents in Norway	Recruited via CYCC in Cape Peninsula region, South Africa	Purposively sampled from the population of all disabled care-leavers in NI to reflect a range of experiences (larger sample frame was based on an earlier survey of the population facilitated by the Health and Social Care Trusts across the region)
Types of impairment	Mental ill health, learning difficulties, autism, physical disability, chronic illness and behavioural disorders	Intellectual disability, autism, mental ill health	Intellectual disability, autism, mental ill health often co-existing with other health conditions (for example, epilepsy) and challenging behaviours
Interview methods	Semi-structured interviews with young people who had dual experiences of care-leaving and disability	Semi-structured interviews were conducted with the young people, some professionals that worked with the young person and their caregivers were interviewed twice at baseline and follow-up interviews	Case studies involved case file reading and interviews with care-leavers, their social worker, carer and, where appropriate, birth parent. Semi-structured interviews with care-leavers were conducted by peer researchers (care-experienced young people) with support from academic researcher when needed
Number of interviews with each young person	One interview (no withdrawals from the study)	Five interviews over an 18-month period as they left care (two left the study during the second wave of interviews)	Three interviews over an 18-month period as they left care (six left the study after the first or second interview)

Table 6.1: Overview of studies (continued)

Country	Norway	South Africa	Northern Ireland (NI)
Adaptations to interview approach	Participants could choose to use Photovoice and life-mode interviews. None chose Photovoice (though several showed photographs when sharing their experiences), but all interviews employed life-mode methods to explore everyday-life experiences	An interview schedule with pictorial support was used. A visual 'life map' was also used to show the transition as well as an ecomap to illustrate significant people in the young person's life. Feelings cards were also to illustrate the young person's emotions about certain aspects interviewed	A shorter, 'All About Me' pictorial version of the interview schedule was provided. Feelings cards were used to illustrate a range of emotions. A visual 'life map' to show the transition from care supported discussions of phases of transition and an ecomap was used to identify key people in their lives

to their own studies. The authors then moved into thematic analysis of these issues to identify three overarching methodological themes. For each of these themes, the authors also collated concrete examples from each study that could be used to illustrate the complexities of researching the transitions of disabled care-leavers in each country and the various strategies used to respond to these challenges to work towards a more inclusive and reflexive research approach. It should be noted that ethical concerns were also discussed including issues relating to consent, confidentiality, capacity and risk of harm. The authors decided that these ethical challenges required separate, in-depth consideration elsewhere and, within the scope and limited space of this chapter, the primary focus would be on methodological issues. The chapter will now provide an overview of the country context for each study followed by discussion of the three core methodological themes that emerged across each of the studies: categorising disabled care-leavers and the effect on recruitment; designing inclusive research tools; and responding to fieldwork challenges.

The impact of country context

It is important to be mindful of the impact of varying country contexts on researching the experiences of disabled care-leavers. How disability is understood within each country's sociocultural context and how disability is categorised within and across child and adult service systems has a significant impact on the experiences of disabled care-leavers but also the approach to researching their transitional experiences. The policy and service structure for aftercare support for youth leaving care is also important when seeking to recruit research participants within these service systems.

In NI, under the Children (Leaving Care) Act (NI) (2002) and Children (Leaving Care) Regulations (NI) (2005), health and social care service providers have clear duties to maintain contact with youth leaving care and provide aftercare until age 21 or 24 if they are still in further education and training. A regional strategy also outlines the role of the state as a Corporate Parent for children in its care with responsibility for promoting their wellbeing and welfare as any parent would be reasonably expected to act (Department of Health and Department of Education, 2021). However, as disabled youth age out of children's services and seek support from adult services there is a shift from a focus on parental models of care to services with eligibility criteria based on type and severity of impairment that is more aligned with the medical model (Kelly et al, 2016). A disabled care-leaver, therefore, is entitled to leaving and aftercare support until at least the age of 21 but may not be able to access adult disability or mental health services (Kelly et al, 2022).

In Norway, a similar division between child and adult disability or mental health services is reported (Bennwik and Oterholm, 2021). Under the Child Welfare Act (1992), aftercare can be offered from the age of majority until the young person reaches 25 years old with the aim of supporting their transition to independence in adulthood. Aftercare consists of the same services that are offered before these young people reach the age of majority, including foster care, financial support, counselling and housing services. The Norwegian welfare system does not have a strong, targeted, legislative framework for the transition to adulthood, neither for care-leavers from the child welfare system nor for disabled young people. There are no national aftercare programmes, but there seems to be an expectation that child welfare services, in combination with high-quality universal support and services for adults, should be sufficient to meet individual care-leavers' needs in the transition to adulthood (Munro et al, 2016). If a care-leaver needs disability-related support, child welfare services are responsible for assisting the young person to connect with relevant services and coordinating support. However, Norwegian studies show that care-leavers facing more complex challenges are often transferred to adult services instead of receiving aftercare from child welfare services (Oterholm, 2009).

In South Africa, care-leaving is referenced in the Children's Act (2005), however, aftercare support is not mandatory and there is no funding for aftercare programmes (Kelly et al, 2020a; Strahl et al, 2021). The absence of a legal duty to support young people leaving care is concerning, particularly as the socioeconomic context in South Africa is characterised by high youth unemployment rates, poverty, homelessness and poor quality education that further exacerbates the challenges facing care-leavers (van Breda and Dickens, 2016). In South Africa the *White paper on the rights of people with disabilities* (Department of Social Development, 2016) is explicitly grounded in a commitment to the social model of disability. However, disabled young people leaving care face significant barriers to accessing adult disability services and transitional support for care-leavers is unregulated, often managed by the Child and Youth Care Centres (CYCCs) providing care. Several providers have noted the absence of support for care-leavers and are developing transitional supports, however, these do not specialise in transition support for disabled care-leavers (Tanur, 2012).

Across all three country contexts, therefore, disabled care-leavers are vulnerable to being unsupported due to significant gaps in policy and service provision. The varying policy and country contexts outlined reflect the complex challenges disabled care-leavers are likely to encounter as they navigate their way from care into young adult life and underline the importance of addressing the experiences of disabled young people in care-leaver research. These issues also indicate that the categorisation of disabled care-leavers within these complex and often inadequate service systems is likely to impact on researchers' efforts to identify and recruit disabled care-leavers as research participants.

Categorisation of disabled care-leavers and the impact on recruitment

The implications of these varied country contexts for recruitment and sampling of disabled care-leavers in each of our studies were multiple. Each study sought to recruit disabled care-leavers via the main child welfare or care/aftercare service providers. However, these service providers in each country initially indicated that disabled young people would not be within their service remit. On the other hand, disability and mental health service providers indicated that disabled care-leavers would not be within their services as they should be located within services for youth leaving care. This dual lack of recognition for disabled care-leavers highlights how this population can fall between the gaps in services with no service taking lead responsibility for their welfare.

The researchers in all three countries, therefore, had to spend considerable time working with service providers to help them to identify disabled care-leavers within their services. At times, this required use of medical model language that service providers used, including clarity about types and levels of impairment. Across the studies, researchers were asked by gatekeepers to stipulate the range of conditions/disorders that could be included in the study, often with a narrow focus on a clearly diagnosed medical condition or severe impairment. While this may help to guide gatekeepers with their identification of study participants, it may also serve to exclude those with unspecified conditions, those not yet formally diagnosed and those with less severe levels of impairment. This use of medical language also evoked theoretical and methodological challenges that required ongoing, sensitive negotiation with gatekeepers.

Opportunities to discuss study inclusion criteria and the complexities of defining disability with individual gatekeepers usually helped to address these issues and identify disabled care-leavers within the service system, however, researchers were also often told that the potential participant was 'too impaired' or 'vulnerable' to participate in research, indicating an over-protectionist stance. This required further negotiation with service providers. For example, sometimes the social worker's concern about the vulnerability of the young person could be allayed when the researcher explained more about the participatory approach being used or if the timing of the invitation to participate was delayed to avoid current issues (for example, the young person was recovering from an illness or had recently moved to new housing).

A further issue impacting on recruitment was the extent to which young people who were approached to participate in the study self-identified as disabled. Across our studies, we were aware of this issue and ensured that study recruitment materials did not place an over-emphasis on disability or impairment. Many young people contacted to participate in the three studies did not use the term disability to describe their own identity or identify as being disabled, even if they could describe many disabling experiences. As an example, one care-leaver who did not consider themselves to be disabled and did not wish to use disability services was denied access to generic job-training and the regular housing market and found that they had no choice but to receive support from disability services. This presented a clash between the research and service categories of disabled youth leaving care and the young people's own self-identities. In some instances, young people were happy to confirm they were in receipt of disability services which helped to confirm eligibility for the study but did not self-identify as disabled. This disassociation with categories of disablement is unsurprising given the dominance of the medical model focus on impairment-related deficits, the social oppression of disabled people and the cultural stigma associated with disability (Rohwerder, 2018). However, it should be noted that there may be multiple other reasons for this disassociation including lack of knowledge of disability-related terminology or own diagnosis or, indeed, integration of disability-related experiences as a normative part of the young person's identity/daily experience that does not require a label or identification as disabled (Kelly, 2005). In parallel to this disassociation with disability, young people leaving care can also be keen to shed their identity as a care-leaver due to the stigma of being a former child in care (Frimpong-Manso, 2018). For disabled care-leavers rejecting these intersecting social identity categories is understandable as young people are keen to minimise the risk of further stigma and marginalisation (Kelly et al, 2020a).

The researchers, therefore, were acutely aware of how the categories 'disabled' and 'care-leaver' are embedded in discourses of oppression and the potential risk and, by relying on such categories, researchers can inadvertently reproduce dominant understandings of disability and care that are not beneficial to the young people participating in research (Stone and Priestley, 1996). In contrast, we have learnt that the onus is on the researcher to use this insight to enable socially marginalised young people to transform oppressive categories and open new understandings of the intersections of disability and leaving care. This encourages the researcher to reflect critically upon how they work with these categories in research and how research can potentially counteract disabling effects. A positive experience from the researchers' dialogue with professionals was that new understandings of disability could emerge that challenged practice grounded in the medical model and encouraged a deconstructed understanding of disability that recognised the political processes of classification and drew attention to social structures rather than the individual attributes. Likewise, it was fruitful to discuss how these 'disabled' and 'care-leaver' identities may intersect and/or obscure other forms of social and personal difference.

In summary, therefore, several stages of the recruitment process developed into a negotiation with service providers and potential participants about what it means to be disabled, what terms could be used to describe disability and leaving care, and how self-identification can be promoted within the research rather than used as a strategy to exclude young people. These conversations led to an enhanced understanding of both disability and care-leaving among the research teams, but also within the professional community facilitating each study. This ongoing process of critical reflection and negotiation of categories informed the theoretical approach to the research, drawing on ideas from critical disability studies to stay close to the language used by study participants while maintaining a commitment to understanding disability as a matter of social justice (McNeilly et al, 2021). While inclusive and open understandings of disability was helpful in the recruitment stage, as it both avoided imposing categories on young people and helped include those with borderline/undiagnosed disability, the researchers recognise the need to approach this carefully to ensure participants have relevant experiences to address research questions. For example, in the Norwegian study young people who did not self-identify as disabled were only included in the study if they had experiences relevant to the study's core research questions and gave clear accounts of experiences relevant to disability issues, such as experience of disablism, use of disability services or categorisation as disabled by service providers.

Designing an inclusive research approach

Various strategies may need to be employed to enable an inclusive and reflexive approach to involving disabled care-leavers in research. Researchers will need to consider adaptations to their usual interviewing methods and make refinements to interview guides and communication tools to accommodate a range of participants (Teachman, 2019). Such adaptations and preparatory work are aimed at equipping the researcher with a range of skills and tools that can be used reflexively to meet individual participant needs/ preferences rather than a disablist focus on individual levels of incapacity or lack of cognition. The emphasis is on how the researcher can facilitate the engagement of disabled care-leavers in the interview process rather than the participant's individual limitations (McNeilly et al, 2021).

In our studies, a range of adaptations and communication aids were utilised to facilitate the inclusion of disabled care-leavers in interviews. Carefully piloting of interview guides and communication tools with disabled young people was essential to test out the range of options available and different levels of interview schedules. Such piloting exercises also provide an opportunity for disabled young people to assist with the design and development of the research tools. For example, in the Northern Irish study a Young People's Advisory group with members who had experience of disability and leaving care guided the development of the research tools and assisted with the piloting of interview schedules (Kelly et al, 2016). This helped to create a more inclusive approach that enabled participation, but avoided a paternalistic or age inappropriate approach.

We also found that it was important to have at least two different versions of the interview schedule to reflect a range of literacy, comprehension and concentration abilities, but still enable the collection of useful data relevant to the study's aims and objectives. For example, in the Northern Irish study, a longer interview schedule was shortened to produce a more accessible version that still addressed the same core themes but used shorter question styles and more accessible language. Across our studies, visual representations of transitions or interview themes also helped to introduce more creative ways for disabled young people to engage with the interview. Graphics, ecomaps, sentence completion and drawing or writing activities also prompted further discussion to enable disabled young people to share their perspectives (Teachman, 2019). For example, on the South African study, visual life-maps aligned with the interview questions about how they envisioned their lives after care helped to identify hopes and goals for the future (Mupaku et al, 2021). Similar pictorial techniques were used in the NI study which used an 'All About Me' booklet that had a page for each theme on the semi-structured interview schedule that was visually presented to invite discussion, inclusion of photographs and writing or drawing activities (Kelly et al, 2016). This study also found it helpful to use visual cards to depict like/dislike, yes/no and a range of feelings were used to illustrate emotions. These alternative interview approaches and aids helped to provide a 'communication toolbox' offering a range of ways to participate that could be used by young people with different levels of capacity. In introductory visits, young people were shown these tools and could decide with the researcher which approaches would be most helpful to facilitate their interview.

In the Norwegian study, user organisations for care-leavers and disabled youth were consulted in order to identify potential communication challenges and to seek advice on how best to design an inclusive interview guide. Similar to the other two studies, the Norwegian researcher held an initial meeting with each young person to develop rapport and explore how best to approach each interview including the timing of the interview, where it would be conducted and how to address any potential communication challenges. At this early stage, the researcher tried out different types and levels of questions and adjusted the interview approach according to the needs and preferences of each young person. In this study, the interviews adopted a life-mode interview approach (Haavind, 2014). Here, the young person was encouraged to openly describe their daily everyday lives rather than being asked direct questions about impairment or disability which was particularly helpful when participants did not identify with disability or impairment. This approach enabled the researcher to learn from the young person and use language they preferred to describe bodily experiences or disabling encounters at later stages of the interview process. Reflecting critical disability studies, such experiences highlight how researchers need to adopt an individualised and fluid approach to language that is responsive to the preferences of participants rather than imposing terminology routinely used by service providers.

Responding to fieldwork challenges

Despite all efforts to prepare for interviews and design a range of accessible and inclusive research tools, challenges were encountered during each of our studies, highlighting the need for a reflexive approach as the research progresses. Across all three studies, a key challenge was the need to adapt the interview approach in response to the individual needs of the young person while avoiding the risk of a paternalistic, disablist or age-inappropriate approach.

In most cases researchers had access to information about the young person before the interview, including their impairment type, communication style and any potential issues relating to literacy, concentration, memory or sensory issues. This information was sometimes presented by carers or professionals as a barrier to the young person's participation in the study with a focus on deficits, traditionally aligned with medical model thinking. While it is helpful to have access to information about the young person's support needs or communication preferences, across our studies we found it was important to only use this information as guidance and to still make every effort to overcome barriers to the young person's participation in interviews. In accordance with critical disability studies, the researchers focused on establishing rapport with each young person and developing an effective communication approach that could facilitate their participation in an interview. In South Africa and NI, this involved offering the young person options, showing them the range of visual aids and communication tools available and trying out different levels of question styles or communication methods (including those more familiar to the young person that the research may not have considered) to establish which level of interview schedule might work best. These studies also involved multiple interviews over time which gave the participant and researcher more time to develop their relationship and an opportunity to further refine research tools in advance of follow-up interviews with each participant.

During fieldwork, the researchers also had to be responsive to the everyday context of care-leavers' lives and ensure that interviews were carefully scheduled at times that best suited the young person. For example, avoiding times of the day when they were likely to be busy with other demands or be feeling tired. For some participants, it was also important to remember to offer frequent breaks or shorter, multiple interviews over several visits rather than one lengthy interview. These findings indicate that, at the stage of planning and costing a study involving disabled care-leavers, research teams need to factor in additional time and resources to facilitate their meaningful involvement.

In most cases, across our studies, the researcher was able to proceed with an interview. However, in a very small number of cases, an interview was not possible. These young people had multiple and complex impairments and often exhibited high levels of distress when meeting a researcher who was unfamiliar and not part of their daily routine. In these cases, rather than exclude the young person and their unique experience of leaving care, information was gathered by spending time with the young person, observing their experiences, and collecting information about their transition from those who cared for them and knew them well (often carers/parents or key professionals). While gathering information from other sources by proxy is not ideal, it is important for the researcher to uphold an ethical and sensitive response to individual needs that may mean an interview is not always possible or appropriate (indeed it could be disabling) and alternative methods are needed to more meaningfully capture the experiences of some disabled young people (Kelly, 2007; Teachman, 2019).

The involvement of parents/carers was another key challenge across our studies. Parents/carers usually know the young person well and can provide helpful information about their support needs and communication styles. They can also be a useful source of support for the young person during initial visits and can sometimes help with interpreting sign systems or expressions used by the young person. However, parents/carers may be inclined to speak for the young person and young people may expect their parent/carer to be present during the interview and speak on their behalf. This can be a well-established practice for both the young person and their parent/carer when engaging with professionals over the years (McNeilly et al, 2021). It is important, therefore, for the researcher to explain the boundaries of the parent/carer role in the interview from the outset. If the young person would like their parent/carer to be present, the researcher needs to emphasise that the focus is on the young person's views and experiences rather than the parent/carer perspective. In several cases, following interviews with disabled young people, parents/carers asked the researcher what the young person had said, usually due to a genuine interest in their expressed views that they may not have previously known. However, in these situations, the researcher should explain the boundaries of confidentiality and reassure the young person that their right to confidentiality will be respected.

A further challenge particularly relevant to longitudinal research with disabled young people is the retention of participants. Researchers working on longitudinal studies with care-leavers during their transitions from care are familiar with this challenge (van Breda, 2020). However, for disabled care-leavers there can be additional, often unexpected challenges affecting retention. Across our studies some disabled young people experienced periods of ill health, hospital admissions, adjustments to medication or treatment and changes to their daily routines that significantly disrupted their availability to continue with their participation in the research. In these circumstances, researchers must provide flexible choices for participants about how and when they wish to be interviewed and offer all possible opportunities for participation for those keen to continue their engagement in the study. In our studies, the researchers were flexible and arranged alternative, later dates for interviews. However, delays in follow-up interviews also made it difficult for some disabled young people to recall earlier interviews or details of the study. This could mean spending more time with participants to re-explain the purpose of the research and the nature of their ongoing involvement in the study. Previous studies have used a range of strategies to assist with recall and to maintain a connection with participants during delays in data collection that could also be usefully applied, including: timelines of the research stages; photographs of research activities; pictorial bookmarks depicting the seasons and time span between data collection points; and postcard or web-based updates (Kelly, 2007; Weller, 2012). Across our studies, we have found that staying in regular contact with participants in the time lapse between interviews helps to maintain this rapport over time and encourages retention. We kept in contact with participants by telephone, text or email and found that this ongoing contact: demonstrated a commitment on behalf of the research team to facilitate their involvement of the participant; provided opportunities to update participants on the study's progress; and also gave the researcher further insight into the young person's transitional journey and any changes in their circumstances.

Conclusion

Disabled young people are a significant, marginalised sub-group within the population of youth leaving care across the globe but have been under-represented in the field of care-leaver research (Slayter, 2016; Harwick et al, 2017). This chapter has reflected on the experiences of three studies involving disabled care-leavers in research to inform and encourage others working in this field to engage disabled youth in their future studies of care-leaving. From the outset, how disability is recognised and understood has a profound impact on the attitudes and approaches of service providers, researchers and young people themselves. Researching the experiences of disabled care-leavers requires an understanding of: the misrecognition of disabled youth leaving care within and across service systems; and the impact of stigma and oppression associated with both disability and leaving care on the identities of disabled youth leaving care. These insights underline the need for researchers to commit to inclusive research approaches that challenge and address barriers to the participation of disabled care-leavers. Fundamentally, researchers in the field of leaving care should actively seek to recruit disabled care-leavers and be tenacious in their negotiations with gatekeepers to broaden and deepen opportunities for disabled youth to participate not only as but also potentially as advisors and co-researchers (Kelly et al, 2020b; Curran et al, 2021). Researchers are encouraged to develop inclusive research methods and tools but also to engage in reciprocal dialogue with professionals, parents/carers and young people to push the boundaries of traditional, often paternalistic, approaches to disability and leaving care. Across our studies, participants had diverse experiences of both disability and care-leaving and a wide range of cognitive, social, and communication abilities and preferences. These variances demand a reflexive research approach that is person-centred to facilitate the inclusion of each participant. Our studies also highlight that disabled youth leaving care are not a homogeneous group and we have much to learn from the intersectional and varied experiences of disabled care-leavers in different national contexts across the Global North/South. Informed by a critical disability studies perspective, we encourage others researching in the field of leaving care to learn from the messages from our research to meaningfully engage disabled youth in their research and continue the journey towards a more inclusive care-leaver research agenda that enhances our understanding of the views and experiences of disabled youth leaving care.

Note

[1] In alignment with the social model of disability, this chapter uses the terms: 'disabled young people' (rather than young people with disabilities) to recognise disability as a form of social oppression experienced by people with impairments; and 'impairment' to refer to the bodily lived experience of participants and to reflect impairment-related labels used by service providers. The authors recognise, however, that varied terminology is used across service contexts and by disabled people.

References

Bennwik, I.H.B. and Oterholm, I. (2021) 'Policy values related to support for care leavers with disabilities', *European Journal of Social Work*, 24(5): 884–895.

Campbell, F.K. (2009) *Contours of ableism: The production of disability and abledness*, London: Palgrave Macmillan.

Cheatham, L., Randolph, K. and Boltz, L. (2020) 'Youth with disabilities transitioning from foster care: Examining prevalence and predicting positive outcomes', *Children and Youth Services Review*, 110. Doi: 10.1016/j.childyouth.2020.104777

Crous, G., Montserrat, C. and Balaban, A. (2020)'Young people leaving care with intellectual disabilities or mental health problems: Strengths and weaknesses in their transitions', *Social Work & Society*, 18(3): 1–19.

Curran, T., Jones, M., Ferguson, S., Reed, M., Lawrence, A., Cull, N. and Stabb, M. (2021) 'Disabled young people's hopes and dreams in a rapidly changing society: A co-production peer research study', *Disability and Society*, 26(4): 561–578. https://doi.org/10.1080/09687599.2020.1755234

Dadswell, A. and O'Brien, N. (2022) 'Participatory research with care leavers to explore their support experiences during the COVID-19 pandemic', *The British Journal of Social Work*, 52(6): 3639–3657.

Department of Health and Department of Education (2021) *A life deserved: 'Caring' for children and young people in Northern Ireland*, Belfast: Department of Health and Department of Education.

Department of Social Development (2016) *White paper on the rights of people with disabilities*, Johannesburg: Department of Social Development.

Frimpong-Manso, K. (2018) 'Building and utilising resilience: The challenges and coping mechanisms of care leavers in Ghana', *Children and Youth Services Review*, 87: 52–59.

Goodley, D., Liddiard, K. and Runswick-Cole, K. (2018) 'Feeling disability: Theories of affect and critical disability studies', *Disability & Society*, 33(2): 197–217.

Gundersen, T., Farstad, G.R. and Solberg, A. (2011) *Division of responsibilities for the benefit of children? Children and young people with disabilities in child welfare*, Oslo: Norwegian Institute for Research on Upbringing, Welfare and Aging.

Haavind, H. (2014) 'Who does he think he is? Making new friends and leaving others behind – on the path from childhood to youth', in M. Schott and D.M. Søndergaard (eds) *School bullying: New theories in context*, Cambridge: Cambridge University Press, pp 129–158.

Harwick, R.M., Lindstrom, L. and Unruh, D. (2017) 'In their own words: Overcoming barriers during the transition to adulthood for youth with disabilities who experienced foster care', *Children and Youth Services Review*, 73: 338–346. https://doi.org/10.1016/j.childyouth.2017.01.011

Kelly, B. (2005) '"Chocolate makes you autism": Impairment, disability and childhood identities', *Disability and Society*, 20(3): 261–275. https://doi.org/10.1080/09687590500060687

Kelly, B. (2007) 'Methodological issues for qualitative research with learning disabled children', *International Journal of Social Research Methodology*, 10(1): 21–35. https://doi.org/10.1080/13645570600655159

Kelly, B., McShane, T., Davidson, G., Pinkerton, J., Gilligan, E. and Webb, P. (2016) *Transitions and outcomes for care leavers with mental health and/or intellectual disabilities: Final report*, Belfast: QUB. Available from: https://research.hscni.net/sites/default/files/YOLO%20Final%20Report.pdf

Kelly, B., van Breda, A., Bekoe, J., Bukuluki, P., Chereni, A., Frimpong-Manso, K., Luwangula, R., Pinkerton, J., Ringson, J. and Santin, O. (2020a) *Building positive futures: A cross-country pilot study on youth transitions from alternative care in Africa*, Belfast: QUB. Available from: https://pureadmin.qub.ac.uk/ws/portalfiles/portal/219945215/Building_Positive_Futures_Main_report.pdf

Kelly, B., Friel, S., McShane, T., Pinkerton, J. and Gilligan, E. (2020b) '"I haven't read it, I've lived it!": The benefits and challenges of peer research with young people leaving care', *Qualitative Social Work*, 19(1): 108–124.

Kelly, B., Webb, P., Davidson, G., Pinkerton, J. and McShane, T. (2022) 'Raising the profile of care leavers with mental health and/or intellectual disabilities: A contribution from Northern Ireland', *Children and Youth Services Review*, 136. doi: 10.1016/j.childyouth.2022.106434

Lee, J., Powers, L., Geenen, S., Schmidt, J., Blakeslee, J. and Hwang, I. (2018) 'Mental health outcomes among youth in foster care with disabilities', *Children and Youth Services Review*, 94 : 27–34. https://doi.org/10.1016/j.childyouth.2018.09.025

MacDonald, S., Ellem, K. and Wilson, J. (2016) 'Supporting young people with an intellectual disability transitioning from out-of-home care to adult life in Queensland, Australia', in P. Mendes and P. Snow (eds) *Young people transitioning from out-of-home care: International research, policy and practice*, London: Palgrave, pp 45–69.

McNeilly, P., Macdonald, G. and Kelly, B. (2021) 'Rights based, participatory interviews with disabled children and young people: Practical and methodological considerations', *Comprehensive Child and Adolescent Nursing*, 45(2): 217–226. https://doi.org/10.1080/24694193.2021.1874078

Mendes, P. and Snow, P. (2014) 'The needs and experiences of young people with a disability transitioning from out-of-home care: The views of practitioners in Victoria, Australia', *Children and Youth Services Review*, 36: 115–123. https://doi.org/10.1016/j.childyouth.2013.11.019

Mupaku, W., van Breda, A. and Kelly, B. (2021) 'Transitioning to adulthood from residential childcare during COVID-19: Experiences of young people with intellectual disabilities and/or Autism Spectrum Disorder in South Africa'. *British Journal of Learning Disabilities*, 49: 341–351. http://doi.org/10.1111/bld.12409

Munro, E.R., Mølholt, A.K. and Hollingworth, K. (2016) 'Leaving care in the UK and Scandinavia: Is it all that different in contrasting welfare regimes?', in P. Mendes and P. Snow (eds) *Young people transitioning from out-of-home care*, London: Palgrave Macmillan, pp 199–219.

Oliver, M. (2013) 'The social model of disability thirty years on', *Disability & Society*, 28(7): 1024–1026. https://doi.org/10.11080/09687599.2013.818773

Oterholm, I. (2009) 'How do the child welfare services in Norway work with young people leaving care?', *Vulnerable Children and Youth Studies*, 4(2): 169–175. https://doi.org/10.1080/17450120902927636

Rohwerder, B. (2018) *Disability stigma in developing countries*, Brighton: Institute of Development Studies.

Slayter, E. (2016) 'Foster care outcomes for children with intellectual disability', *Intellectual and Developmental Disabilities*, 54(5): 299–315. https://doi.org/10.1352/1934-9556-54.5.299

Stone, E. and Priestley, M. (1996) 'Parasites, pawns and partners: Disability research and the role of non-disabled researchers', *British Journal of Sociology*, 47(4): 699–716. https://doi.org/10.2307/591081

Strahl, B., van Breda, A.D.P., Mann-Feder, V. and Schröer, W. (2021) 'A multinational comparison of care leaving policy and legislation', *Journal of International and Comparative Social Policy*, 37: 34–49. https://doi.org/10.1017/ ics.2020.26

Tanur, C. (2012) 'Project Lungisela: Supporting young people leaving state care in South Africa', *Child Care in Practice*, 18(4): 325–340. https://doi.org/10.1080/13575279.2012.713851

Teachman, G. (2019) 'Optimizing interviews with children and youth with disability', in P. Liamputtong (ed) *Handbook of research methods in health social sciences*, Singapore: Springer, pp 2023–2040.

Thomas, C. (2007) *Sociologies of disability and illness: Contested ideas in disability studies and medical sociology*, Basingstoke: Palgrave Macmillan.

Van Breda, A. (2018) 'Research review: Aging out of residential care in South Africa', *Child & Family Social Work*, 23(3): 513–521. https://doi.org/10.1111/cfs.12431

Van Breda, A. (2020) 'Patterns of criminal activity among residential care-leavers in South Africa', *Children and Youth Services Review*, 109. https://doi.org/10.1016/j.childyouth.2019.104706welle

Van Breda, A. and Dickens, L.F. (2016) 'Young people transitioning from residential care in South Africa: Welfare contexts, resilience, research and practice', in P. Mendes and P. Snow (eds) *Young people transitioning from out-of-home care: International research, policy and practice*, London: Palgrave Macmillan, pp 349–366.

Weller, S. (2012) 'Evolving creativity in qualitative longitudinal research with children and teenagers', *International Journal of Social Research Methodology*, 15(2): 119–133. 10.1080/13645579.2012.649412

7

Trauma-informed research with young people transitioning from care: balancing methodological rigour with participatory and empowering practice

Jade Purtell

Introduction

There are methodological tensions in research with marginalised populations. Policy makers look to research for solutions to some of our more complex social problems. Research evidence informs public policy with important implications for our generation of knowledge in the social sciences and in social policy. The following discussion looks at sampling and recruitment issues in research with 'hard to reach' cohorts, specifically care-leavers around the world who are unable to be contacted by researchers and those who decline opportunities to participate in research. More 'edgy' research strategies are necessary to attract 'hard to reach' groups to participate in different studies. This chapter is based on the author's challenges in carrying out research on care-leavers and early parenting in Australia. The author attempted to design a study that could demonstrate some of the rigour of quantitative research, that was trauma-informed and sensitive to care-leavers' needs and experiences. The study was also designed to be participatory and empowering to ensure care-leavers could be well represented and draw enjoyment and pride from their participation and contribution to knowledge in this important and under-researched field. The author has developed the 'adaptive participation model' to build on learnings from traditional positivist and interpretivist research approaches, trauma-informed practice and youth participation theory. Research with groups on the edge requires flexibility and responsiveness to participant needs which often requires innovative design and subsequent re-design of data collection approaches. The adaptive participation model seeks to support careful consideration of methodological choices in research targeting 'hard to reach' cohorts anywhere. Here, though, we focus on 'hard to reach' care-leavers in the context of Western democratic welfare states and with the case study being the Australian state of Victoria.

Transitions from care (TfC) policy has undergone major reforms in many states in Australia in the past five years. Many states have adopted extended care and transitions supports policies effectively moving TfC from 18 years of age (or younger) until 21 years of age across foster care, kinship care, residential care and permanent care cohorts in some states (Mendes, 2021). In 2020, approximately 46,000 children were in out-of-home care in Australia – around 3 per cent of 0–17-year-olds nationally (AIHW, 2021). Care type populations vary among age groups with young people in residential care homes making up approximately 5 per cent of the care population for under-15-year-olds, then later nearly 20 per cent of the TfC cohort (15–18-year-olds) (CCYP, 2020). Similarly, Indigenous children make up around 16 per cent of children in care in Australia (AIHW, 2021); but in the state of Victoria Indigenous young people represent approximately 25 per cent of those in the TfC cohort (CCYP, 2020). In Victoria Aboriginal people make up only 0.8 per cent of the overall population, their over-representation in out-of-home care is well recognised as a continuing and serious national concern (Victorian Public Sector Commission, 2019). There are also high rates of disability reported among the TfC population (CCYP, 2020).

With an increasing focus on research with young people transitioning from care, sub-groups of the cohort experiencing some of the worst outcomes are being investigated in more detail. Australian research has recently looked at transition from care issues for a range of care-leaver sub-populations including young people with disabilities (Snow et al, 2014); Indigenous care-leavers (Mendes et al, 2020); care-leavers with youth justice involvement (Baidawi, 2020); and young people transitioning from care with complex needs (Malvaso et al, 2016; Purtell and Mendes, 2016). While further research examining pathways from care for young people facing the most difficult transitions is important, approaches for maximising representation of 'hard to reach' or 'disengaged' groups of care-leavers are rarely discussed in the literature.

There is evidence that young people transitioning from care with the worst pre-care, in-care and post-care experiences are more likely to refuse services or 'disengage' from supports (Stein, 2012; Malvaso et al, 2016; Purtell and Mendes, 2019). This suggests that such young people may also be inaccessible for researchers either because contacting them to invite them to participate in research is not possible or, if contactable, they may not elect to participate in research. Logie (2021) asks who it is that we call 'hard to reach', arguing that we often use the term to explain disengagement or a lack of inclusion. Logie (2021) cites Brackertz (2007) to suggest that people who feel unheard and/or uncared for may actively disengage from support services. As this chapter is based mainly on the author's experience in one state of Australia, a Western democracy with a neoliberal welfare state, 'disengaged' groups are described as those who refuse or avoid TfC services and interventions. The broader argument of this chapter concerns research with care-leavers overall. Young people in other countries, particularly those with an underdeveloped or non-existent welfare states should not be described as 'disengaged' but they can be regarded as 'hard to reach'. Care-leavers who do not or cannot access TfC service provision, may also be excluded from global research on care-leavers, despite evidence that many issues care-leavers face occur universally (Landerer, 2022). Mendes and Rogers (2020) estimate that approximately 20 per cent of care-leavers fall into the disengaged category. This estimate is based on Stein's (2012) typologies of the care-leaver cohort in the United Kingdom, again a Western democracy with a neoliberal welfare state. Stein identified 'strugglers' as being those who had the worst pre-care and in-care experiences and often transition from care to poorer outcomes such as homelessness, substance abuse, criminal offending, mental ill health, and early pregnancy and parenting. Stein's 'survivor' typology was ascribed to TfC experiences of young people with numerous placements and placement breakdowns, poor outcomes and ongoing dependence on the welfare state for their basic needs, despite a self-identity of being 'out on their own in the world' (Stein, 2012). Stein's typology for care-leavers experiencing more positive outcomes was for those 'moving on' from care to develop more normative existences, staying on with carers, finishing school and going to university or finding full-time employment and becoming independent with the assistance of TfC services (Stein, 2012). Realistically, many of these cohorts are likely to either be uncontactable to invite to participate in research or uninterested or unable to participate. In using the term 'hard to reach' in this chapter the author refers to those care-leavers who are unable to be invited to participate in research and those who decline to participate. This definition can be applied across the world when we talk about hierarchies of research and representativeness of research samples of care-leavers as we go on to do here.

The hierarchy of research evidence places the most clinical approaches to research at the top of the quality research index, with systematic reviews and experimental research designs considered most rigorous (Albers et al, 2017). Yet there is little evidence that the samples in many studies would be representative of disengaged care-leavers. Most recruitment strategies involve third parties such as carers and professionals in getting information about research projects to care experienced young people. Young people who are 'disengaged' or 'disengaging' are less connected to carers and professionals and therefore less likely to hear about research participation opportunities. Failing to ensure representation of 'hard to reach' or disengaged care-leavers dilutes the rigour and reliability of research evidence. This has important consequences for the knowledge we have about major social problems and the evidence on which we base important policy decisions. This chapter argues first that increasing representation of disengaged groups is critical to the development of rigorous research evidence, and second, that increasing representation requires more participatory and empowering approaches to research design which incorporate trauma-informed and youth participation theories.

Recruitment and sampling difficulties in research with care-leavers

Many studies of young people's transitions from care experience some difficulty and/or expend significant resources trying to locate care-leavers to invite to be part of their research. A review of response rates for some of the largest and most well-known studies indicates that disengaged cohorts are probably under-represented in many key studies however. The Australian Institute of Health and Welfare (AIHW) conducts research on the views of children and young people in care with the assistance of case managers, departmental staff and other support persons. Their 2018 study had a response rate of only 53 per cent (n = 2,428) (AIHW, 2019). Common difficulties in finding care-leavers once they had been exited from care relate to housing instability, homelessness and frequent changes of phone numbers (Keller et al, 2016; McDowall, 2018). In Australia, agencies cease contact with care-leavers at 18 years or upon the expiry of court care orders. Transition from care services up until 2021 required young people to seek out their local service providers if they needed support. Services otherwise had no contact details for care-leavers unless they had been referred to their services and were engaged with support. Australia's national peak body for the voice of the child in out-of-home care, the CREATE Foundation, maintains a membership programme for care-experienced children and young people who have participated in any of the organisation's events or programmes. Out of 3,293 'ClubCREATE' members in the 18–25 age range identified and contacted during a data collection period spanning around 15 months, only 10 per cent of care-leavers in the sample completed the survey (McDowall, 2018).

In the United States, where populations are much larger, Courtney et al (2018) maintained a response rate of 95.3 per cent for Wave 1 of their longitudinal study (n = 763) and 84.7 per cent of original respondents at Wave 3 of this study (n = 616). The Wave 3 report details the extensive resources allocated to participant recruitment and retention however. Prospective participants were sent a letter introducing the research, five dollars in cash and notice that a researcher would call in the next two weeks. If a researcher couldn't get through to the young person by phone, they were then able to make a home visit. If still unable to contact a young person, the researcher could contact their child welfare worker for assistance. Young people were offered US$60 dollars to complete the survey each time (Courtney et al, 2018). In an Australian longitudinal study of transitions from care without the investments of the Courtney et al (2018) study, 57 per cent of participants dropped out of the study between Wave 1 and 2. The attrition rate between Waves 2 and 3 was 30 per cent (Muir et al, 2019). There are many factors impacting recruitment of care-leavers to various studies and resourcing is only one of them.

What response rates for various studies do not tell us is why some people have not responded or consented to participating in research. It often remains unclear whether invitations have been received and refused, or not received at all. What if nonrespondents share some similar demographic qualities? How many of these young people may be categorised as Stein's (2012) strugglers and how much do we really know about this group of care-leavers? Youth participation theory offers some insights into how different approaches to research may be perceived by young people and how comfortable the 'struggler' cohort may be participating in different kinds of research. Groups we have considered as 'hard to reach' may in fact be groups that traditional approaches to research have unknowingly excluded. Participatory and trauma-informed approaches to research may in fact be key to developing trust with vulnerable groups and to achieving the recruitment, retention and ethical standards necessary for truly rigorous and reliable research findings.

In this section, examining sampling and recruitment issues with people in 'hard to reach' groups, this chapter demonstrates how research methodologies that are typically considered to be most rigorous may exclude research populations that we are often most concerned to find out more about. In the following section we look at how research methods that are considered to be *less* representative, reliable and rigorous may be more effective at attracting 'hard to reach' groups. Youth participation theories are discussed in terms of lessons available to researchers about ways to create more empowering research designs.

Participatory and empowering, trauma-informed methodologies

Youth participation theories are increasingly influential in research and policy with care-experienced young people. These rights-based participation models highlight ways that research has previously been conducted *on* rather than investigated *with* young people. Participatory research is distinct from youth participation theory though both are concerned to reduce power imbalances between researchers and participants and can better enable care-leavers to feel in control of their contribution to a study or consultation (Kellett and Ding, 2004; Briskman, 2014). Moore et al (2018: 93) provide a comprehensive study of how trauma-informed and safe approaches to research on sensitive issues with children and young people needs to be informed by children and young people with one of their children's reference group members articulating: 'I think because you're talking about safety you need to give people lots of choices. They shouldn't feel pressured into talking about things. They should definitely be given a chance to have a say but it has to be their choice.'

As already stated, combining participatory approaches to research with trauma-informed approaches privileges flexibility and adaptability to cater to different styles of engagement and participation among young people. Clinical and standardised approaches to research specifically oppose flexibility because statistical analysis only has external validity under certain sampling standards (Neuman, 2000). Since care-leavers are a heterogeneous group with diverse experiences, abilities and backgrounds, for research to be inclusive it is important to be attentive to stigma when conducting research. Hoffman Cooper (2021: 2), a care-experienced researcher, states that: 'As a youth, I experienced my status in foster care was positioned by others as a deficit identity laden with stigma and approached with morbid curiosity.' Just one example of practical considerations that reduce stigma is that researchers need to ensure attention is not drawn insensitively to literacy issues or hyperactivity disorders. Standardised surveys, for example, can create risk of humiliation for young people who can't read well or sit still and concentrate for long periods of time (Goodwin and Tiderington, 2020). The following youth participation models provide various ways of thinking about young people's agency and power sharing with decision makers more broadly than research contexts. However, these models provide important learnings for researchers in seeking to engage 'hard to reach' groups.

Hart (1992) developed the 'ladder of participation', which highlights the amount of agency afforded to young people in different research and consultation opportunities. The ladder model is divided into eight rungs:

1. manipulation;
2. decoration;
3. tokenism;
4. assigned but informed;
5. consulted and informed;
6. adult-initiated, shared decisions with children;
7. child initiated and directed; and
8. child-initiated shared decisions with adults (Hart, 1992: 8).

The first three rungs – manipulation, decoration and tokenism – are classified as non-participation. Beginning from the fourth rung is actual participation where children and young people understand the purposes of their participation and the context of the work they are being asked to be a part of. These are the basic requirements for informed consent in ethics applications. 'Consulted and informed' describes when children and young people have given informed consent and participate in projects where the scope is pre-determined however their contributions are taken seriously (Hart, 1992). This is akin to non-participatory and positivist research methods which seek to extract information from participants, such as structured and closed question surveys, interviews and focus groups for example (Neuman, 2000; Flynn and McDermott, 2016). The highest rung on Hart's ladder is for 'youth-led' participation where young people develop their own projects and adults assist. Academic research requires that exact details of research procedures and instruments are declared within an application to the ethics committee often before researchers are allowed to speak with young people from the research populations to be studied. This is despite evidence suggesting that developing research projects in partnership with care-experienced youth advisors can improve the participatory nature of the research and has been reported to also increase young people's engagement as research participants (Keller et al, 2016; Kelly et al, 2020).

A more recent model by Lundy (2007) emphasises the need for young people's voices to be heard, and acted upon by decision makers. According to this model, meaningful consultation requires 'space' to be made for young people to contribute and this needs to be safe (free of retribution and inclusive) for children and young people to express their views and experiences or 'voice' freely (Lundy, 2007). Recognising that rights to participate may not equate to a right to outcomes that a child or young person requests, Lundy (2007) argues that an audience must take children and young people's views into account. They can demonstrate this influence (or at least involvement) by reporting back on the decisions they have taken and how they have incorporated what they've heard from children and young people. These principles too can be included in informed consent processes to explain what control researchers have over impact of research findings and outcomes from dissemination strategies. Careful consideration of the best ways to communicate findings to the participants themselves may also be important.

Wong et al (2010) propose that shared power is the ideal form of youth participation with partnerships between decision makers (in this case researchers) and young people leading to empowerment and positive development for young people involved. Wong et al (2010) argue that empowerment is achieved in the progression to shared control between adults and children and young people. Each of these perspectives raises interesting points, with Hart (1992) privileging youth-initiated and youth-controlled participation largely in opposition to traditional research methodologies which position researchers as experts and positivist methods as most reliable for generating evidence-based practical applications from research findings

(Flynn and McDermott, 2016; Albers et al, 2017). Lundy's (2007) work highlights the importance of what happens after research is conducted – what researchers do to promote the implementation of what young people have recommended or suggested needs to happen. Often research funding may run out before findings are published and disseminated and researchers have little control over how broad an audience their work receives, let alone what actions audiences take after considering the evidence. Wong et al (2010) privilege shared control in youth participation. None of these models are concerned with identifying complementary expertise among youth and professionals to consider who may be best placed to undertake which tasks in a given research project. For example, a social work practitioner researcher may have a more developed understanding of practice contexts such as resourcing and reporting requirements for funding bodies whereas a care-leaver is probably best placed to identify how being on the receiving end of services feels, and the impact of this on a young person's motivation, stress levels and general wellbeing. Each of these models is also organised around an ideal type and none are developed for research and consultation specifically with care-experienced people to incorporate trauma-informed approaches.

This chapter argues that there is no ideal type for research and consultation with care-experienced people – context and adaptability are key in this work. No approach is inherently 'better' than another, though one may be better suited to one set of circumstances than another. Methodological approaches that are 'fit for purpose' will most likely serve best. Participation theories, trauma-informed approaches and positivist research methods all lack a framework by which to assess which methods may be most appropriate to the specific research contexts. Trauma-informed practice asks for researchers to consider the trauma context prospective participants *may* have experienced and the reactions they may experience as part of their participation in research. Trauma-informed theories do not dictate what sort of research methods should be used, however. Positivist research has clear standards but lacks reflexive critique of its representativeness, by its own standards. Youth participation theory helps shed light on these issues but holds a naive hierarchical orientation that is not necessarily trauma-informed. Youth participation theories further do not concern themselves with how likely it is that their findings will be engaged with by policy- and decision-makers. This could arguably diminish the participatory dimension if the potential actions and systemic changes recommended go unnoticed. For participatory work to be effective it must have an impact on those with authority to make changes.

The adaptive participation model

The adaptive participation model consolidates the author's learning and practice experience while carrying out their study on care-leaver early parenting with participatory research ambitions and many 'real-world' challenges. The model and its components provide useful tools for considering research designs that are participatory, trauma-informed, rigour-oriented and impactful. The model aims to assist researchers in carrying out challenging projects and to promote greater agency and decision-making power-sharing with research participants and/or lived experience research consultants.

This chapter has detailed two major challenges in attracting representative samples of 'hard to reach' groups to participate in transitions from care studies. There is evidence that finding potential participants to invite to be a part of research studies is difficult when many care-leavers are disengaged from services. Also, when study designs do not incorporate methodological approaches promoting young people's agency and understandings of previous trauma then prospective participants may perceive risks to their wellbeing by insensitive research practice and decline to take part in the research. Representative samples are the cornerstone of rigorous research however response rates for large studies suggest that 'hard to reach' groups are under-represented in many studies. The adaptive participation model looks to ways of designing research to maximise representation, rigour, empowerment and impact in research with vulnerable groups through pragmatic and flexible research design.

The adaptive participation model looks for opportunities within *all* research studies to maximise representation of harder to reach care-leavers by utilising research methodologies that protect wellbeing and seek to increase the impact and reach of the project findings. In this regard the adaptive model disregards hierarchies or linear pathways to best practice and instead looks at how best practice can be incorporated into differing contexts. The adaptive participation model also acknowledges that participatory research methods are not often regarded as particularly rigorous, and this perception may affect the impact of the research in policy making. If young people want their participation in research to have an impact, we then also have a duty as researchers to design research that is respectful and empowering while also being rigorous and reliable enough to attract audiences with power and influence. The adaptive participation model has a number of components including:

- resource mapping
- modes of inquiry for empowering practice
- preparation and risk mitigation
- audience and influence

These components are introduced in the following sections to demonstrate how the adaptive participation model can assist in the development and adaptation of research designs investigating issues for 'hard to reach' and disengaged groups.

Resource mapping

Research design is often decided very early in a project and without the requisite understandings of the research population's general circumstances and how this will affect various, often fixed resources available for a particular project. The author's research on care-leaver early parenting was approved prior to a literature review being conducted, for example, and these early stages of the research changed the researcher's understanding of what data collection methods would actually be possible with a 'hard to reach' group within an already often disengaged group. Researchers may draw on a range of resources both more tangible (such as funding) and less tangible (such as networks) when carrying out different studies. The matrix in Figure 7.1 helps us think about what resources a researcher may have more and less of depending on the nature of their study. The previous discussion has identified the multiple barriers to finding, recruiting and engaging care-leavers in research. Typically, this requires significant time, an experienced research team, adequate funding for reimbursing young people, researchers' travel and expenses – as well as young people to invite to be part of a study. These resources are represented in the resource map in Figure 7.1.

Figure 7.1: Resource map

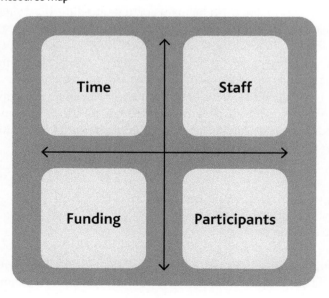

The inter-relationships between these levels of resourcing are complex and context-dependent. The implications of this resourcing for methodological decisions are often not considered as these choices are typically thought to be epistemological rather than pragmatic (Flynn and McDermott, 2016). The author argues that research contexts are far more complex than epistemological positions suggest and without some clarity and contingency planning research project timelines and budgets can start to be derailed by difficulties in participant recruitment. Here we consider a range of different resourcing contexts and participatory and trauma-informed approaches that give thought to research impact.

Time

Research projects can vary greatly in terms of time, and this is often dependent on the length of time the project is funded for. Delays to ethics approval, recruitment of participants and collaboration arrangements with research partners can all be outside of a researcher's control and forward planning at research design stages is likely to facilitate a more time-efficient research experience.

If you have a lot of time, quantitative research may attract a good sample size for useful statistical analysis and these findings may attract a broad and influential audience but without significant time to work closely with carers and caseworkers the sample will most likely be difficult to recruit. Qualitative data may help to contextualise quantitative data in a mixed methods study, or to personalise statistics and this can help policy makers better understand the personal implications of different policies. Again, with ample time, co-production of research design with care-experienced people can assist researchers to develop meaningful indicators and questions for care-experienced research participants and to identify barriers to participation ahead of recruitment. With less time it may be wiser to use a mixed methods design as this may maximise rigour and triangulation options if time runs short or difficulties arise in attracting desired sample/s of participants. With little time available qualitative research may be easier for recruitment and provide a rich data source however transcription costs and data analysis may be resource-intensive. Focus groups or open-ended question surveys may be less resource-intensive ways to collect rich data quickly.

Staff

Where research institutes or universities are involved in a study senior academics may be able to promote the study at managerial and executive levels which can increase practitioner efforts to aid recruitment to research projects. Without senior researcher support researchers may be able to collaborate with organisations supporting transitioning youth to find mutually beneficial approaches to participant recruitment. Reimbursement for participants may assist practitioners to engage with young people so they may be happy to assist you in finding prospective participants even if they are busy and under-resourced. If you have few staff and few relationships with practitioners and service providers, you may need to attend lots of network meetings to build relationships individually with practitioners who can assist you.

Funding

Generous reimbursements for participants may increase recruitment numbers. Stable staffing by researchers specialised in or familiar with TfC and trauma-informed issues may assist with participant engagement and retention in longitudinal studies. Quantitative measures may increase impact of research where statistics can be usefully cited. Where funding is allocated for more event-based participation such as focus groups in partnership with youth advocacy organisations then they may do most of the recruitment work for you and manage some of the duty of care issues for trauma-informed practice and participant safety. Without significant funding, however, organisations and practitioners may not be able to assist with small sample, exploratory projects unless their needs align with the research questions being addressed.

Participants

Where researchers are able to promote their research to large numbers of care-leavers, having the research co-designed by young people may increase perceptions of integrity and increase participant numbers. Focus group phases to inform research design may ensure researchers ask the 'right' questions (questions that care-leavers find relevant and unintrusive, for example). Maximising support options available to young people who experience distress following their participation should be a priority however and attention should be paid to how participant safety will be managed, especially if young people will be consulted in group environments where sensitive issues will be covered. Where researchers have few people to invite to be part of their study, beginning with a more accessible population (such as practitioners) may assist in developing the right questions for transitioning youth to make the most of the small number of people you may be able to consult with.

The adaptive participation model has been designed from the author's learnings across each of the scenarios provided here and seeks to simplify processes that can integrate epistemological orientations with participatory and trauma-informed approaches that seek to create impact while being responsive to research contexts. Table 7.1 presents a reflective checklist

Table 7.1: Resource mapping reflection questions

Resource	Indicate Resource Availability
Time	
How much time is there to complete the project?	
Is co-production with care-leavers possible?	
Can we consult care-leavers before ethics committee applications are completed or only after ethics approval?	
Do we need to establish relationships with care-leaver support services?	
What will be the extent of our relationship with co-design partners and research participants? Will we assist care-experienced collaborators to access psychological or wellbeing support if distress arises?	
Staff	
How many staff will work on the project and will all of them conduct fieldwork?	
How many staff have experience working with care-experienced young people?	
Is the project conducted by a major institution or organisation research populations may be familiar with? Is their reputation with care-leavers positive?	
Will collaboration with services that are in contact with the research population be formal or informal?	
Funding	
Are the researchers employed part-time, full-time or casually? Are they likely to complete the project?	
Are care-experienced people given paid opportunities to assist with the research project?	
Is there budget allowance for researcher travel?	
Are participants offered reimbursement for their time and expenses? How generously?	
Are funds quickly accessible for young people to be paid out quickly?	
Participants	
Do researchers require ethics clearance to speak to young people about participating in co-design of the research?	
Does the research team have existing contact with potential participants or others in contact with care-leavers?	
Are duty of care and risk mitigation strategies well developed and understood by all research partners and collaborators?	
Is research participation accessible to young people with mobility, literacy, mental health, locational and/or technological challenges?	

of planning questions to consider in relation to each of these resourcing categories. Being keenly aware of the availability of given resources should assist in the development of pragmatic and achievable research designs.

Resource mapping focuses on project issues related to the research team which are important for the project's success and research impact. A careful plan can ensure a project is properly resourced for participant safety and empowering experiences. The next adaptive participation component to consider is focused on potential research participants and what their experience of participating in the given research project may be. Modes of inquiry are created by the way that we formulate questions and tasks for our participants. What are we asking participants to reflect on, remember and think about, and then articulate back to us? How will this affect them in the short, medium and longer terms?

Modes of inquiry: 'introspective' or 'extrospective' questioning

Managing duty of care and legal responsibilities can also be complex, especially where researchers are relying on external, free services to provide emotional or psychological support if a participant experiences research involvement as distressing. To mitigate risk to potential research participants a researcher should be aware of common issues experienced by the participant group and develop research methods and questions that avoid dwelling on subjects likely to cause distress. This is particularly so where therapeutic support cannot be offered and may be difficult to access. A researcher should also aim to minimise distressing content in promotional materials and informed consent documentation.

One way to mitigate risk of re-traumatisation is to pay careful attention to the way in which researchers enquire about their topics of interest and the settings they create for people to participate in their research. In keeping with the comment from the children's advisory group quoted in the participatory, empowering and trauma-informed methodologies section in this chapter, it is important to give people choices about how they participate and how much they say. Questions that inquire about personal experience can lead people with experiences of trauma to re-visit traumatic experiences. If you reframe questions to be about less personal issues a person may be able to more easily discuss issues and also think more clearly about what information they may or may not want to disclose in the research setting. For research with children and young people who have been in care, many lines of questioning can lead to discussions about abuse and neglect that young people may not have intended to or had to time to consider disclosing. In group settings these discussions may trigger other participants present also. It is important that researchers consider how much detail about personal experiences they really want to hear about and to then be clear about how they will support young people if they are involved in discussions they find distressing. Personal questions can be thought of as 'introspective questioning' as they invite people to look inwards. 'Extrospective questioning' then can describe lines of questioning that are focused on things *external* to a person. You can garner useful information without asking people to reflect on and relay personal information. For example, in the author's study of care-leavers and early parenting, rather than pose research questions asking about a young person's experience of transitioning from out-of-home care arrangements, pregnancy and parenting, participants were asked what they thought about policies and practices related to young people transitioning from care and becoming parents. Extrospective questioning can also create a more participatory and empowering research setting by asking participants to comment on matters of public importance rather than personal trauma. When researchers show their concern for participant safety and empowerment in these kinds of ways they can build more trust and rapport, but also interest, enthusiasm, ambition and leadership. Youth participation theory reminds us that when we build young people's expectations around the importance of their research participation we have a duty to ensure their contributions are impactful. A further component of the adaptive participation model is the consideration of potential audiences and their influence as outlined in the next section.

Audience and influence

A further tension in research design which is largely disregarded by participatory research methods concerns the audience for research findings and the influence of the researchers and their findings on audiences with power to consider and implement recommendations. Mannay et al (2019) ask us to consider the differences between marginalised groups having a 'voice' in research and being *heard*. One of the major benefits of large, quantitative studies is that their findings are highly regarded, widely read and commonly cited as 'hard' evidence. When we are conducting participatory, trauma-informed and empowering research, how are we also ensuring that this research will find an influential audience and that findings will be taken seriously?

Because many young people are motivated to help improve services for young people transitioning from care after them, being transparent about a realistic assessment of how your research will impact policy making and practice change will assist in developing rapport and will help care-leaver participants understand more about policy-making processes. Young people who feel they have not been respected or told the truth may be reluctant to participate in further research and may feel less confident in support services which can lead to disengagement. Disengagement actively discourages a young person's participation and empowerment. It should therefore be a key goal of trauma-informed research to provide experiences that encourage engagement. Encouraging engagement is both a duty of care and practical consideration as engagement in research is critical to the development of rigorous evidence for policy-making decisions.

Discussion and conclusion

There are many expectations in research which do not necessarily reflect or accommodate the practical realities of recruiting 'hard to reach' or disengaged cohorts to participate in different studies. Research 'on the edge' is critical to our learning and a lack of participation by groups on the edge causes a lack of representation. This is problematic for the generation of knowledge and evidence which may then be used to inform policy development. Any misunderstandings we draw from the evidence we have can lead to inappropriate, ineffective and ultimately inefficient services being developed and implemented with inappropriate practice potentially causing harm to already vulnerable youth. Edgy research methods that incorporate trauma-informed and participatory theories teach us to adapt to the needs of 'hard to reach' cohorts in order to attract them as participants. Research that represents disengaged cohorts will help us build our knowledge and understandings of serious social problems that care-leavers often experience such as homelessness, substance abuse, criminal offending, mental ill health, and early pregnancy and parenting (Stein, 2012). This is true of research with the largest and smallest sample sizes if a given study engages young people who would not otherwise participate in services and research studies. Carrying out research that protects participant safety in vulnerable cohorts is a complex undertaking however this is critical in upholding our duty of care as researchers and as generators of rigorous research evidence. The adaptive research model provides reflections and examples of edgy research practices based on the authors' real-life experience of recruiting and interviewing groups on the edge of society. Care-leavers, especially those who are characterised as 'disengaged', complain that they aren't listened to and that they don't have a 'voice' in their care. When we exclude them from our research processes, we inadvertently extend society's silencing of groups on the edge to the detriment of our social policy planning and implementation.

References

AIHW (Australian Institute of Health and Welfare) (2019) *The views of children and young people in out-of-home care: Overview of indicator results from the second national survey 2018* (Cat. no. CWS 68), Canberra: AIHW.

AIHW (Australian Institute of Health and Welfare) (2021) *Child protection Australia 2019–2020*, Canberra: AIHW.

Albers, B.A.S., Pattuwage, L., Rinaldis, S. and Talor, D. (2017) *Out-of-home care: An evidence and gap map.* Available from: https://www.ceiglobal.org/sites/default/files/uploads/files/Out-of-Home%20Care%20An%20Evidence%20Gap%20Map.pdf

Baidawi, S. (2020) 'Crossover children: Examining initial criminal justice system contact among child protection-involved youth', *Australian Social Work*, 73(3): 280–295. doi:10.1080/0312407X.2019.1686765

Brackertz, N. (2007) 'Who is hard to reach and why?', ISR Working Paper. Swinburne University of Technology.

Briskman, L. (2014) *Social work with indigenous communities: A human rights approach*, 2nd edn. Annandale: The Federation Press.

CCYP (Commission for Children and Young People) (2020) *Keep caring: Systemic inquiry into services for young people transitioning from out-of-home care.* Available from: https://ccyp.vic.gov.au/inquiries/systemic-inquiries/keep-caring/

Courtney, M., Okpych, N., Park, K., Harty, J., Feng, H., Torres-Garcia, A. and Sayed, S. (2018) *Findings from the California Youth Transitions to Adulthood Study (CalYOUTH): Conditions of youth at age 21.* Available from: https://www.chapinhall.org/research/calyouth-wave3/

Flynn, C. and McDermott, F. (2016) *Doing research in social work and social care: The journey from student to practitioner researcher*, Los Angeles: SAGE.

Goodwin, J. and Tiderington, E. (2020) 'Building trauma-informed research competencies in social work education', *Social Work Education*, 41(2): 143–156. doi:10.1080/02615479.2020.1820977

Hart, R. (1992) *Children's participation: From tokenism to citizenship.* Available from: https://www.unicef-irc.org/publications/pdf/childrens_participation.pdf

Hoffman-Cooper, A.E. (2021) 'From foster youth to foster scholar: Suggestions for emancipatory research practices', *Children and Youth Services Review*, 120: 105752. Doi:10.1016/j.childyouth.2020.105752

Keller, S., Strahl, B., Refaeli, T. and Zhao, C.T. (2016) 'Researching care leavers in an ethical manner in Switzerland, Germany, Israel and China', in P. Mendes and P. Snow (eds) *Young people transitioning from out-of-home care: International research, policy and practice*, London: Palgrave Macmillan, pp 241–261.

Kellett, M. and Ding, S. (2004) 'Middle childhood', in S. Fraser, V. Lewis, S. Ding, M. Kellett and C. Robinson (eds) *Doing research with children and young people*, London: SAGE, pp 161–174.

Kelly, B., Friel, S., McShane, T., Pinkerton, J. and Gilligan, E. (2020) "I haven't read it, I've lived it!": The benefits and challenges of peer research with young people TfC', *Qualitative Social Work*, 19(1): 108–124. doi:10.1177/1473325018800370

Landerer, F. (2022) 'The importance and impact of participation and network building in care leaving: The use and significance of the care leaver declaration from the international care leavers convention 2020', *Institutionalised Children Exploration and Beyond*, 9(2): 152–160. https://doi.org/10.1177/23493003221088063

Logie, C. (2021) *Working with excluded populations in HIV: Hard to reach or out of sight?* Cham: Springer.

Lundy, L. (2007) ' "Voice" is not enough: Conceptualising Article 12 of the United Nations Convention on the Rights of the Child', *British Educational Research Journal*, 33(6): 927–942. doi:10.1080/01411920701657033

Malvaso, C., Delfabbro, P., Hackett, L. and Mills, H. (2016) 'Service approaches to young people with complex needs leaving out-of-home care', *Child Care in Practice*, 22(2): 128–147. doi:10.1080/13575279.2015.1118016

Mannay, D., Staples, E., Hallett, S., Roberts, L., Rees, A., Evans, R. and Andrews, D. (2019) 'Enabling talk and reframing messages: Working creatively with care experienced children and young people to recount and re-represent their everyday experiences', *Child Care in Practice: Northern Ireland Journal of Multi-disciplinary Child Care Practice*, 25(1): 51–63. doi:10.1080/13575279.2018.1521375

McDowall, J.J. (2018) 'Out-of-home care in Australia: Children and young people's views after five years of national standards', *Developing Practice: The Child, Youth and Family Work Journal*, 50: 108–109.

Mendes, P. (2021) 'Extending out-of-home care in the state of Victoria, Australia: The policy context and outcomes', *Scottish Journal of Residential Child Care*, 20(1): 97–107.

Mendes, P. and Rogers, J. (2020) 'Young people transitioning from out-of-home care: What are the lessons from extended care programmes in the USA and England for Australia?', *The British Journal of Social Work*, 50(5): 1513–1530. doi:10.1093/bjsw/bcaa028

Mendes, P., Standfield, R., Saunders, B.J., McCurdy, S., Walsh, J., Turnbull, L. and Armstrong, A. (2020) *Indigenous care leavers in Australia: A national scoping study*. Available from: https://apo.org.au/sites/default/files/resource-files/2020-08/apo-nid307306_0.pdf

Moore, T.P., McArthur, M. and Noble-Carr, D. (2018) 'More a marathon than a hurdle: Towards children's informed consent in a study on safety', *Qualitative Research*, 18(1): 88–107. Doi:10.1177/1468794117700708

Muir, S., Purtell, J., Hand, K. and Carroll, M. (2019) *Beyond 18: The longitudinal study on leaving care wave 3 research report: Outcomes for young people leaving care in Victoria*. Available from: https://aifs.gov.au/sites/default/files/publication-documents/1812_b18_wave_3_final_report_0.pdf

Neuman, W.L. (2000) *Social research methods: Qualitative and quantitative approaches*, 4th edn, Boston: Allyn & Bacon.

Purtell, J. and Mendes, P. (2016) 'Stand by me – flexible and holistic support for young care leavers: Smoothing transitions from care', *Children Australia*, 41(3): 208–213. doi:10.1017/cha.2016.18

Purtell, J. and Mendes, P. (2019) *Confident, ambitious and achieving: Care leavers supported by the Westcare Continuing Care program*. Available from: https://www.academia.edu/39146011/CONFIDENT_AMBITIOUS_AND_ACHIEVING_CARE_LEAVERS_SUPPORTED_BY_THE_WESTCARE_CONTINUING_CARE_PROGRAM

Snow, P.C., Mendes, P. and O'Donohue, D. (2014) *Young people with a disability leaving state care. Phase Two Report: Issues, challenges, directions: The young people's perspectives*. Available from: https://www.academia.edu/10745383/_Young_people_with_a_disability_leaving_state_care_Phase_Two_Report?email_work_card=view-paper

Stein, M. (2012) *Young people TfC: Supporting pathways to adulthood*, London and Philadelphia: Jessica Kingsley Publishers.

Victorian Public Sector Commission (2019) *Aboriginal Victoria today*. Available from: https://vpsc.vic.gov.au/html-resources/aboriginal-cultural-capability-toolkit/aboriginal-victoria-today/#:~:text=Victorian%20Aboriginal%20Demographics,to%2037%20for%20other%20Victorians

Wong, N.T., Zimmerman, M.A. and Parker, E.A. (2010) 'A typology of youth participation and empowerment for child and adolescent health promotion', *American Journal of Community Psychology*, 46(1): 100–114. doi:10.1007/s10464-010-9330-0

8

Care foundations: making care central in research with care-experienced people

Róisín Farragher, Petra Göbbels-Koch, John Paul Horn and Annie Smith

Considering a 'caring' view in the research process

The field of leaving-care research has experienced increasing diversity in its philosophies and methodological approaches within social sciences research over the past two decades, but challenges with power imbalances between researchers and participants still exist (Hunter et al, 2011a, 2011b). As care-experienced people often experience limited control over their affairs during their time in care (Sinclair et al, 2005; Unrau et al, 2008) and high levels of relational instability (Avery and Freundlich, 2009; Chambers et al, 2018), the temporary and structural nature of research relationships pose potential harms to this population. Researchers can address this risk of harm by paying attention to how the distance between 'the studied' and 'the researcher' can be closed, sharing power and balancing benefit to participants with benefit to the field. We suggest that these risk-reduction activities create 'care' in the research relationship.

The nature of distance in the research relationship depends on which approach to constructing knowledge (epistemology) the researcher adopts. In the positivist tradition, truth is absolute; there exists one truth and knowledge is generated by observing and analysing evidence (Moon and Blackman, 2014). Distance is necessary to maintain objectivity; getting too close to the research participants invites bias and clouds the ability to see the truth. In constructivist and subjectivist traditions, truth is relative and knowledge is co-constructed between the researcher and the participant. Knowledge is derived by examining either how participants create meaning around different experiences (constructivism) or how reality itself is perceived and shapes the experiences of participants (subjectivism) (Moon and Blackman, 2014). In both traditions, researchers evaluate evidence and generate claims about the lives of participants.

To avoid harms that might come from the inherent power imbalance within relationships (Cohn and Lyons, 2003), research must be free from coercion and conducted with informed consent (respect for persons); minimise harm and maximise benefits to participants and society (non-maleficence and beneficence); and treat all participants as equal, while avoiding overburdening those who are most vulnerable (justice) (National Commission for the Protection of Human Subjects of Biomedical and Behavioral Research, 1978). In a traditional paradigm, research has focused heavily on non-maleficence to participants and beneficence to the field (Pieper and Thomson, 2016). Noticeably missing from this paradigm is the maximised benefit towards participants themselves within the context of the study (positive beneficence); the paradigm sees ethical standards as met, so long as society benefits and participants are relatively unharmed (Ruch, 2014; Pieper and Thomson, 2016).

In a parallel process, the academy and other social institutions evaluate and credential researchers on their ability to secure funding, publish, or affect social change using their research (Hammersley, 2003). Scientific research-funding bodies, editors of high-impact journals and policy-making bodies may privilege positivist research in both academic and practical forms of inquiry (Rogers, 2012; Levitt et al, 2017). In this sense, 'objectivity' in the research process, and the distance this requires, is valued and rewarded.

In our exploration of care, power (by virtue of objective distance) and traditional ethics (due to the lack of attention to positive beneficence) present the greatest barriers to establishing care in the research relationship. When preference is given to distance, the inherent hierarchy of the research relationship positions the researcher as the sole expert. Researchers evaluate the ability of participants to recount or make meaning of their experiences. This power represents a form of *epistemic injustice*; plainly, decisions by those with power (in this context, researchers) about who knows something by virtue of their experiences or credentials and whether they possess the ability to derive meaning or advance inquiry from their experiences (Fricker, 2007; Grasswick, 2017). The voices of participants, their needs as individuals or their stated desires for policy/practice change may be overlooked by the researcher (expert) making meaning of participants' experiences. This represents a specific type of power imbalance; participants' credibility in knowing the field based on lived experience or ability to inform inquiry is limited to what the researchers deem relevant or plausible.

Adding complexity to the matter of epistemic injustice is the case of an insider researcher – a researcher who is also part of the population they study. The ability of insider researchers to remain objective is questioned and their work may be seen as less credible (Grasswick, 2017). This extends to research viewing participants as co-equal partners in the construction of knowledge. Yet excluding research participants' voices may contradict the helping professions' declared aim of producing emancipatory research with vulnerable populations (Rogers, 2012; Ruch, 2014). If the purpose of research within the helping professions is to empower those most vulnerable, we believe a deeper investigation into the concept of care (shared power and positive beneficence) is necessary to explore our ethical conduct of research with care-experienced people.

In this chapter we discuss how 'care' (in research conduct and interactions) can be inserted into the design, conduct and dissemination of research. First, we describe how researchers can attend to the positive beneficence of research by anticipating and planning around the risks and needs of participants in leaving-care research. Second, we illustrate the value of engaging care-experienced people in the analysis, interpretation, drafting and dissemination of research data. Third, the care-experienced authors of this chapter provide reflections of their experiences as both researchers and participants. The chapter concludes with a summary of practical advice for those engaging with care-experienced people in research.

Considering care during research design

How can we implement 'care' as an empathic, caring researcher-researched relationship at the early stages of study design? 'Care' can have different facets as different actors and actions are involved in the planning stage of a research project with care-experienced young people: choosing the research topic, designing and testing the research tools, establishing relationships with care-experienced people and gatekeepers, and ensuring potential participants can make informed decisions about participation. Apart from the common ethical principles, of voluntariness or confidentiality, and methodical considerations, in this section, we consider the relationship between the different actors in leaving-care research and how to establish a caring, trustful foundation in the early stage of the research.

Leaving-care research aims to understand and improve the lives of young people in the transition from care to adulthood. Participants need to be protected from harm such as re-traumatisation, by using, for instance, a trauma-informed research approach (Epp et al, 2022). This applies for researchers as well. A leaving-care researcher may be confronted with sensitive information. Care in the choice of topic addresses the researchers' abilities to keep participants safe while dealing with such topics themselves in terms of self-care and maintaining emotional boundaries. Emotional boundaries are essential considering the risk of secondary trauma for researchers exposed to traumatic reports (Whitt-Woosley and Sprang, 2018; van der Merwe and Hunt, 2019). The challenge is maintaining professional boundaries to protect oneself from secondary trauma while simultaneously being empathic. This balance is important for addressing participants' potential emotional reactions adequately. As many leaving-care researchers have training in social work practice or related professions, their clinical training in how to deal with traumatic content, emotional distress and mental health issues may also be helpful in the role of a researcher (Mendes et al, 2014). A caring professional relationship means that researchers are prepared to deal with this content adequately, for instance, by undertaking extra training to deal with emotional distress occurring during the research process.

As in participatory research, care-experienced young people may get involved in the early research design. If this is not possible, for example, due to limited financial and time resources (Kelly et al, 2020), it is important to consult a small group of care-experienced young people for reviewing the research tools before starting the data collection. The early feedback from care-experienced young people helps to clarify language and emotional reactions. The integration of their ideas and wishes implies a respectful and participatory attitude, which harmonises the roles of researchers and the researched. Consulting people with care experience in advance to develop a common language can increase engagement with gatekeepers and potential participants. For example, among the first steps in designing a leaving-care research project researchers are strongly advised to consult care-experienced people at the beginning of the process to discuss the preferred, inclusive terminology which is suitable for the group they want to address, like 'care-leaver', 'care-experienced people' or 'young people leaving care'.

Furthermore, gatekeepers can be protective of the young people they work with. They may raise concerns about the potential triggering effects and overall safety of children and young people participating in research. It is, therefore, essential to address any concerns raised by gatekeepers and to have a safety plan in place to ensure research participants can receive the support they need if they become distressed as a result of participating in the research process.

The following example is presented by the second author to demonstrate how she addressed safety concerns by gatekeepers whom she approached to collaborate in her PhD research project about suicidal ideation among care-experienced people. I (Göbbels-Koch) will write in the first person about my experiences. For this study, I conducted an online survey and semi-structured interviews with care-experienced adults in England and Germany between July 2020 to June 2021 (see Göbbels-Koch, 2022). As a preparation, I reviewed the literature on triggering, so-called iatrogenic effects of questions about suicidal ideation and suicide risk screening tools in research (DeCou and Schumann, 2018). Current evidence does not suggest that questions about suicidal experiences would be harmful (Bajaj et al, 2008). Moreover, participation in research on sensitive topics can also offer beneficial effects (see Mendes et al, 2014).

Several gatekeepers raised concerns about triggering effects of questions related to this sensitive topic. Having reviewed the literature on those feared effects, I was able to address these concerns with evidence-informed background knowledge and confirm that research on such sensitive topics is safe to conduct while still having safety measures in place, such as having supportive contacts available and a protocol on how to intervene if a participant shows distress or discloses being at imminent risk. In this context, additional training on interventions for addressing emotional reactions or distress, such as disclosure of the acute risk of suicide or traumatic content, can benefit both participants and the researcher's confidence in safely conducting research. Furthermore, a beneficial impact of well-prepared research with a 'caring' principle was confirmed by participants themselves. At the end of the interviews conducted for this study (see Göbbels-Koch, 2022), some of the care-experienced participants reflected on how they felt after talking about their experiences of suicidal ideation:

> 'Yeah, good. Actually, I feel better now 'cause I do like getting stuff off my chest. It has the opposite effect of what you think it would. I actually feel much better now.' (Male, 19 years old)

> 'But actually this is been (-) a lot more pleasant than I sup(-) pleasant [...] would not work, it's been (-) it's been nicer than I thought it would be talking about this stuff actually.' (Female, 30 years old)

These quotes contrast the concerns raised by a few gatekeepers previously. The feedback of previous participants could be discussed with future gatekeepers during the research process. Therefore, being aware of possible concerns may help to have a constructive conversation with gatekeepers to assure them about the safety of participation and that the researcher cares for everyone involved. Being able to address concerns about participants' wellbeing is about creating trusting relationships with gatekeepers.

At the same time, gatekeepers also play an essential supportive role after a young person has participated in a study. They can provide additional support and extended debriefing after participating in a study for which researchers may have only limited resources. Hence, establishing collaborative relationships with gatekeepers is essential in the study design for leaving-care research.

Forming caring relationships in a research project may profit from multiple contacts with (potential) participants. Longer relationships help build rapport to make the young person feel more comfortable, confident and possibly more communicative during the interview (Keller et al, 2016). A meeting or call in advance may be useful when planning to conduct one-to-one interviews with care-experienced young people. Such an introduction provides participants with further information about the research and the opportunity to ask questions before agreeing to participate. Inviting potential participants to ask the researcher questions gives them an empowering opportunity that further balances the roles between the researcher and the researched and builds rapport (Karnieli-Miller et al, 2009).

Furthermore, the researcher and the potential participant can get an idea of how the participant feels about talking about the topic. If investigating a sensitive topic, this would be an opportunity to discuss together a safety net in case of distress (see Keller et al, 2016). This approach would contribute to a caring and trustful relationship where the steps to build rapport start ahead of the first interview.

'Care' in research with care-experienced people can be implemented from an early stage of the study design and provides multiple advantages for the research process. Starting off the research with a 'caring' principle can be reached by engaging with gatekeepers, care-experienced advisors and potential participants during the conceptualisation and design of the study.

Considering care during analysis and dissemination

Youth engagement has been described as the meaningful and sustainable involvement of young people in decisions that affect them (Smith et al, 2009; Checkoway, 2011). This can and should include their engagement in research that affects young people, to ensure they are not just subjects of research, but active participants in knowledge generation and mobilisation. Hawke et al (2020) believe such engagement is a moral imperative and note the particular value of engaging youth as full partners from design to dissemination.

Engaging vulnerable individuals in research projects that relate to their lived experiences and needs increases the quality of the research, as well as its relevance to the target population (Hawke et al, 2020). Effectively engaging vulnerable youth in the research process offers both the youth and the researcher the opportunity to learn from the other's experience and expertise, as they work towards a common goal (Powers and Tiffany, 2006). However, there is a dearth of training and learning opportunities about youth engagement across academic settings, which can result in a failure to engage young people in authentic ways and exclude them from key stages of the research (Hawke et al, 2020).

Ensuring the sustained meaningful engagement of care-experienced young people throughout the research process can be challenging. In addition to many researchers lacking experience in effective youth engagement strategies (Hawke et al, 2018), care-experienced youth often have histories of trauma, have experienced unhealthy relationships with adults and can be struggling with personal and systemic issues that make committing to a lengthy project difficult. Meanwhile, researchers who do engage young people often focus solely on getting their input into the design and data collection for their study and pay little attention to keeping young people engaged post-data collection. For example, a review of 399 studies that considered engaging youth in research found that participants were most likely to be involved in identifying the needs, priorities and goals of research, and in designing or conducting the research; and were least likely to be involved in data analysis, interpretation and dissemination of findings (Jacquez et al, 2013).

The pressure on researchers to publish is often cited as a reason why the time and effort required to successfully sustain youth engagement is too difficult to achieve (Tsang et al, 2020). There is often an assumption that youth are not interested in data analysis or have not yet developed the cognitive skills to understand empirical concepts (Jacquez et al, 2013). However, an evaluation of a project to engage care-experienced youth in research clearly contradicts these assumptions and as one participant noted: 'There were many skills around data analysis and problem solving that I learned. I think the problem-solving skills will be very useful in other situations' (Peled, 2021: 8).

Providing opportunities for care-experienced youth to engage in the post-data-collection process offers them the chance to gain skills in areas such as public speaking, leadership, teamwork, time management, planning and facilitating workshops and creating dissemination materials (McCreary Centre Society's Youth Research Academy, 2016). For example, an evaluation of a project that engaged young people with mental health challenges in data analysis, interpretation and dissemination (Peled et al, 2017) found that all 27 participants stayed engaged until the conclusion of the project and all reported that the experience was meaningful to them. The majority also reported improvements in their research skills, emotional wellbeing and connectedness to other young people and their community.

Similarly, a large-scale survey of homeless youth that included young people in all stages of the research process (Smith et al, 2020) found that the youth not only gained skills in survey design, data collection, creating dissemination materials, workshop facilitation and public speaking, but also noted that the experience improved their employment opportunities, increased their self-confidence, helped them find their career path and made them feel they were making a difference in the lives of other homeless youth. After disseminating the findings, one of the youth researchers stated: 'Sharing what we found felt good and it let people know not all homeless youth use drugs or alcohol, and that the number who do is dropping' (Smith et al, 2015: 13).

Engaging care-experienced young people post-data collection can be challenging. It is important to ensure researchers strike an appropriate balance between honouring youth's abilities and commitment, while also not overwhelming or tokenising their input. There is a need to ensure sufficient time and resources are in place to support the engagement process, nurture relationships between members of the research team, work through challenges and celebrate successes. However, participants in such projects (for example, Peled, 2021: 11) recognise the value of these opportunities: '[T]he information I learned has informed my career choice … I've also realised that I bring value to the table.' Another stated: 'I felt that I was able to participate in a meaningful activity and that I was listened to. The research projects exceeded my expectations' (Peled, 2021).

An example of meaningfully engaging care-experienced youth throughout the research process comes from McCreary Centre Society's Youth Research Academy (YRA) which is based in Vancouver, Canada and was co-developed by author four [AS].[1] The YRA is designed to engage care-experienced youth in community-based research. Trained and supported by experienced community researchers, youth members of the YRA conduct academically rigorous, community-based research projects that address issues of concern to youth in and from care and the agencies that serve them.

Members of the YRA learn to create an analysis plan, conduct data analysis, write reports and disseminate findings. For example, under the guidance of a senior community-based researcher they learn basic SPSS skills (statistical software), including how to set up a data file, run frequencies and crosstabulations, perform data transformation skills such as recodes, and save and interpret the output. Throughout the process, they reflect on their findings and interpret the data (for example, McCreary Centre Society's Youth Research Academy, 2022). As one YRA participant noted: 'Youth in care need a voice and sometimes it's hard for us to speak up and I really think getting us involved and to share research helps. It gives us a voice and helps us to tell a story without making us have to expose our own story' (male youth) (Peled, 2021: 22).

Evaluation results show that the YRA model has not only offered authentic youth-led research to statutory and community agencies but has also offered impactful learning opportunities for youth with care experience (Smith et al, 2019). For example, one youth who analysed data about vaping reflected:

'I learned some new SPSS analysis skills and learned about the various associations between vaping and other aspects of youth health. I learned about opinions that other youth have on vaping, how different things that can happen in your life can affect if you vape or not, and that I had some big misconceptions about vaping' (non-binary youth). (Smith et al, 2019: 35)

YRA members' engagement in the development and delivery of dissemination materials has also been shown to increase their sense of ownership, satisfaction and enjoyment in the process, as well as their sense of optimism and chance to network (Smith et al, 2019; McCreary Centre Society's Youth Research Academy, 2020). As one female youth researcher noted in Peled (2021: 10): 'Before joining the YRA, I had no idea that there was a community of youth from care, and only by going out doing presentations and workshops and things did I find all the other opportunities available to us, and MANY other great connections.'

Learnings from the YRA model show that significant change can occur when young people with care experience are supported and trained to fully engage in the entire research process. For example, having reviewed dissemination materials created by the YRA from a research project about how to better support youth who use substances, the British Columbia Representative for Children and Youth called on the government to create a number of youth-specific supports (Charlesworth, 2018).

Ensuring the sustained meaningful engagement of care-experienced young people throughout the research process can be challenging. However, their lived experience, voice and meaningful participation in the co-production of research is invaluable in enhancing the quality of the topic being researched. Additionally, ensuring dissemination materials accurately capture the challenges, supports and emerging issues of care-experienced young people, which adult researchers without care experience would likely have missed. Such engagement in the research process moves the emphasis beyond the ethical standpoint of doing no harm to a focus on authentic reciprocity.

Reflections on the advantages and challenges of insider researcher: considerations for others

Charmaz (2014) states that the researcher's standpoint shapes how we see participants' stories and may stand in juxtaposition to theirs. We may unconsciously select aspects of their lives or episodes within their stories to illustrate our own and by so doing we can support their voices or distort their realities as we know them. The idea of the researcher position arguably becomes complex when you find yourself researching a community or setting you have direct involvement or connection with. Being an 'insider' can have both advantages and challenges. The two authors of this chapter who have care experience discuss how the role of the researcher in creating caring relationships can become tricky when one is care-experienced. We also report how we mitigated issues related to, for example, power in previous research projects that related to our positions in research. We highlight how we, as insider researchers, are experts of our own experience and how research participants also are experts of their own experience. This allows us to craft a caring means of sharing power, including the power to construct knowledge.

As described earlier, there are many ways in which we can care for those participating in the research from the beginning of the research process to the end. However, during the research process we can deploy several methods to ensure caring, respectful rapport is built. For example, in research

I (Farragher) carried out, I found various ways to ensure care for both my participants and for myself as a care-experienced researcher. The aim of the research was to understand ideas and experiences of 'family' for those with care experience. I never found myself to be fully objective and understood that I had my own preconceptions and bias about family, family relationships and the care system in Ireland, given I spent several years in care. I held assumptions about truth and knowledge that are derived from a variety of social contexts. In line with my constructivist grounded theory research design (Charmaz, 2014), I understood the necessity of acknowledging and examining personal assumptions and values, to not excessively hinder or influence the findings of the study. In conjunction with a postmodern perspective, I also reflected on and was committed to adopt collaborative and participant-centred approaches to the research methodology.

One of the ways I acknowledged my position was through the process of reflecting on my position. I wrote memos and reflective notes (much like a diary) from the early stages of the research process. The recording of the researchers' decisions, emotions and insights along with field notes, memo-writing and personal notes are processes described by Greene (2014) and Probst and Berenson (2014) as exercises in reflexivity. While the meaning of reflexivity can differ depending on the context, reflexivity in qualitative research tends to be understood as an awareness of the influence of the researcher on the research and, simultaneously, how the research process affects the researcher (Greene, 2014; Probst and Berenson, 2014). As Probst and Berenson note (2014: 814), reflexivity is both a 'state of mind and a set of actions' which informs the research experience as it is taking place. Engaging in this allowed me to develop a daily writing habit, take time to stop and notice, and crucially, to reflect on what I had already read, ensuring I did not impose meaning on the data.

Additionally, according to Plesner (2011: 471), the issue of power imbalances 'has been an issue for anthropologists concerned with how to elicit stories from otherwise marginalized groups, feminists concerned with giving voice to silenced groups of women and action researchers concerned with making sure research takes into account the needs and wants of the researched'. Reading Plesner's (2011) and Nader's (1974) ideas about a researcher position made me reflect on my position during the research and how I might be viewed by participants given my insider status. The constructivist grounded theory research design that was used helped me give primacy to the data generated in the interviews and enhanced my awareness of possible bias. I emphasised key principles of respect, informed consent, beneficence, non-maleficence and integrity. I also endeavoured to help participants feel authentically cared for, by giving them a list of contact details for support services should they be upset and wish to speak with someone following an interview.

Another way in which the questions of power imbalance, ethics and control (particularly related to my own care experience and insider status) were handled was through practical steps. Before the participants met with me, they had an opportunity to read that I too had an experience of the care system and so insider status was disclosed. When I met with the participants for the interviews, and fully informed consent was given verbally and in writing, I again disclosed that I had care experience and that the current study was something I had a great interest in. Building this rapport, allowing participants to choose the time and place of interview and viewing the interviews as an occasion for both my and the participants' meaning-making, made me realise that the study was not to be carried out simply from a bottom-up or top-down approach, but with a meeting in the middle approach whereby I understood the participants were experts by experience and a co-producer of knowledge.

In contrast to Farragher, I (Horn) conducted a qualitative study in which I did not immediately disclose my care-experienced status to the participants; rather, I let this disclosure unfold organically as the research interviews progressed by echoing how their experiences matched (or did not match) my own care experience. I made this decision to encourage the participants to engage in rich description of their own experiences of seeking support during their time at university and to decentre my voice in the research relationship. In my view, participants who knew from the outset about my care experience might try to use our shared experiences to develop a shorthand in explaining their experiences, which could lead to miscommunication as care in the United States can be meaningfully different between jurisdictions. This would in turn lead to an issue when centring the voices of participants by not being able to accurately capture the nuance of their experiences in publications. Despite this practice of strategic disclosure, I also recognised, as an analyst of the data, my care experience allowed some insight into how some of the narrative fit together, particularly with regards to settings and how stigma was experienced in other places. While both Farragher and I made different choices about where in the process we would disclose our experiences, we both saw the value of sharing our insider status with participants as we believe sharing who we are as researchers is important in reducing the power imbalance traditionally held between researchers and participants. The value of being an insider researcher was supported by one of the participants in my study of care-leaving college graduates (Horn, 2020): ' "[T]he research I'm doing as a doc student, that sort of insider perspective, that deep empathy from having that lived experience, has been so key in not only getting me through the programme, but maintaining my role in this profession long term" (Sarah).'

Despite using strategic disclosure to ensure the participants' voices stayed central to the work, I also recognised that some in the academy might view my ability to give accurate analysis of the data with great scepticism because of my care experience. Prior to engaging in research, it had been intimated to me that I should make sure I didn't allow my own experiences of care to bleed into my work. During the process of data analysis, I consulted two data auditors and shared draft findings. One of the two data auditors was a care-experienced researcher and the other a subject matter expert. The auditors reviewed three transcripts of interviews and looked at case summaries for each participant. They then reviewed the common themes I reported and determined if the data supported my findings. By adding this level of rigour to the study, I was able to ensure that my voice was placed secondary in the analysis to that of the participants.

The two of us who are care-experienced (Farragher and Horn) have had to undertake these extra steps in the research process to address issues of *participatory injustice*, a form of epistemic injustice in which members of a studied group are denied credibility to contribute to inquiry on issues important to their lives (Grasswick, 2017). Despite being as qualified by virtue of training and education in conducting research as non-care-experienced researchers, we have both been subject to critique about our ability to separate our own perspectives on the topic from those of our participants (in qualitative research) or examined data (in quantitative research). We have both received pushback from colleagues about our approach to integrating care into our research practices. Critiques such as these contribute to the larger issue of epistemic injustice and power imbalance by establishing different criteria for engaging in rigorous research for those with insider perspectives than those without. This type of practice is also reflected in the experiences of our outsider researcher colleagues who have found ways to involve care-experienced young people in their work.

How caring approaches can address and ensure meaningful participant involvement

Our experiences carrying out our own research projects have shown that developing trusting and caring relationships with care-experienced people in research design, collection, analysis and dissemination can take time and resources. Researchers need to consider their position, ethical considerations and how they can co-construct knowledge with participants in a way that is respectful, caring and empowering. Attending to these issues is necessary to practice anti-oppressive research practices (Rogers, 2012). However, we acknowledge this may not be practical or feasible for all researchers, given the constraints some institutions place on the research process, variations in access to research funding between high- and low-resourced countries, and the amount of person-labour these practices require. Our position on the importance of care in research stems from a practical barrier in the research process: participant recruitment and engagement.

When care is not present in the research process, potential participants may distrust the researcher's motivation and commitment to empowerment. They may feel frustrated by the different sense of urgency or focus researchers might place on the challenges care-experienced young people are facing. During a pre-conference convening of researchers of transition-aged youth I (Horn) attended, one panellist during a presentation by care-experienced young adults explained: "We are tired of hearing from researchers what is wrong with us. We already know what's wrong. We want researchers to help us figure out how to fix the problems."

This diverging focus between care-experienced young people wanting more information on how to fix the system and researchers continuing to produce surveillance studies highlighting the challenges care-leavers face, combined with a lack of trust in the researcher or research process to accurately depict their experiences, can lead to care-experienced young people avoiding engaging with researchers. This phenomenon is described as *epistemic trust injustice*, or the practice of a studied group viewing well-meaning, well-intentioned researchers with distrust and withholding their participation in research (Grasswick, 2017). To address this issue with care-experienced young people, researchers can begin by yielding the title of 'expert' and deconstructing the hierarchy to which this title contributes. This requires researchers to be fully committed to the process of engaging care-experienced young people, learning their language, using terms they use and, most importantly, learning what issues are most pressing from care-experienced young people's perspectives. In this way, researchers can leverage their positions to reduce the power gap between academics and participants and produce empowering research (Rogers, 2012).

Researchers must understand the unique circumstances each young person may be experiencing and be attuned to challenges that youth may experience in getting and staying involved in research. These challenges could include lack of access to transportation, lack of food, fear of tokenism, stigma, fear of no change or follow up, previous negative experiences participating in research and fear of sharing their story as it makes the care experience too real. Thus, if we wish to ensure those with care experiences participate and keep participating so that their voices are heard, then we as researchers must do all we can at every stage to ensure young people are cared for within the research process. Attending to these challenges creates conditions where anti-oppressive and caring research can be conducted.

Drawing on our experience, we have generated a practical checklist for researchers to consider when approaching and researching the area of care-leaving (see Table 8.1). While we are mindful that not every step can be

Table 8.1: Checklist for care-leaving researchers

1. What is your position in the research? What are participants' views on your role? How might you be perceived by the participants?

2. What power imbalance and challenges to participation may arise (for example, timing of interview, place, funding)?

3. What steps could you take to establish a more trustful and harmonised relationship with participants?

4. What kind of language or terms do participants use to describe their identities and experiences?

5. How can the participants be supported best, during the research process and in follow-up? Do you have a safety plan in place for if a participant becomes distressed? What are the options of support from collaborating gatekeepers?

6. How can you address concerns (for example, trauma-informed safety) that gatekeepers or prospective participants may raise about getting involved in your research project?

7. What steps can you take to meaningfully engage young people throughout the whole research process, including analysis and dissemination?

8. What is your plan to address the barriers young people may experience to staying meaningfully involved in a research project?

9. How will you support youth who wish to be involved in dissemination activities to ensure this is a safe and positive experience for them?

10. Have you elicited feedback on your research tools from care-experienced young people and implemented their recommendations?

11. Have you made your research findings accessible to care-experienced populations, including your participants?

12. Do you have a mechanism for practising accountability to the care-experienced community to ensure your findings accurately reflect their experiences?

13. Are there other organisations and/or resources you can access that will help support you as a researcher and/or your participants during the research process? In what ways may they be of help?

14. What can you do to ensure your own self-care during the research process?

carried out by all researchers, we suggest that regardless of budget, timeframe or scale of the research project all the questions are worthy of consideration.

Conclusion

Care in research concerns two important aspects of the practice of research: power and knowledge. While there has traditionally been a power imbalance within the relationship between the researcher and the researched, many studies have highlighted how children and young people can feel 'powerless' because they have been subjected to the care system. Children and young people in care have consistently reported feeling unheard and invisible, as though their voices do not matter, and feeling a lack of power over decisions in their lives.

In this chapter, we have provided a rationale as to why attending to issues such as power is not just important for those participating in research but can also lead to a caring research process. We have described the importance of why those with care experiences should have their voices heard. Meaningfully engaging care-experienced young people in all aspects of the research process benefits these youth (for example, skills development, improved education and employment prospects, and increased connections) and their peers whose voices get amplified by having their experiences included from design to dissemination. Such engagement also benefits the researcher, who can learn much from young people whose involvement in research often comes from a motivation to contribute to positive change within the care system and to ensure other young people do not go through the same challenges that they have.

As a mix of authors with a range of different experiences from different parts of the world, we believe that integrating care can be done in many little ways. In this chapter, we have provided examples of how we have implemented a caring approach to studies from design to dissemination and our learnings from this. We also reflect on the dual role of care-leaver and care-leaving researcher, with implications for a caring community of care-leaving scholars. While positions in research can be complex, we have outlined several ways ethical and power issues can be anticipated and addressed in research studies. Drawing on our learnings, we concluded with a checklist particularly aimed at early career researchers (regardless of whether they are an insider or outsider researcher or on a continuum) to consider how they can enable opportunities for care, empowerment, reflexivity and participation to be built into the research process, from beginning to end. This may ensure a 'care process' is adhered to for those participating in research. Finally, while we are mindful that not all the ideas proposed in this chapter can be implemented by every researcher in every study, we encourage all researchers to intentionally move towards a more caring and inclusive research process, by increasing the number of caring measures they build into their research programme.

Note
[1]   https://www.mcs.bc.ca/youth_research_academy

References

Avery, R.J. and Freundlich, M. (2009) 'You're all grown up now: Termination of foster care support at age 18', *Journal of Adolescence*, 32(2): 247–257.

Bajaj, P., Borreani, E., Ghosh, P., Methuen, C., Patel, M. and Joseph, M. (2008) 'Screening for suicidal thoughts in primary care: The views of patients and general practitioners', *Mental Health in Family Medicine*, 5(4): 229–235.

Chambers, R.M., Crutchfield, R.M., Willis, T.Y., Cuza, H.A., Otero, A., Goddu Harper, S.G. and Carmichael, H. (2018) '"It's just not right to move a kid that many times": A qualitative study of how foster care alumni perceive placement moves', *Children and Youth Services Review*, 86: 76–83. doi: 10.1016/j.childyouth.2018.01.028

Charlesworth, J. (2018) *Time to listen: Youth voices on substance use*, Victoria: Office of the Representative for Children and Youth.

Charmaz, K. (2014) *Constructing grounded theory*, 2nd edn, London: SAGE.

Checkoway, B. (2011) 'What is youth participation?', *Children and Youth Services Review*, 33(2): 340–345. doi: 10.1016/j.childyouth.2010.09.017

Cohn, E. and Lyons, K. (2003) 'The perils of power in interpretive research', *The American Journal of Occupational Therapy*, 57(1): 40–48. doi: 10.5014/ajot.57.1.40

DeCou, C. and Schumann, M. (2018) 'On the iatrogenic risk of assessing suicidality: A meta-analysis', *Suicide and Life-Threatening Behavior*, 48(5): 531–543. doi: 10.1111/sltb.12368

Epp, D., Rauch, K., Waddell-Henowitch, C., Ryan, K.D., Herron, R.V., Thomson, A.E., Mullins, S. and Ramsey, D. (2022) 'Maintaining safety while discussing suicide: Trauma informed research in an online focus groups', *International Journal of Qualitative Methods*, 21: 16094069221135972. https://doi.org/10.1177/16094069221135973

Fricker, M. (2007) *Epistemic injustice*, Oxford: Oxford University Press.

Göbbels-Koch, P. (2022) *The occurrence and influencing factors of suicidal ideation among people with care experience: A cross-national comparison between England and Germany*, Royal Holloway, University of London (PhD thesis).

Grasswick, H. (2017) 'Epistemic injustice in science', in I. Kidd, J. Medina and J. Pohlhaus (eds) *The Routledge handbook of epistemic injustice*, London: Taylor & Francis, pp 313–323.

Greene, A. (2014) *The role of self-awareness and reflection in social care practice*, Technological University Dublin (doctoral dissertation).

Hammersley, M. (2003) 'Conversation analysis and discourse analysis: Methods or paradigms?', *Discourse & Society*, 14(6): 751–781.

Hawke, L.D., Relihan, J., Miller, J., McCann, E., Rong, J., Darnay, K., Docherty, S., Chaim, G. and Henderson, S. (2018) 'Engaging youth in research planning, design and execution: Practical recommendations for researchers', *Health Expectations*, 21: 944–949. DOI: 10.1111/hex.12795

Hawke, L.D., Darnay, K., Barbic, S., Lachance, L., Mathais, S. and Henderson, J.L. (2020) 'INNOVATE Research: Impact of a workshop to develop researcher capacity to engage youth in research', *Health Expectations*, 23(6): 1441–1449. doi: 10.1111/hex.13123

Horn, J.P. (2020) '"That piece of paper is your golden ticket": How stigma and connection influence college persistence among students who are care leavers', *Child Welfare*, 97: 101–120.

Hunter, A., Murphy, K., Grealish, A., Casey, D. and Keady, J. (2011a) 'Navigating the grounded theory terrain. Part 1', *Nurse Researcher*, 18(4): 6–10. doi: 10.7748/nr2011.07.18.4.6.c8636

Hunter, A., Murphy, K., Grealish, A., Casey, D. and Keady, J. (2011b) 'Navigating the grounded theory terrain. Part 2', *Nurse Researcher*, 19(1): 6–11. doi: 10.7748/nr2011.10.19.1.6.c8765

Jacquez, F., Vaughn, L. and Wagner, E. (2013) 'Youth as partners, participants or passive recipients: A review of children and adolescents in community-based participatory research (CBPR)', *American Journal of Community Psychology*, 51(1–2): 176–189. doi: 10.1007/s10464-012-9533-7

Karnieli-Miller, O., Strier, R. and Pessach, L. (2009) 'Power relations in qualitative research', *Qualitative Health Research*, 19(2): 279–289. doi: 10.1177/1049732308329306

Keller, S., Strahl, B., Refaeli, T. and Zhao, C. (2016) 'Researching care leavers in an ethical manner in Switzerland, Germany, Israel and China', in P. Mendes and P. Snow (eds) *Young people transitioning from out-of-home care: International research, policy and practice*, London: Palgrave Macmillan, pp 241–246.

Kelly, B., Friel, S., McShane, T., Pinkerton, J. and Gilligan, E. (2020) '"I haven't read it, I've lived it!": The benefits and challenges of peer research with young people leaving care', *Qualitative Social Work*, 19(1): 108–124. https://doi.org/10.1177/1473325018800370.

Levitt, H.M., Motulsky, S.L., Wertz, F.J., Morrow, S.L. and Ponterotto, J.G. (2017) 'Recommendations for designing and reviewing qualitative research in psychology: Promoting methodological integrity', *Qualitative Psychology*, 4(1): 2–22. Doi: 10.1037/qup0000082

McCreary Centre Society's Youth Research Academy (2016) *Unspoken thoughts & hidden facts: A snapshot of BC youth's mental health*, Vancouver: McCreary Centre Society.

McCreary Centre Society's Youth Research Academy (2020) *Supports in the spotlight: A youth-led research project into supporting BC youth in and from government care*, Vancouver: McCreary Centre Society.

McCreary Centre Society's Youth Research Academy (2022) *The mental health of BC youth with government care experience*, Vancouver: McCreary Centre Society.

Mendes, P., Snow, P. and Baidawi, S. (2014) 'Some ethical considerations associated with researching young people transitioning from out-of-home care', *Community, Children and Families Australia*, 8(2): 81–92.

Moon, K. and Blackman, D. (2014) 'A guide to understanding social science research for natural scientists', *Conservation Biology*, 28(5): 1167–1177. doi: 10.1111/cobi.12326

Nader, L. (1974) 'Up the anthropologist: Perspectives gained from studying up', in D. Hymes (ed) *Reinventing anthropology*, New York: Vintage, pp 284–311.

National Commission for the Protection of Human Subjects of Biomedical and Behavioral Research [The Belmont Report] (1978) *The Belmont report: Ethical principles and guidelines for the protection of human subjects of research*, Bethesda: Author.

Peled, M. (2021) *Youth Research Academy: An evaluation of a model of youth participatory action research*, Vancouver: McCreary Centre Society.

Peled, M., Smith, A. and Martin S. (2017) 'Engaging experiential youth in a youth-led positive mental health research initiative', paper presented at the 6th Conference of the International Society for Child Indicators (ISCI), Montreal, Canada.

Pieper, I. and Thomson, C.J. (2016) 'Beneficence as a principle in human research', *Monash Bioethics Review*, 34: 117–135.

Plesner, U. (2011) 'Studying sideways: Displacing the problem of power in research interviews with sociologists and journalists', *Qualitative Inquiry*, 17(6): 471–482.

Powers, J. and Tiffany, J. (2006) 'Engaging youth in participatory research and evaluation', *Journal of Public Health Management and Practice*, 12: S79–S87. doi: 10.1097/00124784-200611001-00015

Probst, B. and Berenson, L. (2014) 'The double arrow: How qualitative social work researchers use reflexivity', *Qualitative Social Work*, 13(6): 813–827. doi: 10.1177/1473325013506248

Rogers, J. (2012) 'Anti-oppressive social work research: Reflections on power in the creation of knowledge', *Social Work Education*, 31(7): 866–879. doi: 10.1080/02615479.2011.602965

Ruch, G. (2014) 'Beneficence in psycho-social research and the role of containment', *Qualitative Social Work*, 13(4): 522–538.

Sinclair, I., Wilson, K. and Gibbs, I. (2005) *Foster placements*, London: Jessica Kingsley Publishers.

Smith, A., Peled, M., Hoogeveen, C., Cotman, S. and McCreary Centre Society (2009) *A seat at the table: A review of youth engagement in Vancouver*, Vancouver: McCreary Centre Society.

Smith, A., Stewart, D., Poon, C., Peled, M., Saewyc, E. and McCreary Centre Society (2015) *Our communities, our youth: The health of homeless and street-involved youth in BC*, Vancouver: McCreary Centre Society.

Smith, A., Horton, K., Beggs, M.K., Martin, S. and McCreary Centre Society (2019) *Beyond a dreamcatcher: Improving services for Indigenous justice-involved youth with substance use challenges—A youth led study*, Vancouver: McCreary Centre Society.

Smith, A., Peled, M. and Martin, S. (2020) 'Meaningfully engaging homeless youth in research', in C. Warf and G. Charles (eds) *Clinical care for homeless, runaway and refugee youth intervention: Approaches, education and research directions*, Cham: Springer, pp 405–417.

Tsang, V., Fletcher, S., Thompson, C. and Smith, S. (2020) 'A novel way to engage youth in research: Evaluation of a participatory health research project by the international children's advisory network youth council', *International Journal of Adolescence and Youth*, 25(1): 676–686. doi: 10.1080/02673843.2020.1716817

Unrau, Y., Seita, J. and Putney, K. (2008) 'Former foster youth remember multiple placement moves: A journey of loss and hope', *Children and Youth Services Review*, 30(11): 1256–1266. doi: 10.1016/j.childyouth.2008.03.010

Van der Merwe, A. and Hunt, X. (2019) 'Secondary trauma among trauma researchers: Lessons from the field', *Psychological Trauma: Theory, Research, Practice, and Policy*, 11(1): 10–18. doi: 10.1037/tra0000414

Whitt-Woosley, A. and Sprang, G. (2018) 'Secondary traumatic stress in social science researchers of trauma-exposed populations', *Journal of Aggression, Maltreatment & Trauma*, 27(5): 475–486. doi: 10.1080/10926771.2017.1342109

PART III

Theory and conceptualisation of leaving care

9

Stability in residential out-of-home care in Australia: how can we understand it?

Jenna Bollinger

Introduction

Within Australia, out-of-home care (OOHC) is governed by the individual states and territories. Residential care in Australia is enacted via the provision of care by paid staff, who work on a rotating roster, and care for up to four young people in a house, typically aged between 12 and 18 years. Residential care is often considered to be a placement of last resort, meaning that it is often a young person's final placement before they leave care and young people may be in residential care for many years, despite attempts to limit the duration of it. The participants in the study to be discussed in this chapter spent between two and eight years in residential care, with an approximate mean of 3.9 years. This number is approximate because one young person was unable to determine how long he had been in residential care for. They entered residential care between the ages of 10 and 15 years, with a mean age of 13.1 years. A detailed review of how residential care is enacted in Australia is beyond the scope of this chapter, however, those interested may read Ainsworth and Hansen's (2005) article entitled 'A dream come true – no more residential care: A corrective note'. Furthermore, for a more complete theoretical foundation regarding the issues of stability, see the author's earlier publication, 'Examining the complexity of placement stability in residential out of home care in Australia: How important is it for facilitating good outcomes for young people' (Bollinger et al, 2017).

Stability in OOHC has been explored across many jurisdictions, largely indeed in the United States (for example, Koh et al, 2014; Newton et al, 2000; Ryan and Testa, 2005) and United Kingdom (for example, Rock et al, 2015; Schofield et al, 2017), as well as in Australia (for example, Barber and Delfabbro, 2004; Cashmore and Paxman, 2006). In almost every case, however, these studies have examined foster care and/or kinship care, wherein a child or young person resides with a family. Stability has never directly been studied in residential care in the English-based literature and indeed, the concept of 'stability' has only been given cursory consideration in the extant literature. Stability has been operationalised by a placements-over-time paradigm, wherein a young person's placement history is considered to be stable or unstable based on how many placements they have experienced, therefore, someone who has experienced one or two placements would be considered to have had a stable care experience, while someone who has had 15 would likely be considered to have had an unstable care experience. Cashmore and Paxman (2006) identified that 'stability' based on placement numbers was less associated with outcomes than a sense of felt security within the placement, however the authors continued to operationalise stability and instability by the numbers of placements, however, their findings also identified that those with fewer placements had greater levels of felt security than those who had higher numbers of placements.

Placement 'instability', that is the experience of multiple placements, has been found, with marked consensus, to be linked to increased difficulties, such as contact with the justice and mental health systems in a range of different areas, both while in care and once the young people have left care (for example, Jonson-Reid and Barth, 2000; Newton et al, 2000; Taylor, 2006; Cusick et al, 2010; Barn and Tan, 2012; Fawley-King and Snowden, 2013; Pritchett et al, 2013). Some studies of care-leavers have explicitly considered placement numbers and found that greater placement numbers lead to worse outcomes once the young people have left care (for example, Muir et al, 2019).

While there is ample evidence of the negative impact of placement instability, there does not appear to be any significant reparative power of placement stability; that is, stability does not appear to bring about positive outcomes. Tarren-Sweeney (2008) argued that, for many young people in OOHC, a stable placement may merely lead to less deterioration than may have otherwise occurred, rather than improvements. The reason for this finding may become apparent when we examine how stability has been measured within the literature.

This chapter argues that a nuanced understanding of stability has not been examined in the literature; rather, what has been measured is a time in which a child has not changed placements. I aim to argue that stability requires more than a young person not experiencing a placement move, rather there are likely to be many factors that contribute to an experience of stability. I will explore how participants in my PhD research in New South Wales, Australia, construct stability based on their experiences. I will then propose a new conceptualisation of placement stability and identify how this can be used as a format for identifying whether stability can provide repair of harm.

Previous operationalisation of stability in out-of-home care

There has not been particular consensus on how stability or instability have been operationalised. In 2007, a review was completed that examined, in part, the measurement of stability in foster care (Unrau, 2007). The review found that, across 43 studies, stability was measured in multiple different ways, each of which amounted to varying forms of counting the placements a young person had and determining whether that was stable, such as one or two placements constituted stability, more than this constituted instability. This approach to measurement can be considered a 'placements-over-time' approach to measurement.

Cashmore and Paxman (2006), however, reported that the feeling of security is more important than a placement period during which a young person does not change placements; though these two often co-occur. Within their New South Wales, Australia-based study, felt security was operationalised by collating the feelings, for the young people, of being loved, belonging and having one's needs met within the placement. The authors found that, in general, lower placement numbers correlated with greater feelings of security within the placement. Therefore, the feelings of security are likely to have developed within attachment relationships that have a platform of stability and predictability. Notably, it was theorised that the need for stability functions as a way for individuals to form relationships with people that may become secure through the development of positive attachment. Without an ongoing placement, those attachments cannot be formed.

Connections between stability/instability and outcomes

In multiple studies in the US the link has been investigated between the use of mental health services and OOHC placement instability (for example, Rubin et al, 2004; Park et al, 2009; Fawley-King and Snowden, 2013). Fairly consistently, over large sample sizes ranging from 1,362 (Park et al, 2009) to over 19,000 children and young people (Fawley-King and Snowden, 2013), the results have demonstrated that placement instability is linked to greater use of mental health services such as psychiatric facilities. Fawley-King and Snowden (2013), with a very large sample size, examined incidences of placement change and emergency psychiatric hospitalisation within the first 90 days of a foster placement. The authors indicated that those who used mental health services more frequently had greater rates of instability.

While it has been found to be a consistent predictor of placement disruption, externalising behaviour (such as property damage, aggression, sexual acting out) has also been found to be a consequence of placement instability (Newton et al, 2000). Newton et al (2000) found that for 173 children of a total sample of 415 children in OOHC, who were initially rated as having no behavioural problems, the number of placements they experienced across the study period consistently predicted increased internalising, externalising and total behaviour problems 18 months later.

The authors also found that placement number was a 'weak but consistent' (Newton et al, 2000: 1372) predictor of internalising and externalising behaviour problems 18 months later.

A number of researchers have investigated the impact of placement instability on executive functioning, such as an inability to inhibit behaviour, an inability to consider consequences before acting and an inability to take an alternative perspective (De Bellis et al, 1999; Snyder et al, 2015). For example, Lewis et al (2007) compared 102 children in the United States aged between five and six who were in one of three groups: 33 adopted children who had previously had multiple foster placements (based on discrete numbers of placements), 42 adopted children who had previously had one foster placement and 27 children who had never been placed into foster care and were living with their biological parents. The authors found that those children who had experienced multiple placements performed worse on an inhibition task than those who had been in a stable placement. Furthermore, Pears et al (2010) discovered that as unique foster placement numbers (that is, each new placement) increase, a child's ability for inhibitory control decreases, suggesting that a child's ability to inhibit behaviour, such as taking something that is not theirs or stopping a behaviour that is inappropriate, reduces as placement instability increases.

Stability has not been found to advance more positive outcomes. Indeed, Tarren-Sweeney (2017) and Tomlinson (2008) both hypothesised that positive outcomes may simply be related to a lack of deterioration, or that youth experienced lesser adversity than they may have done had they remained in the family home. Devaney and colleagues made the salient point that stability involves 'children's feelings of connectedness and belonging that are characterized by steady emotional attachments to adults and members of peer networks' (Devaney et al, 2019: 635), however, they also used the placements-over-time paradigm in their analysis.

My PhD research sought to examine whether a lack of apparent improvement in previous studies was connected to Tarren-Sweeney's (2017) and Tomlinson's (2008) hypotheses, or whether it was related to the general operationalisation of stability. The focus of the research was in examining whether, by developing an understanding of stability that incorporated the views, feelings and experiences of young people and staff who lived and worked in residential care, greater benefits of stability can be found. This is an exploratory and novel way of examining stability. While Cashmore and Paxman (2006) and Devaney et al (2019) have made arguments regarding the need for connectedness to safe others as forming a significant part of stability, no researchers have explicitly sought to understand what elements contribute to a feeling of stability and this research has never explicitly been examined in residential care. This research contributes a novel examination of an issue that has received widespread attention, in a new population. Furthermore, research in residential care must take into account how stability may work in residential care, an environment with many moving parts including a rotating roster of staff, multiple co-residents and organisational structures that impact the stability of a given placement. The elements of inconsistency, such as rotating rosters of staff, that are inherent in the day-to-day experiences of young people in residential care, make providing stability challenging, given the lack of a single consistent caregiver, consistent people living in the house and consistent routines.

There appears to be a link between later functioning and the experiences of placement instability, with respect to mental health, contact with the criminal justice system, and drug and alcohol concerns. It stands to reason, then, that by understanding what constitutes stability and thereby implementing strategies to increase stability, then leaving-care outcomes may improve with respect to later functioning.

Methodology

The view of stability as being related to placement numbers led to an overarching aim of understanding what elements contribute to stability, as considered by staff and young people who work and live in residential care (respectively). To that end, an exploratory approach was taken to identifying potential variables associated with placement stability in residential care. Exploratory research, according to Flynn and McDermott (2016), is primarily used when there is little research on a particular topic. There are many individuals involved in residential care, from the other residents, to a rotating roster of staff, to a management structure and overseeing funding bodies, all of whom play a role in the life of a young person in residential care. Merely counting a child's placements and examining their outcomes on that basis fails to capture that complexity. This is because an individual may not experience a vast number of placements, but if the staff and other residents continue to change, the individual's experience of stability may be different and more akin to a young person who experiences multiple placements. Therefore, this research seeks to develop a specific understanding of what constitutes stability for a young person in residential care. This in-depth understanding is best sought through qualitative interviews with experts in their field, consisting of staff and young residential care-leavers, to deeply understand the experiences of stability and instability.

Sampling and data collection

In the current research, two approaches were taken to sampling: purposive and snowball sampling. Purposive sampling is driven by the researcher to select cases that may be useful to the study (Flynn and McDermott,

2016). In this case, this was targeted at identifying participants from different organisations who had different work histories, ideally in different geographical locations, to allow for greater heterogeneity of the participants. In regards to recruitment of young care-leavers, participants were sought who ideally experienced different levels of instability, from different organisations, in different geographical locations. Further, certain groups were deliberately over-sampled (Rubin and Babbie, 2013), also known as maximum variation sampling (Flynn and McDermott, 2016) – a specific type of purposive sampling, as discussed earlier, to ensure that different perspectives were heard. For example, while the majority of staff working in residential care tend to be floor staff, however, in order to ensure that varied perspectives were heard, management, upper management and clinician perspectives were deliberately sought. The second approach was snowball sampling, which involved seeking an individual who fits the research criteria and asking that individual or those initial individuals to identify further participants who meet the study criteria. Staff and young people were not directly approached to be interviewed, however, those who referred participants were requested to identify participants who may meet the particularly sought-after criteria, such as experience in upper management or greater levels of placement instability.

Structured questions regarding the demographics of the participants were administered at the commencement of the face-to-face interview. Staff were asked for information on their experience working in residential care including their specific work roles and length of time working in residential care. For young people, demographic information was collected on the time spent in residential care and OOHC generally, their numbers of placements, and their current experiences regarding mental health, education and living situations. This provided detail about their pre-care, in-care and post-care experiences. Given that young care-leavers, and particularly those in residential care, have poorer outcomes than their peers who were not in OOHC (Baldry et al, 2015), understanding the participants' experiences of mental health, education and housing were deemed important so as to compare the current participants to what is generally known about residential care-leavers.

Ethics approval was granted by Monash University's human ethics committee. Semi-structured interviews were conducted with recent care-leavers and current and former staff members who had worked in residential care in New South Wales. The interview schedule was developed by the primary researcher, in concert with the supervisory team. It was designed to elicit information about experience living or working in residential care, experiences of placement changes, either as a young person or staff member, and experiences of or beliefs about the impact of stability or instability. Interviews lasted approximately one hour and young care-leavers were thanked for their time and participation with a AU$30 gift card. In the final sample were 13 staff members, with a variety of positions including two clinicians, two senior managers, six managers or co-ordinators and three youth workers; and eight young people ranging in age from 18 to 24.

The following vignettes have been written as an amalgam of many young people to highlight what can be typical experiences in residential care. The young people described have experienced varying degrees of 'stability' when considering the number of placements they experienced as well as varying degrees of relationship stability.

Vulcan, a 12-year-old Indigenous boy, was removed from his family when he was eight. He spent three years in foster care, going through seven different placements. He then entered residential care at 11 years of age and has been in one placement in that time. He will regularly leave his placement and go home to his family, resulting in being considered a missing person until he is sighted by the police. He is then returned to his placement where he feels fairly disconnected from his caregivers because he does not spend enough time in the placement to build a relationship.

Lily is a 15-year-old girl who was removed from her family when she was two. She spent most of the next nine years in a single foster family, until she was given up again by her foster carers due to extreme behaviour problems. She has since been in nine residential care placements, over the last four years. She has been in her current placement for nine months, the longest she has spent in a placement since leaving her foster placement. Her co-residents have been inconsistent since she moved in, however, the staff have been fairly consistent. She has a good relationship with one staff member, however, she only works part-time.

Trevor is 17 years of age. He has been in his residential care placement for the last three years and has positive relationships with all the staff members. He feels closely connected to them, however, has no real relationship with the other young people in the placement. He has managed to maintain some employment for the last month, after being out of education for the last three years. He has begun to feel extremely anxious about his impending 18th birthday when he will have to leave the placement. He does not have any family he can live with and is unsure where he will live.

Data analysis

Qualitative interviews were analysed using thematic analysis across a six-step process (Braun and Clarke, 2006; Braun et al, 2015). For the present study, interviews were transcribed into Microsoft Word and then uploaded into QSR NVivo to assist with data analysis. In order to ensure that the data analysis was trustworthy and credible, a number of approaches were used. First, member checking was used, particularly during the interviews, to ensure that meaning was understood and clear, for example, the following exchange took place with one of the participants:

Interviewer: OK, so you said that house worked quite well because of the staff are all really solid and there was a sense that you were generally cared for?

Respondent: Cared and loved as two different words, you felt loved.

Interviewer: By all of the staff?

Respondent: Yes.

By rephrasing what was said and confirming that was the intention of the speaker, the interviewer was able to confirm the meanings conveyed by the speaker. This approach was taken with all participants. Second, peer review was used by providing the supervisory team with copies of the transcripts and discussing coding approaches. Once the interviews were transcribed, specific transcripts were discussed with the supervisory team to ensure that coding was consistent. Third, purposive sampling and maximum variation sampling was used and driven by the research problem to bring both typical and divergent cases to broaden the range of data gathered. In this case, that meant that a spectrum of 'instability' was sought out, from those with one residential care placement to 28 placements, with a variety of pre-residential care experiences, from no foster placements prior to their residential care placement to 32 prior foster placements.

Who are the participants?

The young people ranged in age from 18 to 24, with a mean age of 21.1. Three participants were female, four were male and one identified as a transgender male. Three of the eight, all males, identified as Indigenous. Half of the sample had achieved year 12 qualifications, with a further half of the sample being young parents. These groups did not overlap, that is, those who had completed year 12 did not have young children; those who did not complete year 12 did. Further, everyone in the sample reported having a disability or mental health condition and everyone in the sample at the time of the interview had safe housing. Some participants struggled with recalling detail about their time in care and prior to it, so were unable to provide precise numbers. This makes accurate estimates of average numbers of placements, schools and even age of entry into the care system difficult to assess. It is notable that almost all the participants who entered residential care via foster care reported that they entered residential care because of a lack of further foster placements. Further, the smallest number of total placements had by one participant was two, the highest number of total placements was 36. The smallest number of residential care placements was one, with the highest being 28. Of those who had been in foster care, the smallest number of foster care placements was two with the highest being 32. The mean number of placements was difficult to elicit as some participants could not recall the exact number. This cohort had mixed care experiences, with most experiencing foster care and residential care, however, a small subset experienced only residential care.

Staff participants had a mean age of 44.4 years (min. 20, max. 51), with eight males and five females participating. As is evident, there is a wide range of experience held by the participants, with the mean number of years of experience as 10.8. Most participants have a degree (either undergraduate or postgraduate) from a range of disciplinary backgrounds including psychology, social work and youth work. It is notable that the sample is highly educated, with nine out of 13 (69.2 per cent) staff participants holding at least an undergraduate degree, and 23 per cent holding postgraduate degrees. Those that hold lower qualifications, such as a qualification from a technical college (TAFE) or high school degree, dominated the youth work/floor staff roles. One participant with a TAFE qualification worked as a coordinator, however. Those who worked in clinical roles or management positions all held at least an undergraduate degree.

Novel findings

Remarkably, both staff and young people agreed on the fundamental elements of stability that are necessary. Both groups also identified some elements that were unique to their own experiences that flew under the radar of the other group. For example, young people identified the need for ongoing contact with staff once they left care. Staff identified the need for supervision and training. Before discussing the discrepant findings, let us examine some of the main findings that were unanimous and subsequently the discrepant findings, all of which contribute to an entirely new and previously unconsidered understanding of stability.

Staff consistency

'For me a stable placement means that there are not frequent changes in the staffing and other young people coming and going and their case worker and clinician and other people around them. I think that stability is the people that are involved in their life or constantly there, even if they stay in the house, [change] is just as unsettling for them as moving frequently, which is a worst case scenario.' (KI, coordinator)

Staff and young people both identified the need for consistent staffing as being vital. Consistency applied to both the staff members and constancy within the house, including staff interpretation and enactment of the rules and routines and how the staff managed various situations, such as maintaining routines or addressing behavioural difficulties like property damage or self-harm. It is notable that for both sets of participants, this is considered to be one of the most vital elements that brought stability to a placement, and it may encompass both the house staff as well as the ancillary staff such as caseworkers, managers and clinicians.

Some of the young people reported they had had a great deal of instability of staff, even while remaining in a single placement, or two placements, which led to feelings of disconnection and a fundamental sense that the placement was not positive. For example,

> '[W]ith stability there's kind of got to be that permanency, like we went through probably three clinicians in the two and a half, three years that I was there, two educational consultants, two house managers. So there was never permanence and even with permanent staff, they rotated a few times as well but ... and the staff have to be able to build a connection with the kids: one, it would make working easier and two, it's much more effective.' (E, 18 years, male)

One participant noted she experienced the instability as leaving her feeling that there was "no point in being on this earth ... not having stability ... ma[de] me feel like no one on earth cared ... or the people that tried to and I did would then leave" (B, 18 years, female).

Other young people who reported a greater number of placements, but still had placements within which there was stability of staff with whom they felt connected, reported more positive experiences within residential care: "Well I still talk to them to this day. So I must have had a good connection with them because I still see them and talk to them. Like, they know my kids and stuff" (D, 21 years, female). This finding has not previously been made in the existing literature on stability. However, this can be explained by the previous literature being based on foster care, as such there has been no need to explore the role of a rotating roster of staff. The key difference between foster care and residential care is that foster care is a family-based model, in which the young person resides with the family, as part of the family. Therefore, for a placement to be consistent, the caregivers also, by definition, are consistent and known to each other and those in the placement. This difference between the placement types highlights the need for researchers to specifically examine stability in residential care. Within residential care there is no guarantee of consistent caregivers, nor that these caregivers are known to each other, as in the case of new employees or casual staff. Thus, this particular finding needs specific consideration.

Co-resident stability

Surprisingly, co-resident stability was not raised by either group with regularity. When asked about co-resident stability, the answers were largely equivocal, with some staff and young people acknowledging that it was detrimental to have co-residents change, others indicated that it had little impact and others noted that it could be positive for co-residents to change. Some young people provided their differing views on co-resident changes:

'Oh definitely, you feel the difference in the atmosphere when someone [young person] moves out, you know. You don't feel as cheery as when they were around, kind of thing.' (A, 24 years, male)

'I never really got along with most of my housemates, so when they left it was fantastic. Got peace and quiet. I've had housemates to the point where I had a room downstairs, they had a room upstairs and they've been jumping on the floor all night. So, I'm just like "yep, bye, I can sleep now".' (A, 24 years, male)

'[Regarding placement moves for young people] It doesn't [matter], you get more time if you're in a house where there is two staff members and two kids. Once they leave, you get two staff members so it's better. Until, that's for as many hours [as] there is not another kid shoved in straight away after, which usually happens.' (M, 22 years, male)

It appears that co-resident stability is relevant only when the relationships are positive between the residents in the house. This finding further highlights the need for positive relationships to be at the centre of the stability argument, as without positive relationships, consistency cannot be sufficient. The experience of negative peers, or peers who can be frightening, detracts from the experience of stability, however, positive peers can enhance that experience.

Casual staff

'The same way they were, like a kid wouldn't be OK for you to go look after some other baby and just leave your kid. That's how we feel, these people were like our parents, so we want consistency. We don't want you here one day of the week and then back the next, then you know, off for two weeks and then drop back in again.' (M, 22 years, male)

Both sets of participants identified the presence of casual staff as destabilising for the placement. The participants, as a group, noted that casual staff are unfamiliar both with the residents themselves and the routine. This leaves the young people feeling unsettled. The consistency provided by regular staff is, according to Cashmore and Paxman (2006: 238), the conduit by which 'meaningful and trusting relationships' are formed. The presence of casual staff inhibits the development of meaningful and trusting relationships because they are not consistently there. The young people likened the presence of some casual staff with feeling akin to being abandoned by their parents.

This finding is notable, in that it wholly expands the understanding of stability as extending beyond a paradigm of placements over time. The experience for both groups of casual staff as destabilising, as reducing the stability of the placement, highlights that simply being in a placement over a period of time is insufficient as an operationalisation of stability. For a young person, if simply remaining in one residential house for an extended period of time were a sufficient experience of stability, the presence of casual staff, while all else remains the same, should not detract from the stability of the placement. The fact that, according to the young people and staff participants in the current study, it has a significant effect, enhances the understanding of what it means to be in a stable placement.

Safety

'Yes, that's the main thing, that they feel safe. Because I've heard young people say that they've been at home and that people have come into the house, broken into the house and there's no one there to look after them. Where here where I've worked, I've had young people come to attack other young people and we've stopped them at the front and they know someone cares about them.' (IE, youth worker)

According to the staff and young people, the development of a sense of stability relied upon the experience of both felt and actual safety within the placements. This means that the young people were physically safe from harm within the placement, but also felt safe while they were there. The discussion by both staff and young people highlights that the feeling of safety is as important as the experience of being physically safe. Both the staff and young people cited the need for physical safety within the placement. However, notably, the young people referenced safety almost exclusively in the context of safe peers rather than safe staff, or feeling safe with staff. Staff typically, however, discussed safety in the context of healing. They expressed the view that young people who felt safe had greater opportunities to heal the harm to which they had been subjected and to participate in therapeutic interventions.

Organisations, therefore, have a responsibility to provide an environment within which a young person can experience safety and stability and staff can provide a safe and stable environment. This environment will begin to allow young people to heal, through developing emotional regulation skills, a positive view of themselves and a sense of belonging in a positive and safe environment. The development of these skills and attributes can only occur within a stable environment, through stable and positive relationships with others who genuinely care for them and think well of them.

Ongoing staff contact

'We felt like a lot of these blokes, you know, they still speak to you to this day and have met my kids, you know. All these blokes, they still keep in contact, you know. They've offered hands when I need it, they're part of my family that I see.' (M, 22 years, male)

One important element of stability that only the young people focused on was the staff contact that continued beyond their time in residential care. They commented that the relationships formed with staff were similar to positive relationships with family. They stated these provided ongoing practical and emotional support after their time in care had ended. Some young people asserted that residential care staff taught them about parenting and made them feel loved. Residential care agencies may need to focus more on the importance of ongoing contact after leaving care. They could do this by not only supporting but encouraging this contact and making provisions for the staff to be able to maintain it.

Training and supervision

'I've got a good manager who makes me feel supported because she's always working hard to keep the team together and she's always working with the team and she has the same goals we have – trying to make it like a family environment as best we can. So, my manager is really good like and the rest of my team are really good but it's a hard struggle sometimes for the team.' (AB, youth worker)

Staff identified training and supervision as important. The young people tended not to raise this as a salient issue for them, probably because this is not part of their day-to-day experience. Nonetheless, the staff identified that ongoing training and supervision was valuable in assisting them to continue their work with young people. This is particularly so during difficult times, such as when a poor match between co-residents increases stressors in the house, or if a young person displays particularly challenging behaviours.

Staff noted that training, such as specific training in trauma-informed care, allowed them to understand what was occurring with the young people and develop strategies to more effectively assist them. Further, ongoing supervision provided support to the staff. They noted that, without support, staff tend towards burnout and may take advantage of their leave entitlements. This, in turn, creates greater instability for the young people. The staff, at all levels, spoke of the need for training and support so they could cope better with their demanding work role. The support provided by management appeared to assist the staff to manage the ongoing difficulties within the residential houses, such as challenging behaviour or difficult dynamics between residents. This support helped staff commit to remaining consistent with the young people. Without such support, the consistency of staff would be compromised.

Discussion and practice implications

The findings from both groups highlighted an intricacy associated with an experience of stability that extend far beyond the experience of a single placement equating to an experience of stability. Indeed, it is likely that fewer placements, ideally a single placement, is an ideal outcome for a young person in residential care. A single placement gives rise to a likelihood of a consistent set of carers with a greater likelihood of an experience of consistency with rules, a familiarity with the neighbourhood, and so on. It does not, however, guarantee any of the other elements discussed here. The elements identified by the staff and young people are separate to a singular placement, they are required *as well as* fewer placement changes. Therefore, in order to create an experience of stability, a young person requires consistent caregivers, few casual staff, a safe environment and, ideally, an ability to have ongoing contact with the staff once they have left care. In order to provide this, the staff need the opportunity to be provided with training and supervision. The organisation's responsibility to facilitate support for the staff providing the day-to-day care cannot be understated, despite it not being an obvious or visible element of stability. Staff noted that the work they do is difficult, particularly when there are young people in the placement who are poorly matched or there is a great deal of externalising behaviour occurring. Therefore, being provided with close supervision and support from their managers can make any placement viable.

The conceptualisation of attachment stability can be highlighted by the finding that casual staff can destabilise the placement. Furthermore, that co-residents can change and not affect the residents left behind when there is either no relationship or a negative relationship also enhances the argument that positive relationships, attachment security, is a fundamental need for stability to be present. When the relationships are absent, such as with co-residents with whom there is no bond, or casual staff who are not known, or unfamiliar, there is an absence of stability. An ongoing, consistent placement is insufficient for a young person to feel stable.

There are multiple layers to stability. These include the continuity of a placement, the continuity and quality of the relationships within the placement, as well as the internal sense of stability and feelings of belonging and safety. Staff across all levels identified that with instability, there is often an increase in risk-taking behaviour, negative impacts on an individual's sense of self and disengagement from the house and school. The staff noted that when there is instability, the young people may become involved in the juvenile justice system and use alcohol and/or other drugs (AOD). The young people equally identified that when they were disengaged from the staff they may get in trouble with the law, engage in AOD use, and that their sense of self may be hurt. The young people reinforced the findings of the staff that when there is instability, a young person is likely to suffer its ill-effects and may experience long-term consequences, particularly if there has been juvenile justice or AOD involvement. It is therefore imperative that we consider the implications for this research. Stability, as considered here, as being fundamentally related to positive relationships, with staff and other residents, needs to be prioritised. A consistent placement is a necessary but insufficient condition for a young person to feel stable and for the benefits of stability to be seen. Therefore, we must find ways to ensure that young people have the opportunity to build significant and genuine relationships with those that are caring for them and living with them. A relational approach will require support from management, to provide ongoing training and supervision to the staff on the front lines, increased engagement between the staff and young people to assist the young people to build relationships with each other and the opportunity for young people to remain in a placement with continuous staff and co-residents to be able to do so.

Limitations of the research

The research discussed has some limitations of note, particularly that the research was all conducted in one state in Australia, namely New South Wales. Furthermore, the somewhat small sample size, while not inappropriate for a qualitative study, cannot express the breadth of experience. Both limitations could benefit from being addressed with a broadening of place-based scope, such as expanding the research across Australia, with a larger sample size. Both approaches would provide greater support to the findings.

Conclusion

The case studies discussed previously in the sampling section, Vulcan, Lily and Trevor, support the findings that stability, as understood and constructed in this chapter, is vastly more complex than the experience of a singular placement and the provision of stability needs to take into consideration the elements discussed in this chapter.

Based on the findings in the current study, stability relates to vastly more than a single placement. On the basis of previous operationalisations of stability, the young people, Vulcan and Trevor, would have been considered to have experienced stability; however, would they feel that way? Upon reflection, Trevor may acknowledge the stability he experienced, however it is likely that he is not feeling stable in this time. Vulcan has a stable address, however, he has no quality relationships on which to build. Lily has experienced marked instability, however, may be working towards a feeling of stability if she is able to continue to build on the relationship she has established with one staff member.

The notion of stability *must* be considered as involving the elements discussed in this chapter, rather than an assumption that remaining in a singular placement provides stability. Some of the key findings in this chapter highlighted that a single placement is insufficient for the experience of stability, particularly the struggles reported when casual staff are on shift. Young people experienced increased disconnection and increased dysregulation with the presence of casual staff, which strongly suggests that a single placement is an insufficient factor for providing an experience of stability. Without ongoing, stable, predictable and genuine relationships provided by the placement, all that is provided for the young people is accommodation. Furthermore, the participants identified that when 'stability' is understood as genuinely caring relationships, there appear to be improvements in outcomes. The extant literature that has measured stability purely in terms of placements has failed to find improved outcomes. Therefore, by engaging in measuring and providing stability in the forms of both ongoing placements and consistent relationships, we are able to begin meeting the fundamental needs of stability that a young person has. That is, a felt sense of stability within a placement appears to be related more strongly to a safe, consistent placement within which the young people can forge and maintain (beyond their time in care) genuinely caring relationships with staff who are, in turn, supported by the management of the organisation. This research provides a new and edgy understanding of what constitutes stability. The findings have shed new light on how we consider stability for young people in residential care, through research that has not been undertaken in any jurisdiction. The findings can be utilised by organisations to begin to identify the areas of focus to provide greater stability for young people, such as through supporting staff members to be able to provide greater consistency and be happier in their workplaces, or developing more appropriate models of using casual staff to ensure that there is greater familiarity for the young people with who is taking care of them. By taking such elements into account, an organisation will be better equipped to provide greater feelings of stability and, in turn, potentially allow for better outcomes for the young people they seek to care for.

References

Ainsworth, F. and Hansen, P. (2005) 'A dream come true – no more residential care: A corrective note', *International Journal of Social Welfare*, 14 : 195–199.

Baldry, E., Trofimovs, J., Brown, J., Brackertz, N. and Fotheringham, M. (2015) *Springboard evaluation report*, Victoria: Department of Health and Human Services.

Barber, J.G. and Delfabbro, P.H. (2004) *Children in foster care*, London: Routledge.

Barn, R. and Tan, J. (2012) 'Foster youth and crime: Employing general strain theory to promote understanding', *Journal of Criminal Justice*, 40: 212–220.

Bollinger, J., Mendes, P. and Flynn, C. (2017) 'Examining the complexity of placement stability in residential out of home care in Australia: How important is it for facilitating good outcomes for young people', *Scottish Journal of Residential Child Care*, 16(2): 1–15.

Braun, V. and Clarke, V. (2006) 'Using thematic analysis in psychology', *Qualitative Research in Psychology*, 3(2): 77–101.

Braun, V., Clarke, V. and Terry, G. (2015) 'Thematic analysis', in P. Rohleder and A.C. Lyons (eds) *Qualitative research in clinical and health psychology*, London: Palgrave Macmillan, pp 95–113.

Cashmore, J. and Paxman, M. (2006) 'Predicting after-care outcomes: The importance of "felt" security', *Child and Family Social Work*, 11: 232–241.

Cusick, G., Courtney, M., Havlicek, J. and Hess, N. (2010) *Crime during transition to adulthood: How youth fare as they leave out-of-home care*, Washington, DC: National Institute of Justice.

De Bellis, M., Keshavan, M.S., Clark, D.B., Casey, B.J., Boring, A.M., Frustacti, K. and Ryan, N.D. (1999) 'Developmental traumatology part II: Brain development', *Society of Biological Psychiatry*, 45: 1271–1282.

Devaney, C., McGregor, C. and Moran, L. (2019) 'Outcomes for permanence and stability for children in care in Ireland: Implications for practice', *British Journal of Social Work*, 49: 633–652.

Fawley-King, K. and Snowden, L.R. (2013) 'Relationship between placement change during foster care and utilisation of emergency mental health services', *Children and Youth Services Review*, 34: 348–353.

Flynn, C. and McDermott, F. (2016) *Doing research in social work and social care: The journey from student to practitioner researcher*, London: SAGE.

Jonson-Reid, M. and Barth, R.P. (2000) 'From placement to prison: The path to adolescent incarceration from child welfare supervised foster or group care', *Children and Youth Services Review*, 22(7): 493–516.

Koh, E., Rolock, N., Cross, T.P. and Eblen-Manning, J. (2014) 'What explains instability in foster care? Comparison of a matched sample of children with stable and unstable placements', *Children and Youth Services Review*, 37: 36–45.

Lewis, E.E., Dozier, M., Ackerman, J. and Sepulveda-Kozakowski, S. (2007) 'The effect of placement instability on adopted children's inhibitory control abilities and oppositional behavior', *Developmental Psychology*, 43(6): 1415–1427.

Muir, S., Purtell, J., Hand, K. and Carroll, M. (2019) 'Beyond 18: The longitudinal study on leaving care', Australian Institute of Family Studies, Research Report 019.

Newton, R.R., Litrownik, A.J. and Landsverk, J.A. (2000) 'Children and youth in foster care: Disentangling the relationship between problem behaviours and number of placements', *Child Abuse and Neglect*, 24: 1363–1374.

Park, J.M., Mandell, D.S. and Lyons, J.S. (2009) 'Rates and correlates of recurrent psychiatric crisis episodes among children and adolescents in state custody', *Children and Youth Services Review*, 31(9): 1025–1029.

Pears, K.C., Bruce, J., Fisher, P.A. and Kim, K. (2010) 'Indiscriminate friendliness in maltreated foster children', *Child Maltreatment*, 15: 64–75.

Pritchett, R., Gillberg, C. and Minnis, H. (2013) 'What do child characteristics contribute to outcomes from care: A PRISMA review', *Children and Youth Services Review*, 25: 1333–1341.

Rock, S., Michelson, D., Thomson, S. and Day, C. (2015) 'Understanding foster placement instability for looked after children: A systematic review and narrative synthesis of quantitative and qualitative evidence', *British Journal of Social Work*, 45: 177–203.

Rubin, A. and Babbie, E. (2013) *Essential research methods for social work*, 3rd edn, Belmont: Thomson Brooks/Cole.

Rubin, D.M., Alessandrini, E.A., Feudtner, C., Localio, A.R. and Hadley, T. (2004) 'Placement changes and emergency department visits in the first year of foster care', *Pediatrics*, 114: 354–360.

Ryan, J.P. and Testa, M.F. (2005) 'Child maltreatment and juvenile delinquency: investigating the role of placement and placement instability', *Children and Youth Services Review*, 27: 227–249.

Schofield, G, Larrson, B. and Ward, E. (2017) 'Risk, resilience and identity construction in the life narratives of young people leaving residential care', *Child and Family Social Work*, 22 : 782–791.

Snyder, H.R., Miyake, A. and Hankin, B.L. (2015) 'Advancing understanding of executive function impairments and psychopathology: Bridging the gap between clinical and cognitive approaches', *Frontiers in Psychology*, 6: 328.

Tarren-Sweeney, M. (2008) 'The mental health of children in out-of-home-care', *Current Opinion in Psychiatry*, 21(4): 345–349.

Tarren-Sweeney, M. (2017) 'Rates of meaningful change in the mental health of children in long-term out-of-home care: A seven- to nine-year prospective study', *Child Abuse and Neglect*, 72: 1–9.

Taylor, C. (2006) *Young people in care and criminal behaviour*, London: Jessica Kingsley Publishers.

Tomlinson, P. (2008) 'Assessing the needs of traumatised children to improve outcomes', *Journal of Social Work Practice*, 22(3): 359–374.

Unrau, Y.A. (2007) 'Research on placement moves: Seeking the perspective of foster children', *Children and Youth Services Review*, 29: 122–137.

10

Living an unstable life: exploring facets of instability in the lives of care-leavers in Denmark

Anne-Kirstine Mølholt

Introduction

Social policy, research and social work practice often emphasise that vulnerable young people, such as care-leavers, live unstable lives and that this instability limits their possibilities of reaching long-term goals (Schoon and Bynner, 2003; Wulczyn et al, 2003; Stein, 2008; Ward, 2009; Clemens et al, 2017). The young people's lives are often characterised by fluctuating circumstances and life-changing decisions are made swiftly, such as prematurely leaving school or causing changes in employment, education and relationships (Schoon and Bynner, 2003; Antle et al, 2009; Mølholt, 2017). Ward (2009: 1113) highlights that experiences of instability are one of the primary reasons why welfare outcomes such as educational achievements and emotional wellbeing for children in out-of-home care often are disappointing. She emphasises that instability affects care-leavers not only while in care but also after they have left care to embark on their independent lives. However, there is limited knowledge on how care-leavers experience instability, incorporate it into their lives and assign meaning to it.

The aim of this chapter is to explore facets of instability in the lives of care-leavers by examining their experiences of everyday life. Theoretically, the chapter is inspired by the concept of a 'habitus of instability' as formulated by Justin Barker (2016). Based on his studies of homeless young people, Barker (2016: 680) emphasises that the habitus of vulnerable young people is shaped by precarious and unstable conditions of existence and that they can recreate these conditions in different contexts. Thus, many of their strategies and actions are ways of adapting to the uncertainty and instability in their past as well as their present lives. Methodologically, the study is based on a qualitative longitudinal study that follows a group of care-leavers over a two-year period (Mølholt, 2017). The qualitative longitudinal study makes it possible to follow the care-leavers' experiences of instability prospectively.

The first section of the chapter introduces the field of instability in the lives of care-leavers and presents the concept of a habitus of instability. In the second section, the qualitative longitudinal methodology used to analyse the everyday life among a group of care-leavers in Denmark is introduced. The third, fourth and fifth sections, respectively, present facets of how the young people position themselves in relation to experiences of instability in their everyday life. These findings are analysed in relation to the theoretical framework of a habitus of instability. The chapter closes with a discussion about the facets of the care-leavers' experiences of instability and points to new fields of research to be explored.

Instability as a circumstance in life

Instability in life is often emphasised as a characteristic of youth in general, but whereas the instability of young people in general is often framed by concepts such as 'identity development', 'exploration' and 'possibilities' (Arnett, 2000), instability in the lives of young people in vulnerable life circumstances is framed by concepts such as 'insecurity', 'marginalisation' and 'short-term life planning' (Ward, 2009; Barker, 2016). In a similar vein, the transition for young people into an adult life is in general framed as 'emerging adulthood' (Arnett, 2000), consisting of possibilities to explore adult life before taking on the responsibilities associated with adulthood. However, the transition of young people leaving care is framed as 'instant adulthood' (Antle et al, 2009) as when leaving care, young people must take on adult responsibilities immediately, thus missing out on the preparatory and exploratory opportunities within this transition stage. Consequently, conditions seem to differ depending on the young people's social status. These different conditions not only affect and determine the lives of the young people while young and in the phase of transitioning into adulthood but seem to affect their life in a long-term perspective.

Research highlights that experiences of instability in the lives of care-leavers are connected to factors such as insecure attachments and a lack of stable relationships during their upbringing; frequent changes of household before entering care, sometimes while in care and often after leaving care; frequent changes in social workers; and disruption and discontinuity regarding their education, training and employment (Ward, 2009; Emond, 2014). These factors collectively result in the young care-leavers experiencing a lack of connectedness and belongingness (Ward, 2009; Bengtsson and Mølholt, 2018).

Not all care-leavers live unstable lives. Stein (2012) presents three different outcome pathways for care-leavers, distinguishing between the 'moving on' group, the 'survivors' and the 'strugglers'. The moving on group is likely to have had stability and continuity during their upbringing as well as secure and supportive relationships. They have achieved some educational success before gradually transitioning out of care to live independent lives, often with support from former carers. For the survivor's group, the time in care has been characterised by instability, movement and disruption, and they have likely experienced breakdowns of placements and have, to a lesser degree, obtained educational qualifications. After leaving care, they are likely to experience periods of homelessness, short-term job affiliations, unemployment and disconnected relationships. As for the strugglers, they tend to have had the most destructive pre-care family experiences, for which care is unable to compensate. Their time in care is often characterised by a high degree of placement moves with an associated disruption in relationships and education. After leaving care, they are often unemployed and have great difficulties in maintaining accommodation. Additionally, they are likely to be isolated and experience mental health difficulties.

Bengtsson et al (2020) add additional knowledge to the transitional pathway groups by focusing on the care-leavers' experiences of agency and use of time horizons. Their first group, 'from care to societal insiders', is comparable to the 'moving on' group and is characterised by making long-term-plans that they can follow. The second group, 'from care to societal in-betweeners', is comparable to the survivors. They represent the most inconsistent transitions as they emphasise an ability to exercise agency with goals for the future but at the same time are under pressure from social and psychiatric problems that force them to give up plans and goals. The third group, 'from care to societal outsiders', is comparable to the strugglers. They experience being forced into situations that they have no control over. They act according to a pragmatic agency considering the here-and-now, with little consideration of long-term consequences. These actions often have a negative impact on their lives and further their exclusion from relationships, accommodation and employment.

Thus, there are different pathways for care-leavers when transitioning out of care and into adulthood depending, among other things, on their experiences of instability before, during and after care. As highlighted, stability in life is a central component in the experiences of the 'moving on' group, and experiences of stability thus seem fundamental as to whether the young care-leaver becomes a societal insider or outsider. Care-leavers characterised by instability through their upbringing and during their transition out of care can develop a 'pattern of transience', where they extend the instability into their everyday adult lives (Ward, 2009: 2514). This compromises their life chances and enhances their vulnerable life situation.

This pattern of transience can be elaborated through the concept of the 'habitus' (Bourdieu, 1984). Habitus refers to a person's taken-for-granted and unreflective ways of thinking and acting, which are formed by accumulated experiences through their upbringing and social relationships, thus mediating between the past and the present. It places each person in a social field of differentiated logics and possibilities, and thus the concept of habitus consists of a dispositional theory of action that considers the person's social position.

Inspired by the concept of habitus, Barker (2016) develops the concept of a 'habitus of instability' to give insight into how former patterns of instability in everyday life during their upbringing can be internalised and recreated in the everyday lives of young people. The concept outlines how conditions of existence are internalised and how instability and uncertainty become an organising theme in their lives. Consequently, this affects their life chances in the present and in the future. The concept is based on ethnographic research into the experiences of homeless young people and, as emphasised by Barker (2016), a large number of homeless young people have former experiences with out-of-home care. The concept addresses the internalisation and naturalisation of experiences of instability, insecurity and marginalisation, and how people can come to subjectively aspire to what 'they are socialised to see as objectively probable or "for the likes of them"' (Barker, 2016: 665). The concept of a habitus of instability thus accounts for the regularities of social action while also accounting for individuals' capacity for and experiences of agency. Moreover, these are united as a group habitus when individuals share common conditions of existence and thus share social position. Changes in habitus are most likely to happen when there is a disjuncture between the expectation of the habitus and external opportunities and conditions. Thus, to enact change there must be supportive and resourceful conditions present (Barker, 2016).

A study of the everyday lives of care-leavers in Denmark

In Denmark, approximately 1 per cent of all children aged 0 to 17 are in out-of-home care. Most are taken into care as teenagers, and thus there is not an even distribution across ages. Most young children are placed in foster families, which is the predominant form of placement. However, teenagers are also often placed in residential care (Mølholt, 2017). Out-of-home care ends when the young people turn 18, but aftercare support can be given until they turn 23. Approximately 60 per cent of young people leaving care receive aftercare support, but the provision of aftercare support decreases quickly from age 18 onwards. The most common form of support is a continuation of placement (Deloitte, 2017).

The empirical data is based on the author's PhD study conducted in Denmark with eight care-experienced participants (Mølholt, 2017). While some of the participants had been in care almost all their lives, others were placed as teenagers. Often, they were briefly placed in care as infants or young children and then re-entered care in their teens. As to the placement settings, all participants have stayed in foster families. Two of the participants have stayed with the same foster family throughout their placement, while the rest have experienced greater instability during their time in care and have lived in foster families as well as residential care. They were between the ages of 17 and 20 when they left care. Those that remained in care after the age of 18 were able to do so because Child Welfare Services supplied them with aftercare support. At the beginning of the data collection, participants ranged from 20 to 33 years of age. All the participants were native Danish, and none was married or had any children.

The focus of the study was the participants' past and present experiences of everyday life and their expectations for the future. To gain an insight into the complexities of everyday life a qualitative longitudinal design was used with interviews being conducted at approximately six-month intervals over a period of two years (Neale, 2019). The findings of the PhD study are presented in four analytical chapters in a monograph-based thesis and relate to experiences of their upbringing, family relationships, social relationships and everyday life (Mølholt, 2017). The chapter presents findings that stem from the insight into and curiosity about the nuances of the instability in the lives of the participants found through the longitudinal data collection. The aim is thus to explore and structure the empirical finding of unstable lives in the contexts of the theoretical concept of a habitus of instability.

Five rounds of in-depth interviews were conducted with seven of the participants, five women and two men, and three rounds of interviews were conducted with one female participant as she joined the study a year later than the rest. The first interview was inspired by biographical interviewing and focused on their upbringing and present everyday life. At the subsequent interviews, the starting point was "What has happened since the last time we met?" Different themes such as the experiences of social relationships and perceptions of a good life guided the interviews while facilitating small narratives that are 'the ones we tell in passing, in our everyday encounters with each other, and which I considered the "real" stories of our *lived* lives' (Bamberg, 2004: 267, italics in original). Additionally, the interviews were inspired by interviews that focus on everyday life by having the participants elaborate on the previous day (Haavind, 1987). This elaboration gave insight into practices that often are not articulated as they are seen as common-sense and generalities.

The interviews ranged from one to two hours in length and were conducted either at the participants' homes or, more frequently, at an organisation for care-leavers. This organisation was founded by care-leavers with the aim of supporting other care-leavers. It was also through this organisation that the participants initially were recruited. The study was conducted in accordance with national and university guidelines regarding ethical conduct and data protection (for elaboration on ethical considerations when conducting the

PhD study, see Bengtsson and Mølholt, 2016). To ensure anonymity of the participants, all names have been replaced with pseudonyms.

Facets of instability

Care-leavers are characterised by different pathways but, nonetheless, are, as a group, characterised by unstable lives that challenge their ability to engage in successful long-term and life course planning (Ward, 2011). However, research exploring the linkage between past and present experiences of instability among care-leavers and experiences of everyday life and agency is limited. The following three sections examine facets of how a habitus of instability is presented and incorporated into care-leavers' experiences of everyday life. The stories of care-leavers in the three sections are chosen to give insight into how the young people either adapt to a life characterised by instability, that is, they perceive instability as an uncontrollable circumstance in life, or actively strive to change an unstable life to make it more stable. The focus is on how unstable circumstances affect the everyday lives of care-leavers and how instability in life is a dominating factor in their experiences of the past and the present as well as affecting their plans for the future. As presented in the following sections, the unstable nature of everyday life among the care-leavers is associated with different forms of meaning-making and experiences of agency in life.

Adapting to an unstable life

Mette is in her early 20s at the first interview. She came into care the first time when she was age six, then she moved back home to her parents at age 12 and then returned into care when she was age 14. She has mostly been placed in residential institutions and at a boarding school, but at the end of her placement period she lived with a foster family, with whom she still was in contact at the time of the interviews. She left care when she was age 19 and received aftercare support. She has contact with her biological mother, her father is deceased. During the two years of data collection, Mette maintained a relationship with the same partner but during interviews she was always unsure whether they would still be together at the next interview (six months later). She was the participant with the highest degree of instability in life during the interview period as she changed both living arrangements and affiliation to educational training or employment between each interview.

During the first interview, Mette talks about how living an unstable life has become a part of her self-image, thus pointing to a habitus of instability:

Mette: I'm beginning to accept that this is how my life is. I like stability, but I can't ... I can't figure it out, I guess. And a situation like I'm in right now, where I don't get any money by the 1st. It's freaking unpleasant, it freaking frustrates me, but … if I must be honest, I think it is a feeling that I like. I like that I must take action to work it out and that I'm afraid that things won't work out. I like being on shaky ground.

Interviewer: Why?

Mette: It's how it's always been. Unpredictable. Especially, when I lived at home but also at the residential care. (Mølholt, 2017: 273, all translations in the chapter by author)

Mette has accepted that her life is and always has been characterised by a high degree of instability and, in her present life, she even partly prefers her life as unstable. She has become accustomed to the fluctuating circumstances of life and the unpredictability. Later during the same interview, she nuances her experiences of instability:

'I'm glad that no one moves me around anymore because it was unpleasant to be moved around all the time, but it is also something that I have become addicted to. I mean, I don't like when things stand still because then I become insecure and think, "something terrible is about to happen".' (Mølholt, 2017: 274)

Mette experiences an ambiguity. Unstable living conditions threaten her fundament of living, such as being thrown out of her apartment as she does not have the money to pay the rent. At the same time, however, stability in life causes her to feel insecure and unnerved as stability is unfamiliar to her. It is in the fluctuating and unstable patterns of everyday life that she finds familiarity and a sense of recognition. In her stories of an unstable everyday life, she draws on stories of the past where she was brought up with fragile family relationships as her parents had an alcohol addiction and were mentally ill, so she was placed in different out-of-home care settings. In her present life, she has incorporated these often-shifting circumstances in life, and she is even herself causing changes if life becomes too stable. This illustrates how her habitus of instability is not only characterised by her former experiences during her upbringing but also reinforced by her present actions.

During the third interview, Mette again reflects upon the unstable circumstances in her life. She stresses that children taken into care often feel neglected and in trying to better their own self-esteem and create a new position for themselves, they move physically. Changing the outer context thus becomes a way in which they seek to change the inner context of feelings: '[Y]ou always move around your physical surroundings in trying to get closer to something else. I think that's the primary consequence of being a residential child' (Mølholt, 2017: 275). Changing the physical surroundings can thus be a way for the young people to try to change their circumstances in life through the given possibilities and from their social position. Another participant, Camilla (early 30s), highlights a similar point during her third interview as she stresses that the unstable circumstances during care-leavers' upbringing, with many changes in their care environment, lead to difficulties relaxing and finishing things they have started. To move physically is also a way for Camilla to move mentally and to 'move on in life' (Mølholt, 2017: 275).

During the last and fifth interview, Mette stresses that it is important to be in control in life and, to her, this means creating the unstable patterns in her everyday life. By creating her own unstable living circumstances, she controls and defines the instability she experienced through her upbringing, but which was caused by external factors:

> 'During my childhood, I often had no say in things. I was moved to one place, then I was moved to another place. And when a social worker had to go on maternity leave, I was assigned a new contact person without any say in it. You know, all the time.' (Mølholt, 2017: 275)

Mette touches upon the central point that even though her life appears unstable and with ever-changing circumstances, she feels that she is in control, and she finds a familiarity and security in these ever-changing patterns of life. Stability is unnerving for Mette as it creates in her a pervasive sense that the stable conditions are not going to last, and therefore she causes changes to gain control over the instability and uncertainty characterising her life. By gaining control over the instability in her life, Mette demonstrates agency, and she usually predicts the changes in her life between each interview. For example, at one interview she would state that she would not be living in the same place by the next interview. Instead, she would live there and do this, and typically she was right. By the following interview, she would be living where and doing what she had predicted.

Barker emphasises that stability to young people with a habitus of instability can be experienced as 'ironically unsettling' (Barker, 2016: 675). For Mette, taking control and causing instability in her life is to her a sensible and pragmatic practice framed by how things have been in the past. This gives insight into the strategies and actions developed through her experiences of living an unstable life during her upbringing and the extended influence of a habitus of instability.

Instability as an uncontrollable circumstance in life

Trine is in her early 20s at the first interview. She comes into the study a year later than the other participants and thus the data consist of three interviews with Trine following her over one year. When she was age 14, she was taken into care. At first, she was placed in kinship care, but after a short while, she moved to a foster family where she stayed until she was age 20, thus receiving aftercare support in terms of prolonged placement. During her time in care, she also lived at a boarding school. Trine has limited contact with her mother and no contact with her father. During the data collection period, she lost contact with her foster family because of disagreements. She received financial support in the form of governmental cash benefits at the time of the first interview, but by the next interview, she was enrolled in a bachelor's programme in social education. She lived at the same place, and she did not have a boyfriend at any point during the interview period.

Characterising her life before the interview period, Trine stresses in the second interview that it was 'very unstable. I have never been engaged in the same thing for more than five months maximum' (Mølholt, 2017: 276). She emphasises that her life until recently had been unstable and that she had no money and was at risk of losing her apartment. Being enrolled in the bachelor's programme, she receives educational financial support, and she experiences herself as having 'the best possibilities for the future' (Mølholt, 2017: 276). However, when she is asked what her status will be at the next interview (six months later), she answers: 'I hope I'll still be engaged with the bachelor's degree. And that I like it. Now I'm becoming a bit nervous because I've dropped out of so many things, and usually early on. But I don't know. I try not to think about the future, because it stresses me' (Mølholt, 2017: 276).

Trine experiences her life as becoming more stable, which pleases her since she feels that it betters her life chances, but she is uncertain whether her life will remain stable and whether she can adapt to the stability. When asked how she feels about her life becoming more stable, she explains: 'I think it's important. Because it isn't pleasant not knowing where I'll be in six months. I've often been in that situation in my life. Also, when I was taken into care. So, I think it's important because it provides me with a sense of security' (Mølholt, 2017: 277).

Like Mette, Trine refers to her upbringing when emphasising the unstable nature of her life. When asked about her plans for the future, Trine chooses not to answer as it is her experience that plans for the future and her present life can quickly change. Unlike Mette, Trine seeks a higher level of stability in life and to limit the instability, but it seems somewhat out of her hands to create a more stable life as she emphasises that she is unsure what the near future will bring and whether she will remain in the bachelor's programme.

At the final interview, Trine was still enrolled in the bachelor's programme, which surprises her as she often changes plans and gets new ideas. Like Mette and Camilla, Trine stresses that she has created a behavioural pattern where she seeks new physical surroundings as a way of changing her psychological wellbeing. Getting a bachelor's degree is for Trine a way of getting rid of the social services and moving on in life. However, it is obvious from Trine's stories that she does not experience herself as being in a position where she can control the stabilising factors. She is insecure about whether she can finish her bachelor's degree as her experience tells her otherwise, and she is constantly debating with herself whether she will continue.

Her experiences of instability are characterised by an ambiguity towards a stable life as she believes that a more stable life will better her life chances, but, at the same time, she usually seeks new possibilities to create a different life for herself in the present. Therefore, she seems to a greater extent than Mette to 'go with the flow', and thus there is a lack of agency in Trine's stories of her everyday life. When she is asked whether she will still be enrolled in the bachelor's programme at the time of the next interview, she is unsure, but she hopes so. Her stories consist of a constant attempt to balance a focus on future plans (for example, achieving a bachelor's degree) with a focus on the here-and-now, where she usually changes her educational enrolment because she gets restless. She wishes to live in accordance with the normative expectations of young people getting an education. It is, as she emphasises, extremely important to better her life chances in a society focused on educational performance. However, she is characterised by a habitus of instability, which limits her ability to make long-term plans.

Christian (in his mid-20s) is another participant who seems to lack control over his life and its circumstances. He experiences his everyday life as depending on the status of his surroundings as he highlights that circumstances such as his mother's wellbeing, his relationships and his finances affect the stability, or lack thereof, in his life. There are frequent changes in these circumstances, thus causing Christian's life to change as well. When characterising his life, he emphasises that it is ever- and quickly changing. Therefore, he stresses during the first interview that what he says about his everyday life during one interview might have changed two months later because 'it depends on how things develop as to family and money and relationships. But in general, it is probably a bit more unstructured than other people's lives' (Mølholt, 2017: 272). Whether or not his life has changed by the next interview is not the point in this story but rather that Christian experiences his life as consisting of a high degree of instability and that this is an instability that he himself cannot control.

Seeking to stabilise an unstable life

Line is, like Trine, seeking a more stable life. She is in her mid-20s at the beginning of the data collection. Her care experience started when she was placed first in residential care as an infant and later in a foster family. After that, she moved back to her mother at age nine but was then taken into care again at age 12. She characterises her family as a nomad family, moving from place to place, often to avoid social authorities, and during her time in care, she lived with three foster families and in two residential institutions. Both her parents are deceased, and she has no contact with any of her former foster families. For the first three interviews, Line was living in a different place each time, she was in unstable relationships and was engaged with different educational and training situations. At the last two interviews, she lived in the same place, was not involved in any relationships and was enrolled in and about to finish her public-school examination.

In the stories of the behavioural pattern in her family, Line stresses nomad tendencies and that her mother moved locality each time she had to deal with challenges in life. Line has adopted these patterns, and she describes during the fourth interview how she has a 'throw away and get new' mentality, whether concerning an apartment, boyfriend, friends or educational engagement.

> 'I have never thought that I should have friendships that lasted for years, but now I've had some that have lasted for 10 years. It's impressive because I've always had friends for one year, and then I had to move, or something happened in my life which made me throw away my friends. I've done that for years, met someone and then pushed them away after approximately a year because that's what I've learned. That's what I know of and have done through my childhood, so where should I have learned to hold on to something and fight for it, also through difficult times?' (Mølholt, 2017: 278–279)

Even though her experience reflects that she has friendships that have lasted through half her lifetime, she emphasises instability as the dominating behavioural pattern in her life. It is a pattern of transience, which she highlights has been taught to her through her upbringing and therefore is the only way of acting she is familiar with. Thus, a mediation between past and present experiences in a habitus of instability is accentuated, and as Barker emphasises: 'People can come to see their circumstances as natural and inescapable, habitual, rather than blame the objective order for their disadvantage, unable to conceive the change in the social order which could abolish the cause of their suffering' (Barker, 2016: 681).

However, at the end of the interview period, she finds that her life is changing towards a greater degree of stability as she has realised that the behavioural pattern of 'throwing away and getting new' does not solve her problems in the long run. She actively seeks to change the instability in her life, thus demonstrating agency. For example, she describes at the fifth interview how she is close to achieving her public-school graduation: 'I'm so close at accomplishing something, and I think, I'm doing it. I mean, I *am* doing it. There is no way out. Usually, I would have stopped by now on everything I've started the past years' (Mølholt, 2017: 279, emphasis added).

To change her self-image from one whose behavioural pattern is characterised by instability to one whose life is characterised by stability is a long and difficult process. For Line to take control over and change her behavioural pattern from instability to find peace with stable living conditions also means changing her perspective from an ad hoc perspective to more long-term life planning. However, to assist in this change in habitus, Line must experience herself in a position to change the unstable circumstances in her life through changed structural conditions and opportunities. Barker (2016: 680) argues that 'the habitus of instability reminds us that human action is the culmination of personal histories, external environment and living conditions'. For example, in Line's case, it is relevant not only to examine her motivation for going to school and getting an education but also to consider the general rise in required grades and curriculum to get into education and training. These requirements can limit the possibilities for young people who are older than the general population before getting on an educational pathway.

Another participant, Thomas (in his mid-30s), highlights his wishes for the future, which are formed against the background of his experiences. He wants to find peace and live a quiet life. When asked during the third interview what his future dreams are, Thomas reflects:

'So far, my dream is to get a decent job and own a house or something like that. Get a small family. Actually, not a whole lot. I mean, relax. Enough has happened in my life. It's been disquieting times, so not a whole lot has to happen. I want to relax with people surrounding me.' (Mølholt, 2017: 296)

Thomas's and the rest of the participants' dominating wish for their future lives is to find peace in terms of accepting their care background and to experience that their background is accepted by others so that they feel comfortable revealing their background without the risk of experiencing social stigma. Their wish for a peaceful life also entails the acceptance of a stable and quiet life in which they stand strong and are not easily affected by, for example, their parents' troubling times or other forms of distress in their social surroundings.

To find peace in life is a wish most people can relate to. However, in the stories of these young people with their care backgrounds, the wish for a quiet life is formed in opposition to how their life has been (and perhaps still is) and especially how it was during their upbringing. Thus, the wish for a quiet life is clearly formulated based on their habitus of instability.

Conclusion

Initially, it was emphasised that unstable living conditions and experiences of instability are one of the primary reasons why welfare outcomes are so disappointing for young people who have been in out-of-home care (Ward, 2009). However, as illustrated through the story of Mette, living an unstable life can be a way to demonstrate and experience a sense of control in life. Mette evaluates her life to be founded on unstable living conditions but instead of the instability being caused by external influences, she herself defines and creates the unstable circumstances. Thus, her actions might be evaluated as counter-productive regarding long-term planning and achieving goals, but they must be understood as strategies derived from accumulated experiences. 'Habitus reminds us that what appear to be the choices or practices of individuals can obscure what is actually the structural conditions and limitations from which they have emerged and exist. It reminds us that structural and institutional settings have an impact on decisions and practices' (Barker, 2016: 681).

The young people try to better their lives through the given opportunities for example by moving around in their physical surroundings to experience a change in their psychological wellbeing. Nevertheless, as discussed throughout the chapter, a habitus of instability challenges their possibilities of reaching long-term goals and life course planning and thus adds to their vulnerable living circumstances while in care and in their life after leaving care.

A habitus of instability is relevant to discuss in relation to young people who have been in out-of-home care. The findings reflect that even when they tell stories of stability and continuity in their lives, whether in their present life or in relation to their hopes and dreams for the future, these stories are based upon what they view as a normal and familiar situation, namely unstable living conditions. Barker (2016: 672) highlights that the young people live with a sense of impending instability and insecurity as their habitudinal approach.

The findings emphasise how the young people have limited control over the development of a habitus of instability as it develops through their upbringing and is affected by the instability caused by insecure family relationships as well as being part of a child welfare system where they often experience changes in placement as well as in professionals. They come to aspire to what is expected of them and what is probable. Thus, when they tell their stories of a habitus of instability, these stories are personalised, and it is often emphasised as their own defect and lack of competence if they do not manage to live stable lives that follow normative life course patterns and developments.

The stories presented in the three empirical sections illustrate different facets of incorporating experiences of instability from the past into one's present everyday life. The young people have better life chances when they do not live unstable lives, which centralises the question of how their lives can become more stable. As Barker (2016) emphasises, a habitus of instability can be changed given the right and supportive stable circumstances. Thus, there seem to be two policy points to note. The first point is that measurements are taken to ensure that care-leavers are given the best possible opportunities based on a knowledge of their habitus of instability. It must be ensured that care-leavers are incorporated into their social surroundings and find security in stable living conditions after leaving care. The second point is to ensure that care-leavers do not develop a habitus of instability in the first place. A habitus of instability is derived from experiences in the past, and thus a crucial question is how their lives can become more stabilised during their upbringing to limit the unstable nature of their lived experiences. This must be done through stable and long-term living conditions during their upbringing both in terms of placement conditions and in terms of social relationships with caregivers as well as professionals. The two points can preferably be discussed from the perspective of ensuring social relationships. Gilligan (2012) emphasises a need to focus on young people's bonding relationships to close and familiar networks as well as their bridging relationships that tie them to their local communities and social surroundings. Strong and weak relationships have different ways of offering support and opportunities.

To analytically conclude on which pathway group each of the young people primarily belongs to is difficult. Trine has, for example, experienced stability during her time in care and she is on her way to educational achievement, but she lacks supportive social relationships, and she is unsure whether to continue her education. The findings emphasise that from a qualitative longitudinal perspective the pathway groups must be viewed as flexible and overlapping. Each care-leaver has different ways of handling and acting upon a habitus of instability. Additional research is needed to investigate how a habitus of instability changes over the course of the lifetime and whether the habitus of instability is reflected differently by care-leavers from different pathway groups. It is important to examine, for example, whether young people from the moving-on group are characterised by a habitus of instability. It could be that experiences of unstable living conditions form their fundamental stance but stable social relationships during their upbringing have supported them in changing these conditions and in adapting to stable living conditions, or perhaps experiences of unstable living conditions have been less of an issue for them.

More research into how a habitus of instability affects young people's lives is essential as the experiences of an unstable life seem to affect their life chances not only in the present but also in their future. A habitus of instability seems to limit their sense of belonging and their possibilities of creating a meaningful 'being in the world' with linkages between the past, the present and the future (Bengtsson and Mølholt, 2018). In future research, it is important to examine how it can be ensured that the young people do not develop a habitus of instability and, if they do, how it is possible to help them feel secure in stable and unfamiliar living conditions – thus, to help them create a life in which they may find peace.

References

Antle, B.F., Johnson, L., Barbee, A. and Sullivan, D. (2009) 'Fostering interdependent versus independent living in youth aging out of care through healthy relationships', *Families in Society, the Journal of Contemporary Social Services*, 90(3): 309–315.

Arnett, J.J. (2000) 'Emerging adulthood: A theory of development from the late teens through the twenties', *American Psychologist*, 55(5): 469–480.

Bamberg, M. (2004) 'Talk, small stories, and adolescent identities', *Human Development*, 47(6): 366–369.

Barker, J. (2016) 'A habitus of instability: Youth homelessness and instability', *Journal of Youth Studies*, 19(5): 665–683.

Bengtsson, M., Sjöblom, Y. and Öberg, P. (2020) 'Transitional patterns when leaving care: Care leavers' agency in a longitudinal perspective', *Children and Youth Services Review*, 118: 105486.

Bengtsson, T.T. and Mølholt, A. (2016) 'Keeping you close at a distance: Ethical challenges when following young people in vulnerable life situations', *Young-Nordic Journal of Youth Research*, 24(4): 359–375.

Bengtsson, T.T. and Mølholt, A. (2018) 'Creation of belonging and non-belonging in the temporal narratives of young people transitioning out of care in Denmark', *Nordic Social Work Research*, 8(S1): 54–64.

Bourdieu, P. (1984) *Distinction: A social critique of the judgement of taste*, London: Routledge.

Clemens, E.V., Klopfenstein, K., Tis, M. and Lalonde, T.L. (2017) 'Educational stability policy and the interplay between child welfare placements and school moves', *Children and Youth Services Review*, 83: 209–217.

Deloitte (2017) *Efterværn og den gode overgang til voksenlivet. Undersøgelse af efterværnsområdet i Danmark* [Aftercare and the good transition to adulthood: A study of aftercare in Denmark], Odense: Socialstyrelsen.

Emond, R. (2014) 'Longing to belong: Children in residential care and their experiences of peer relationships at school and in the children's home', *Child & Family Social Work*, 19(2): 194–202.

Gilligan, R. (2012) 'Children, social networks and social support', in M. Hill, G. Head, A. Lockyer, B. Reid and R. Taylor (eds) *Children's services: Working together*, Harlow: Pearson, pp 116–126.

Haavind, H. (1987) *Liten og stor: Mødres omsorg og barns utviklingsmuligheter* [Motherly care and children's developmental potentials], Oslo: Universitetsforlaget.

Mølholt, A. (2017) *Når man har været anbragt. En sociologisk undersøgelse af fortællinger om fortid, nutid og fremtid hos unge, der har været anbragt uden for hjemmet* [When you have been in out-of-home care], Aalborg: Aalborg Universitetsforlag (PhD thesis).

Neale, B. (2019) *What is qualitative longitudinal research?* London: Bloomsbury Publishing.

Schoon, I. and Bynner, J. (2003) 'Risk and resilience in the life course: Implications for interventions and social policies', *Journal of Youth Studies*, 6(1): 21–31.

Stein, M. (2008) 'Transitions from care to adulthood: Messages from research for policy and practice', in M. Stein and E.R. Munro (eds) *Young people's transitions from care to adulthood: International research and practice*, London: Jessica Kingsley Publishers, pp 289–306.

Stein, M. (2012) *Young people leaving care: Supporting pathways to adulthood*, London: Jessica Kingsley Publishers.

Ward, H. (2009) 'Patterns of instability: Moves within the care system, their reasons, contexts and consequences', *Children and Youth Services Review*, 31(10): 1113–1118.

Ward, H. (2011) 'Continuities and discontinuities: Issues concerning the establishment of a persistent sense of self amongst care leavers', *Children and Youth Services Review*, 33(12): 2512–2518.

Wulczyn, F., Kogan, J. and Harden, B.J. (2003) 'Placement stability and movement trajectories', *Social Services Review*, 77(2): 212–236.

11

Understanding the risk of suicide among care-leavers: the potential contribution of theories

Petra Göbbels-Koch

Introduction

Suicide is a leading cause of death among young people worldwide (World Health Organization, 2021). Studies have found that care-experienced people are more likely to experience suicidal ideation and behaviour as well as to die by suicide compared to peers without care experience (Hjern et al, 2004; Vinnerljung et al, 2006; Evans et al, 2017). However, suicide risk assessments are not standardised in care systems like in the United States, and if conducted, the existing tools to assess suicidal ideation and behaviour are not specifically designed for care-experienced young people (Katz et al, 2023).

Although the previously mentioned studies have provided important insights, it remains unclear why care-experienced young people are at greater risk, what impact the transition from care has on this risk and, importantly, which factors can ameliorate this risk, beckoning further investigations. Especially the risk of suicide among care-leavers remains poorly understood.

Interestingly, most of the existing studies about the risk of suicide among care-experienced young people have neglected to consider theories of suicide for investigating the phenomenon in greater depth. This theoretical gap in the research on the risk of suicide among care-experienced people, particularly those leaving care, may be due to different disciplinary origins (like social work and psychology) of (leaving-)care research and theories of suicide resulting in a so-far missed opportunity to deepen the understanding of this phenomenon.

However, a better theoretical understanding of suicide is necessary to guide future research and understand its underlying psychological mechanisms (Grewal and Porter, 2007; Khazem et al, 2015). Bringing together two research fields, suicidology and leaving-care research, will help translate empirical and theoretical findings into practical applications for the benefit of young people leaving care. Closing the theoretical gap underneath the increased risk for suicidal ideation and behaviour could, thus, open up new opportunities in the practical work contributing to much-needed suicide prevention tailored to young people in and leaving care.

Therefore, this chapter discusses how far theories of suicide can help better understand the elevated risk of suicidal ideation and behaviour among care-leavers. As an example, Joiner's Interpersonal-Psychological Theory of Suicide (IPTS) is examined in light of empirical findings from leaving-care research. The IPTS features three factors that influence the development of suicidal thoughts and behaviour: thwarted belongingness (like isolation); perceived burdensomeness (like feeling like a burden to others); and acquired capability of being able to harm oneself lethally (Joiner, 2005). Further details and examples are presented in the section on 'Examples from empirical leaving-care studies and the link to the Interpersonal-Psychological Theory of Suicide'.

Although no published study has applied this theory to care-experienced people yet (see, however, Göbbels-Koch, 2022), examples from previous empirical studies show that for some young people, the experience of leaving care matches closely with the theory's key factors, backing its relevance. While this presents one approach to how the elevated risk of suicide can be better understood, a socio-ecological perspective helps complement this theoretical understanding from individual to societal levels (Cramer and Kapusta, 2017).

This chapter aims to inform practitioners about potential risks and protective factors that could help prevent suicide among care-leavers. I argue that tools based on suicide theories could be applied to advance future leaving-care research to address this issue, improve the assessment of suicidal ideation and contribute to evidence-informed guidelines for working with care-experienced young people.

The chapter is structured as follows: After presenting a review of the hitherto known risk of suicidal ideation and behaviour among care-experienced young people, the key concepts of the IPTS are outlined thereafter. In the next step, the factors of the IPTS – thwarted belongingness, perceived burdensomeness and acquired capability – are linked to examples from empirical studies with care-leavers. The examples demonstrate that key factors of the IPTS are found in the reported experiences of leaving care. After reflecting on the findings within a socio-ecological context, the conclusions of the presented analysis are summarised, and implications and challenges for future research and practical applications are discussed.

Background: care-leavers' risk of adverse experiences in early adulthood

During the development from adolescence to adulthood, young people are confronted with social expectations of achieving independent living. For care-leavers, this is particularly challenging as they often have fewer social resources to rely on and face this transition at a younger age than their peers without care experience (Stein, 2006, 2012). This trajectory often coincides with critical phases of adolescence and young adulthood associated with instabilities and uncertainties regarding future and identity (Arnett, 2007).

The outcomes of former looked-after children are diverse. Taking a resilience-centred perspective, Stein (2006) proposed to distinguish between three typified groups with different experiences of leaving care: those with a smooth transition and ongoing stability in their lives ('moving on'); those who face more challenges like financial and housing instabilities but mask this by presenting themselves as strong ('survivors'); and those who experienced most disruptions before entering care and while in care and struggle in several areas of life after leaving care ('strugglers') (Stein, 2006, 2012). Whether a care-leaver transits smoothly and successfully to an independent life with positive experiences or rather has a disruptive and insecure period with the risk of social exclusion is dependent on a complex interplay of factors (see Mendes and Moslehuddin, 2006; Daining and DePanfilis, 2007; Dixon, 2008; Gypen et al, 2017; Sulimani-Aidan and Melkman, 2018; Bengtsson et al, 2020). Care-experienced young people face higher risks of not being in education, employment or training, experiencing periods of housing instability, early parenthood or mental health difficulties compared to their peers who grew up with their birth family (Dixon, 2008; Simkiss, 2012; Gypen et al, 2017; Cameron et al, 2018). These challenges increase the risk for disruptive transitions and may initiate a chain of problems mutually reinforcing one another. For example, challenges in attending school or training regularly can make it difficult to find appropriate jobs, possibly resulting in struggles with finances and securing housing. Sometimes, the complexity of such issues can impact their mental health and even affect their will to live.

Suicidal experiences can occur not only after leaving care but while in care. Several studies showed that children or adolescents in care have an elevated risk of suicidal ideation and behaviour compared to peers without care experience. For instance, a US study by Taussig et al (2014) found that already from a very young age (9–11 years old), care-experienced pre-adolescent children were more likely to experience suicidal thoughts and behaviour compared to their peers without care experience. This trend continues in later developmental stages, including adolescence and early adulthood. Evans et al (2017), for example, estimated the prevalence of suicidal ideation and suicide attempts among care-experienced adolescents based on three previous studies from the United States (Pilowsky and Wu, 2006), Australia (Sawyer et al, 2007) and Canada (Katz et al, 2011). The authors calculated that care-experienced adolescents under the age of 18 were about twice as likely to experience suicidal ideation and more than four times as likely to attempt suicide compared to youth without care experience (Evans et al, 2017). The report by Brandon et al (2013) mentions that young people in England who died by suicide often had a history of neglect or maltreatment, and many were involved with agencies like children's social services. The authors highlight that abandonment, isolation and limited support were evident in the serious case reports about those young people (Brandon et al, 2013).

The statistics on suicide attempts among care-leavers show a large variation depending on the study's focus and methods: Dixon (2008) reported that 4 per cent of a sample of 106 care-leavers from seven English local authorities attempted suicide within ten months after leaving care; in Goddard and Barrett's (2008) study, 16 per cent of 70 participating care-leavers from England and Wales attempted suicide. A case-file study investigating the risk among care-leavers in Northern Ireland found that 18 per cent of 164 care-leavers experienced suicidal thoughts, 27 per cent engaged in self-harm and suicidal behaviour, and 7 per cent attempted suicide (Hamilton et al, 2015). A study among former long-term foster children in Sweden also found an increased risk for suicidal behaviour with a moderate gender difference: 9 per cent of male and 14 per cent of female former foster children attempted suicide in adulthood compared to 1 per cent of the male and 2 per cent of the female general population (Berlin et al, 2011). Vinnerljung et al (2006) estimated that compared to their peers, care-leavers had a four to five times higher risk of being hospitalised due to a suicide attempt. Another Swedish study showed that former long-term foster children, other former child welfare recipients and adoptees had a three to four times higher risk of dying by suicide than their peers in the general population (Hjern et al, 2004). Interestingly, the risk for suicidal behaviour seems to be highest in the first year after leaving care: a small-scale longitudinal study with care-leavers from Australia showed variations of reported suicide attempt rates dependent on the time after leaving care: 29 per cent reported suicide attempts after three months, 36 per cent after 12 months and 13 per cent after four to five years after leaving care (Cashmore and Paxman, 2007).

Part of this variation likely results from the studies being conducted at different times and countries, small sample sizes and methodological differences. Despite the variation, the consensus emerging from these studies indicates that care-experienced young adults have an increased risk of suicidal ideation and behaviour. However, a deeper understanding of which factors influence the risk is still needed to address this issue.

Theories of suicide and their links to care-leavers

Theories of why a person dies by suicide (or attempts suicide) exist in various disciplines, including philosophy, sociology, neurobiology and psychology.

Understanding why some people die by suicide while others do not requires a perspective recognising the complex interplay between multiple factors (World Health Organization, 2014).

There appears to be a lack of applying established suicide theories to care and leaving-care research despite the potential of allowing a deeper understanding of factors that influence the development of suicidal ideation and behaviour. One of the few examples of theoretical application in empirical leaving-care research is the exceptional study by Cashmore and Paxman (2007). Cashmore and Paxman's study was the first to apply Beck's Hopelessness Theory to care-leavers in Australia using Beck's Hopelessness Scale (BHS). The BHS can help to predict eventual suicide attempts and death by suicides by assessing the grade of hopelessness (Beck et al, 1974, 1989). In the small-scale longitudinal study, the authors used, among other things, the BHS to assess mental wellbeing and the risk of suicide. The researchers reported that four to five years after leaving care, fewer care-leavers reported suicide attempts than at previous time points and were more hopeful about their future concerning getting more settled, a good job, marriage, family or travelling. High levels of positive feelings, self-efficacy and purpose in life were reported at that time (Cashmore and Paxman, 2007). Although the results cannot be generalised because of the sample size and characteristics, they support the idea that hopelessness plays a role in the occurrence of suicidal ideation and behaviour among care-leavers.

Interestingly, the scores on the BHS were significantly correlated with the satisfaction with the level of social support that care-leavers received. Care-leavers who perceived more satisfying social support, for example, from family and friends, were less likely to experience suicidal thoughts and attempt suicide, which came along with more favourable scores on the BHS (Cashmore and Paxman, 2007). Social factors and interpersonal relationships play an essential role in the theory of suicide presented next.

The study by Cashmore and Paxman is an exceptional example of applying an established suicide theory to leaving-care research. Such theoretical foundations and applications seem to play a relevant role in deepening our understanding of risk and protective factors influencing suicidal ideation and behaviour among care-leavers.

In the following, one rather new cognition-based suicide theory is described in more detail and used as an example to link to reported experiences of the process of leaving care: Joiner's IPTS. This theory has been chosen for several reasons. First, cognitions are well known to have a significant influence on the emotions and behaviour of people. As shown in what follows, its focus is relevant to many cognitions associated with the living conditions of many care-leavers. Second, this theory has been applied successfully in research or clinical contexts. For this chapter's purpose, it has been essential that the theory has led to the development of established and clinically relevant tools (questionnaires) with the following characteristics. First, the assessment tool needs to be easily accessible and suitable to be used by any profession working with care-experienced young people. Second, it does not ask about suicidal desires and thoughts directly. Still, it assesses interconnected factors associated with acute suicidal ideation to identify those at risk who might try to mask their thoughts, such as those belonging to Stein's (2006) group of 'survivors'. Third, specific interpersonal experiences are unique due to the care experience itself, which come along with changes in the social environment and relationships like separation from the birth parents and access to social resources.

Joiner's Interpersonal-Psychological Theory of Suicide

The IPTS was proposed by Joiner in 2005. It recognises the wish to die by suicide and a person's ability to fulfil this longing. Thereby, the theory draws a clear distinction between suicidal ideation and suicidal behaviour. The IPTS postulates a three-way interaction of the following components (see Figure 11.1; Göbbels-Koch, 2022: 35): thwarted belongingness (TB), perceived burdensomeness (PB) and acquired capability (AC) (Selby et al, 2014).

TB is defined as the individual perception that one does not belong to an appreciated group or relationship and indicates social isolation and alienation. The lack of social integration and the experience of withdrawal from others can result in psychological pain. Based on Joiner's theory, social isolation can result from lacking trust in other people or the absence of long-lasting relationships, for example, due to childhood maltreatment (Joiner, 2005; Joiner et al, 2009).

PB is defined by Joiner (2005) as the individual perception of being ineffective and incompetent, thereby constituting a burden for those held dear. This perception is related to shame and the focus on one's death as the only possible solution in favour of the interests of loved ones. Consequently, social interaction is influenced negatively.

Both PB and TB are associated with suicidal ideation. According to the theory, both factors must co-exist at the same time to develop suicidal thoughts. In other words, if a person does not perceive oneself as a burden to others and/or feels socially integrated, the will to live remains solid, according to the IPTS (Joiner, 2005). Additionally, research on IPTS also indicates that hopelessness about TB and PB 'may play an important role in the activation of suicidal desire including planning a suicide attempt' (Tucker et al, 2018: 431). Furthermore, when a person develops the desire to die (TB + PB) and the person has additionally the ability to execute lethal self-harm (AC), the risk of a suicide attempt or death by suicide is high (Joiner, 2005).

Figure 11.1: Three-way interaction of Joiner's Interpersonal-Psychological Theory of Suicide explaining the development of suicidal ideation and behaviour

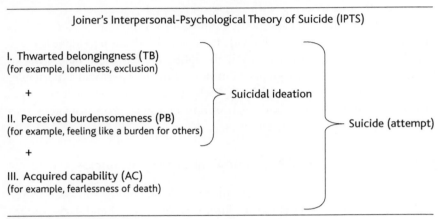

Joiner's Interpersonal-Psychological Theory of Suicide (IPTS)

I. Thwarted belongingness (TB)
(for example, loneliness, exclusion)

+

II. Perceived burdensomeness (PB)
(for example, feeling like a burden for others)

+

III. Acquired capability (AC)
(for example, fearlessness of death)

Suicidal ideation

Suicide (attempt)

Source: Göbbels-Koch (2022: 35)

Questionnaires for assessing the three IPTS factors, the Interpersonal Needs Questionnaire and the Acquired Capability for Suicide Scale, have been developed, tested and validated among different groups, except care-experienced people (Van Orden et al, 2012; Ribeiro et al, 2014; Chu et al, 2017; Ma et al, 2019). Examples from previous studies indicate that the factors outlined in the IPTS are relevant to care-leavers.

Approach

This review presents the link between the potential factors influencing the risk of suicide among young people leaving care and suicide theories focusing on IPTS. Following the presentation of the main aspects of the IPTS, examples from empirical studies with care-leavers link the theoretical constructs to reported experiences.

Cited empirical studies were selected from a wider literature review (see Göbbels-Koch, 2022) based on topics such as care-leavers, care-experienced young adults, outcomes of former looked-after children concerning mental health, their risk of suicide, their social networks and future perspective. Included articles were published in English in a peer-reviewed journal or as official research reports after the year 2000.

The following empirical examples were selected if they link to at least one of the factors of the presented theory of suicide reported as part of the experience of leaving care: TB, PB and AC. The predominant focus on qualitative studies helped include parts of the published original statements of care-experienced young people, particularly their expressed feelings and thoughts.

This approach was chosen to identify links between empirical data about mental health experiences among care-leavers and the presented suicide theory. The IPTS is used as an example to explore the value that suicide theories can contribute to further investigating this issue. Apart from the IPTS, also other suicide theories are recommended to consider for future research about the risk of suicide among care-experienced people to gain a better understanding of underlying mechanisms. However, the IPTS shows relevant parallels to care experience as presented in the next section. Developing a deeper understanding of this topic has the potential to inform policy and practice.

Examples from empirical leaving-care studies and the link to the Interpersonal-Psychological Theory of Suicide

Thwarted belongingness

Schofield's (2002) psychosocial model of long-term foster care emphasised the importance of belongingness for care-experienced young people. She described that a positive experience of belongingness could contribute to a young person's resilience and optimistic future perspective (Schofield, 2002). Keeping this in mind, how would TB affect young people leaving care? Several studies mentioned care-leavers' experience of social isolation, loneliness or the lack of belongingness (see Mallon, 2005; Ward, 2011; Häggman-Laitila et al, 2018; Sulimani-Aidan and Melkman, 2018). An example of an expressed experience of TB is the following quote from a young care-leaver from Israel: 'When I was in the army service I felt it the most. You don't belong anywhere. You are all alone. Although I had many people around me ... still I was very, very lonely' (Sulimani-Aidan, 2017: 335).

Young people ageing out of care are usually supposed to leave their living space and the people they lived with. Returning to either the previous foster family or residential care home is often not possible. Ties established during care, for example, with carers or cohabitants, will break for many young people after having left, often leading to feelings of loneliness (Ward, 2011). The following quote from a care-leaver from Romania reflects this situation:

'I used to live somewhere locked and then they let me out and you say "go"; inside a bird cage and you say "go away"... but I don't know where to go, I'll fly away but I have no place to go; they give you your bags and say "go away", but where should I go, I've got no family, no friends, where should I go?' (Dima and Skehill, 2011: 2535)

In addition to this uncertainty, Dima and Skehill (2011) mentioned that some care-leavers perceived that they had to leave very suddenly. The researchers reasoned that some young people in care possibly neglect the reality of the inevitable moment when they have to leave (Dima and Skehill, 2011).

Finding and integrating into a new social group can be difficult for some, and they struggle with loneliness. Care-leavers who live in more isolated placements are at a greater risk of engaging in suicidal behaviour (Hamilton et al, 2015). Additional to isolation, Slater et al (2015) found that especially older care-leavers who are not in touch with their social workers anymore are at greater risk of suicide attempts.

Adley and Jupp Kina (2017) mentioned that care-leavers missed the support to establish long-lasting, trustful relationships despite the importance of an emotional support network. The authors also found that some care-leavers felt alienated from their peers, even friends, due to their care experience (Adley and Jupp Kina, 2017). The following quote from a care-leaver describes the perceived alienation:

> 'Five close friends from school, they've grown up with me through my different families, it's nice to have them but only problem is that none of them been in care so sometimes when you're down about stuff it's hard to relate to them. I only have one friend who lives on their own who is older than me, all my other friends live with their parents, I feel like oh my god is this honestly just me.' (Adley and Jupp Kina, 2017: 102)

Interestingly, Fulginiti et al (2018) showed correlations between suicidal ideation and social connectedness with caregivers and peers among a sample of adolescents involved in the child welfare system in the United States. Their study is an exceptional example of research on suicidal ideation among care-experienced adolescents which connects Joiner's concept of TB. Although the researchers did not use the Interpersonal Needs Questionnaire, their study highlights that TB can be relevant to suicidal ideation in the context of (leaving) care experience.

Perceived burdensomeness

The perception of being a burden to others may seem at odds with the experience of isolation and exclusion that some care-leavers face. Yet, some empirical studies about care-leavers' experiences in early adulthood provide hints that not despite, but because of a poor social network, some care-leavers may feel that they are a burden to others. The Care Inquiry highlights that '[s]ome of [the interviewed care-leavers] said they felt at their most vulnerable because, if things went wrong, there were few people to turn to, and they felt like a burden' (2013: 19). For instance, a care-leaver expressed the PB even within an existing social network:

> 'I had a lot of friends, I made a lot of friends but I wouldn't really rely on them, at the end of the day they're your friends, things can happen so

I don't want to put my everything in that, I'm more of a private person, I try to deal with my issues myself.' (Adley and Jupp Kina, 2017: 101)

Avoiding becoming a burden for others despite the need for help is expressed in the following quote from a care-leaver from Israel:

'I have only my self [*sic*] to rely on [...] my sister is my anchor. I know that she will be there for me if I really need her. But [*sic*] has her own daily survival with her husband and kids ... I don't want to burden her. We help each other in our everyday reality. But how can she help me?! She needs help in herself.' (Sulimani-Aidan, 2019: 252)

Increased self-reliance may protect a person from feeling like a burden to others. However, the fear of being a burden to others may hamper the acceptance of necessary help and increase the risk of suicidal thoughts. Asking for help is often described as difficult for some care-experienced young adults because of shame or the feeling that they need to prove themselves. Three examples from interviews that Adley and Jupp Kina (2017: 101) conducted with care-leavers demonstrate this kind of burden:

'[A said] some people feel shame to say they need help, it's easier to say no. I felt ashamed 'cos [sic] I'm not good at budgeting.'

'[B said] I didn't want to say I needed help with budgeting because a lot of the stuff they said about me was negative so then they'd say "she can't manage living on her own".'

'[C said] I'm not comfortable talking about what I need, it can be hard to ask, you don't want to look like you're not coping.'

These short extracts from interviews with three care-leavers show the complexity of their living conditions. The lack of trust highlighted earlier often includes the professional support system such as the personal advisor. Despite difficulties and not having dealt successfully with challenges, it can be an obstacle to making themselves dependent on others due to the fear of possible reactions by professionals and disappointing former carers and themselves. The feeling of being a burden is likely to cause emotional stress.

Acquired capability

The capability of harming oneself lethally due to fearlessness of death and pain tolerance (Van Orden et al, 2008; Ribeiro et al, 2014) is consistent with reported self-harming practices of care-experienced young people. For instance, Stanley et al (2005) found high levels of self-harm among care-experienced young people. According to Evans (2018), most self-harming behaviour among looked-after children and adolescents is non-suicidal self-harm used to deal with their identity within the care system. However, non-suicidal self-harm is considered a risk factor for suicide and can result in a lower threshold of fearing pain or death, thereby AC (Van Orden et al, 2008; Joiner et al, 2012). Wadman et al (2017) showed that fearlessness of death and isolation were considered influencing factors for self-harm among care-experienced adolescents compared to their peers. The authors referred to Joiner's concept of AC (Wadman et al, 2017).

Socio-ecological perspective

Why some people experience suicidal ideation and behaviour or die by suicide while others do not is a complex phenomenon with several existing theories trying to find explanations. Due to its complexity, so far, no single theory seems to be able to explain all suicidal experiences in total. Therefore, a multi-theoretical perspective widening from an individual to a societal level might contribute to a deeper understanding of why care-leavers are at higher risk of experiencing suicidal ideation and behaviour than others without care experience. The following framework shows that the IPTS can be integrated into other suicide theories complementing a socio-ecological explanation of the risk of suicide. This concept reflects the relevance of multiple suicide theories to investigate the risk of suicide among care-leavers and prevention options.

Cramer and Kapusta (2017) presented a socio-ecological framework that links several suicide theories and informs a multi-level suicide prevention model. Their socio-ecological framework looks at four tiers of risk and protective factors: individual, interpersonal/relational, community and societal. They provide examples of suicide theories complementing the four tiers of the socio-ecological framework: the theory of psychache by Shneidman, Joiner's IPTS, the Military Transition Theory and Durkheim's suicide theory (Cramer and Kapusta, 2017).

On the individual level, the suicide theory by Shneidman (1998) explains the risk of suicide through the experience of psychache. Psychache is an unbearable psychological pain due to negative emotions that a person tries to escape by suicidal behaviour (Shneidman, 1998). Regarding the elevated risk of suicide among care-experienced people as mentioned earlier, some experience particularly great challenges during the transition from care that may also cause negative, in some cases intolerable, emotions related to the concept of psychache. As described by Joiner et al (2009: 57), psychological pain could also be experienced due to negative cognitions on relationships, such as TB or PB. The potential links between IPTS and leaving care have already been discussed. The IPTS can, therefore, be dealt with on both individual and interpersonal levels (Cramer and Kapusta, 2017).

Turning to the community level, Cramer and Kapusta (2017) refer to the Military Transition Theory presented by Castro and Kintzle (2014), which focuses on the transition to a new position and identity within the community. The authors highlight the transition process that results in either a successful integration into the community or an elevated risk of suicide with links to IPTS's factors of TB and PB. Despite major differences in the situation of soldiers due to, for example, combat experiences that are also linked to IPTS's AC, the particular challenges experienced in the transition to integrate into the community with a new role may also pose cautious but interesting parallels to some transitional experiences from care. For instance, the transition from care to early adulthood might be related in terms of building a new social identity from a child in care to a care-experienced adult, from being part of a foster family or residential group to the new inter- or assumed independent role within a community. Relationships and an often extended formal support network while being in care change because dependencies from and responsibilities of previous carers and support services for children in care often break away when leaving care at the age of 18 years. However, as Castro and Kintzle (2014) use this theory as an example for the community tier of their framework and its links to how PB or TB may be developed, the transferability of this theory to the context of leaving care, keeping in mind that this theory focusses on the transition from military to civilian culture, has to be dealt with caution. Nevertheless, it may help reflect on the changes in roles and integration into the community during the transition from care that may influence a young person's attitude towards life.

Finally, at the societal level, the sociological suicide theory by Emile Durkheim considers the interplay of individual integration and regulations by norms and rules within society as an explanation for why some people may react with suicidal behaviour (Durkheim, 1897; Lester, 1999; cited in Cramer and Kapusta, 2017). The degree of social integration, for example, experiencing a lack of social connection within society, would result in suicidal intentions (Van Orden et al, 2010). Here, links to Joiner's IPTS are also drawn, for example, by presenting similarities between Durkheim's concept of altruistic suicide and PB (Joiner, 2005: 34). Reflecting on the care system and leaving care process within a society, the feeling of social integration may be influenced by some challenges of the transition from care, for example, higher unemployment rates. Therefore, integrating a young adult with care experience in education or employment and providing this person with a contributing role within society may pose a relevant resource and protection factor concerning suicide prevention.

As the socio-ecological framework by Cramer and Kapusta (2017) offers a multi-level perspective on potential explanations of the elevated risk of suicide among care-leavers, the authors also present a socio-ecological suicide prevention model addressing individual, rational, community and societal levels. Referring their model to the (leaving) care system, suicide prevention on the individual level would involve building and strengthening resources, including teaching the young people in (or leaving) care positive health behaviours, coping strategies, and providing mental health courses to all young people with care experience. On the relational levels, carers, social workers and personal advisors would receive special training on this topic, and access to psychotherapy would be possible for every child in care or care-leaver. Suicide prevention on a community level for young people in care and care-leavers would consider connections to the whole care-experienced community and systems like schools. Noteworthy on this level is opportunities for free mental health screenings and crisis support lines, mainly designed with and for people with care experience. Finally, on the societal level, awareness of suicide prevention in the form of campaigns would be raised to reduce the stigma of seeking professional support.

All in all, considering a socio-ecological perspective shows that, on the one hand, the risk of suicide among care-leavers can be viewed on multiple levels with links to interpersonal factors as considered by Joiner's IPTS seeming to play an important role throughout. On the other hand, suicide prevention within the care system may involve multiple levels reflecting on the role of relevant stakeholders like carers, social workers, teachers and other professionals working with care-experienced young people. Applying these recommendations would postulate structural conditions and available resources on professional, organisational and political levels.

Conclusion

Fortunately, many young people who leave care manage to achieve an independent and progressed life and positive mental wellbeing. Yet, some care-leavers struggle to cope with the multitude of challenges they face. Although multiple studies have demonstrated higher rates of suicidal ideation and behaviour among care-experienced young people compared to peers without care experience, a detailed psychological understanding of the underlying reasons is still missing. The role of the transition from care to young adulthood concerning this phenomenon has not been much explored in depth yet. This chapter showed that Joiner's IPTS provides promising theoretical explanations for the elevated risk of suicide among care-leavers, relevant not only for researchers investigating this topic but also for alerting practitioners, service providers and policy makers. The cited examples from various empirical studies demonstrate that the issues described by the concepts and factors of the theory are highly pertinent to the experience of many care-leavers. Further empirical research (quantitative and qualitative) is needed to directly examine the relevance of suicide theories among the care-experienced population.

Obviously, no single theory can explain all suicidal ideation and behaviour. As previous research indicated, combining theories in future studies could help identify the potential interplay between social factors and hopelessness and future perspective (Kleiman et al, 2014; Tucker et al, 2018). A multi-theoretical and socio-ecological perspective is valuable to gain a more comprehensive picture. As shown in this chapter, links to the IPTS can often be found across several theories that make this theory particularly interesting. A deeper understanding of the risk for suicide based on clarified and refined theoretical models is essential for developing evidence-informed prevention programmes and intervention guidelines (Stellrecht et al, 2006; Tucker et al, 2018).

From a practical point of view, Joiner's IPTS has been chosen because it has led to the development of a validated and widely available questionnaire. Should the theory prove useful, the questionnaire could easily be implemented in the support for care-leavers. Assessing care-leavers' perceptions of interpersonal factors and AC may help identify those most at risk for suicidal ideation and behaviour. This assessment is particularly relevant for social workers or personal advisors who are in regular and direct contact with care-leavers to address the young people's needs more precisely. For instance, possible implications for practical work would include long-term relationship-based approaches to promote the feeling of belongingness and reducing the perception of burdensomeness. Social work and care need to support developing and fostering the young person's resources and resilience based on evidence-informed knowledge. In fact, many care-experienced young people have relevant resources and are resilient against suicidal thoughts and acts.

Using such theories and their tools in a complementary fashion to identify what makes care-experienced young people resilient could help build up resources and coping strategies from an early stage. Closing the theoretical gap underneath the increased risk for suicidal ideation and behaviour could, therefore, open new opportunities in the practical work with care-experienced young people.

References

Adley, N. and Jupp Kina, V. (2017) 'Getting behind the closed door of care leavers: Understanding the role of emotional support for young people leaving care', *Child & Family Social Work*, 22: 97–105. https://doi.org/10.1111/cfs.12203

Arnett, J.J. (2007) 'Emerging adulthood: What is it, and what is it good for?', *Child Development Perspectives*, 1: 68–73. https://doi.org/10.1111/j.1750-8606.2007.00016.x

Beck, A.T., Weissman, A., Lester, D. and Trexler, L. (1974) 'The measurement of pessimism: The hopelessness scale', *Journal of Consulting and Clinical Psychology*, 42: 861–865.

Beck, A.T., Brown, G. and Steer, R.A. (1989) 'Prediction of eventual suicide in psychiatric inpatients by clinical ratings of hopelessness', *Journal of Consulting and Clinical Psychology*, 57: 309–310.

Bengtsson, M., Sjöblom, Y. and Öberg, P. (2020) 'Transitional patterns when leaving care: Care leavers' agency in a longitudinal perspective', *Children and Youth Services Review*, 118: 105486. https://doi.org/10.1016/j.childyouth.2020.105486

Berlin, M., Vinnerljung, B. and Hjern, A. (2011) 'School performance in primary school and psychosocial problems in young adulthood among care leavers from long term foster care', *Children and Youth Services Review*, 33: 2489–2497. https://doi.org/10.1016/j.childyouth.2011.08.024

Brandon, M., Bailey, S., Belderson, P. and Larsson, B. (2013) *Neglect and serious case reviews: A report from the University of East Anglia commissioned by NSPCC*, University of East Anglia/NSPCC. Available from: https://learning.nspcc.org.uk/media/1053/neglect-serious-case-reviews-report.pdf

Cameron, C., Hollingworth, K., Schoon, I., van Santen, E., Schröer, W., Ristikari, T., Heino, T. and Pekkarinen, E. (2018) 'Care leavers in early adulthood: How do they fare in Britain, Finland and Germany?', *Children and Youth Services Review*, 87: 163–172.

The Care Inquiry (2013) *The views and recommendations of children and young people involved in the Care Inquiry*. Available from: https://thecareinquiry.files.wordpress.com/2013/04/ci-views-recommendations-of-yp.pdf

Cashmore, J. and Paxman, M. (2007) *Wards leaving care: Four to five years on. A longitudinal study*, Social Policy Research Centre, University of New South Wales.

Castro, C.A. and Kintzle, S. (2014) 'Suicides in the military: The post-modern combat veteran and the Hemingway effect', *Current Psychiatry Reports*, 16: 460. https://doi.org/10.1007/s11920-014-0460-1

Chu, C., Buchman-Schmitt, J.M., Stanley, I.H., Hom, M.A., Tucker, R.P., Hagan, C.R., Rogers, M.L., Podlogar, M.C., Chiurliza, B., Ringer, F.B., Michaels, M.S., Patros, C.H.G. and Joiner, T.E. (2017) 'The interpersonal theory of suicide: A systematic review and meta-analysis of a decade of cross-national research', *Psychological Bulletin*, 143: 1313–1345. https://doi.org/10.1037/bul0000123

Cramer, R.J. and Kapusta, N.D. (2017) 'A social-ecological framework of theory, assessment, and prevention of suicide', *Frontiers in Psychology*, 8: 1756. https://doi.org/10.3389/fpsyg.2017.01756

Daining, C. and DePanfilis, D. (2007) 'Resilience of youth in transition from out-of-home care to adulthood', *Children and Youth Services Review*, 29: 1158–1178.

Dima, G. and Skehill, C. (2011) 'Making sense of leaving care: The contribution of Bridges model to transition to understanding the psycho-social process', *Children and Youth Services Review*, 33: 2532–2539.

Dixon, J. (2008) 'Young people leaving care: Health, well-being and outcomes', *Child & Family Social Work*, 13: 207–217. https://doi.org/doi:10.1111/j.1365-2206.2007.00538.x

Evans, R. (2018) 'Survival, signaling, and security: Foster carers' and residential carers' accounts of self-harming practices among children and young people in care', *Qualitative Health Research*, 28: 939–949. https://doi.org/10.1177/1049732318759935

Evans, R., White, J., Turley, R., Slater, T., Morgan, H., Strange, H. and Scourfield, J. (2017) 'Comparison of suicidal ideation, suicide attempt and suicide in children and young people in care and non-care populations: Systematic review and meta-analysis of prevalence', *Children and Youth Services Review*, 82: 122–129.

Fulginiti, A., He, A.S. and Negriff, S. (2018) 'Suicidal because I don't feel connected or vice versa? A longitudinal study of suicidal ideation and connectedness among child welfare youth', *Child Abuse & Neglect*, 86: 278–289. https://doi.org/10.1016/j.chiabu.2018.10.010

Göbbels-Koch, P. (2022) *The occurrence and influencing factors of suicidal ideation among people with care experience: A cross-national comparison between England and Germany*, Royal Holloway, University of London (PhD thesis).

Goddard, J. and Barrett, S. (2008) 'Guidance, policy and practice and the health need of young people leaving care', *Journal of Social Welfare and Family*, 30: 31–47.

Grewal, P.K. and Porter, J.E. (2007) 'Hope theory: A framework for understanding suicidal action', *Death Studies*, 31: 131–154. https://doi.org/10.1080/07481180601100491

Gypen, L., Vanderfaeillie, J., De Maeyer, S., Belenger, L. and Van Holen, F. (2017) 'Outcomes of children who grew up in foster care: Systematic-review', *Children and Youth Services Review*, 76: 74–83.

Häggman-Laitila, A., Salokekkilä, P. and Karki, S. (2018) 'Transition to adult life of young people leaving foster care: A qualitative systematic review', *Children and Youth Services Review*, 95: 134–143. https://doi.org/10.1016/j.childyouth.2018.08.017

Hamilton, D.J., Taylor, B.J., Campbell, K. and Bickerstaff, D. (2015) 'Suicidal ideation and behaviour among young people leaving care: Case-file survey', *Child Care in Practice*, 21: 160–176. https://doi.org/10.1080/13575279.2014.994475

Hjern, A., Vinnerljung, B. and Lindblad, F. (2004) 'Avoidable mortality among child welfare recipients and intercountry adoptees: A national cohort study', *Journal of Epidemiology and Community Health*, 58(5): 412–417.

Joiner, T.E. (2005) *Why people die by suicide*, Cambridge, MA and London: Harvard University Press.

Joiner, T.E., Van Orden, K.A., Witte, T.K. and Rudd, M.D. (2009) *The interpersonal theory of suicide: Guidance for working with suicidal clients*, Washington, DC: American Psychological Association. https://doi.org/10.1037/11869-000

Joiner, T.E., Ribeiro, J.D. and Silva, C. (2012) 'Nonsuicidal self-injury, suicidal behavior, and their co-occurrence as viewed through the lens of the interpersonal theory of suicide', *Current Directions in Psychological Science*, 21: 342–347.

Katz, C.C., Gopalan, G., Wall, E., Leoni-Hughes, H., Pargiter, T. and Collins, D. (2023) 'Screening and assessment of suicidal behavior in transition-age youth with foster care involvement', *Child and Adolescent Social Work Journal*. https://doi.org/10.1007/s10560-023-00913-4

Katz, L.Y., Au, W., Singal, D., Brownell, M., Roos, N., Martens, P.J., Chateau, D., Enns, M.W., Kozyrskyj, A.L. and Sareen, J. (2011) 'Suicide and suicide attempts in children and adolescents in the child welfare system', *CMAJ*, 183: 1977–1981.

Khazem, L.R., Jahn, D.R., Cukrowicz, K.C. and Anestis, M.D. (2015) 'Physical disability and the interpersonal theory of suicide', *Death Studies*, 39: 641–646. https://doi.org/10.1080/07481187.2015.1047061

Kleiman, E.M., Law, K.C. and Anestis, M.D. (2014) 'Do theories of suicide play well together? Integrating components of the hopelessness and interpersonal psychological theories of suicide', *Comprehensive Psychiatry*, 55: 431–438.

Ma, J.S., Batterham, P.J., Calear, A.L. and Han, J. (2019) 'Suicide risk across latent class subgroups: A test of the generalizability of the interpersonal psychological theory of suicide', *Suicide and Life-Threatening Behavior*, 49: 137–154. https://doi.org/10.1111/sltb.12426

Mallon, J. (2005) 'Academic underachievement and exclusion of people who have been looked after in local authority care', *Research in Post-Compulsory Education*, 10: 83–104.

Mendes, P. and Moslehuddin, B. (2006) 'From dependence to interdependence: Towards better outcomes for young people leaving state care', *Child Abuse Review*, 15: 110–126.

Pilowsky, D.J. and Wu, L.-T. (2006) 'Psychiatric symptoms and substance use disorders in a nationally representative sample of American adolescents involved with foster care', *Journal of Adolescent Health*, 38(4): 351–358. https://doi.org/10.1016/j.jadohealth.2005.06.014

Ribeiro, J.D., Witte, T.K., Van Orden, K.A., Selby, E.A., Gordon, K.H., Bender, T.W. and Joiner, T.E. (2014) 'Fearlessness about death: The psychometric properties and construct validity of the revision to the Acquired Capability for Suicide Scale', *Psychological Assessment*, 26(1): 115–126. https://doi.org/10.1037/a0034858

Sawyer, M.G., Carbone, J.A., Searle, A.K. and Robinson, P. (2007) 'The mental health and wellbeing of children and adolescents in home-based foster care', *Medical Journal of Australia*, 186(4): 181–184. https://doi.org/10.5694/j.1326-5377.2007.tb00857.x

Schofield, G. (2002) 'The significance of a secure base: A psychosocial model of long-term foster care', *Child & Family Social Work*, 7(4): 259–272. https://doi.org/10.1046/j.1365-2206.2002.00254.x

Selby, E.A., Joiner, T.E. and Ribeiro, J. (2014) 'Comprehensive theories of suicidal behaviors', in M.K. Nock (ed) *The Oxford handbook of suicide and self-injury*, Oxford: Oxford University Press, pp 286–307.

Shneidman, E.S. (1998) 'Perspectives on suicidology: Further reflections on suicide and psychache', *Suicide and Life-Threatening Behavior*, 28: 245–250.

Simkiss, D. (2012) 'Outcomes for looked after children and young people', *Paediatrics and Child Health*, 22: 388–392.

Slater, T., Scourfield, J. and Greenland, K. (2015) 'Suicide attempts and social worker contact: Secondary analysis of a general population study', *British Journal of Social Work*, 45: 378–394. https://doi.org/10.1093/bjsw/bct112

Stanley, N., Riordan, D. and Alaszewski, H. (2005) 'The mental health of looked after children: Matching response to need', *Health & Social Care in the Community*, 13: 239–248. https://doi.org/10.1111/j.1365-2524.2005.00556.x

Stein, M. (2006) 'Research review: Young people leaving care', *Child & Family Social Work*, 11: 273–279.

Stein, M. (2012) *Young people leaving care: Supporting pathways to adulthood*, London and Philadelphia: Jessica Kingsley Publishers.

Stellrecht, N.E., Gordon, K.H., Van Orden, K., Witte, T.K., Wingate, L.R., Cukrowicz, K.C., Butler, M., Schmidt, N.B. and Fitzpatrick, K.K. and Joiner, T.E. (2006) 'Clinical applications of the interpersonal-psychological theory of attempted and completed suicide', *Journal of Clinical Psychology*, 62(2): 211–222. https://doi.org/10.1002/jclp.20224

Sulimani-Aidan, Y. (2017) 'To dream the impossible dream: Care leavers' challenges and barriers in pursuing their future expectations and goals', *Children and Youth Services Review*, 81: 332–339. https://doi.org/10.1016/j.childyouth.2017.08.025

Sulimani-Aidan, Y. (2019) 'Qualitative exploration of supporting figures in the lives of emerging adults who left care compared with their noncare-leaving peers', *Child & Family Social Work*, 24: 247–255. https://doi.org/10.1111/cfs.12609

Sulimani-Aidan, Y. and Melkman, E. (2018) 'Risk and resilience in the transition to adulthood from the point of view of care leavers and caseworkers', *Children and Youth Services Review*, 88: 135–140. https://doi.org/10.1016/j.childyouth.2018.03.012

Taussig, H.N., Harpin, S.B. and Maquire, S.A. (2014) 'Suicidality among preadolescent maltreated children in foster care', *Child Maltreatment*, 19: 17–26.

Tucker, R.P., Hagan, C.R., Hill, R.M., Slish, M.L., Bagge, C.L., Joiner, T.E. and Wingate, L.R. (2018) 'Empirical extension of the interpersonal theory of suicide: Investigating the role of interpersonal hopelessness', *Psychiatry Research*, 259: 427–432. https://doi.org/10.1016/j.psychres.2017.11.005

Van Orden, K.A., Witte, T.K., Gordon, K.H., Bender, T.W. and Joiner, T.E. (2008) 'Suicidal desire and the capability for suicide: Tests of the interpersonal-psychological theory of suicidal behavior among adults', *Journal of Consulting and Clinical Psychology, Suicide and Nonsuicidal Self-Injury*, 76: 72–83. https://doi.org/10.1037/0022-006X.76.1.72

Van Orden, K.A., Witte, T.K., Cukrowicz, K.C., Braithwaite, S.R., Selby, E.A. and Joiner, T.E. (2010) 'The interpersonal theory of suicide', *Psychological Review*, 117: 575–600. https://doi.org/10.1037/a0018697

Van Orden, K.A., Cukrowicz, K.C., Witte, T.K. and Joiner, T.E. (2012) 'Thwarted belongingness and perceived burdensomeness: Construct validity and psychometric properties of the interpersonal needs questionnaire', *Psychological Assessment*, 24: 197–215.

Vinnerljung, B., Hjern, A. and Lindblad, F. (2006) 'Suicide attempts and severe psychiatric morbidity among former child welfare clients: A national cohort study', *Journal of Child Psychology and Psychiatry*, 47: 723–733.

Wadman, R., Clarke, D., Sayal, K., Armstrong, M., Harroe, C., Majumder, P., Vostanis, P. and Townsend, E. (2017) 'A sequence analysis of patterns in self-harm in young people with and without experience of being looked after in care', *British Journal of Clinical Psychology*, 56: 388–407. https://doi.org/10.1111/bjc.12145

Ward, H. (2011) 'Continuities and discontinuities: Issues concerning the establishment of a persistent sense of self amongst care leavers', *Children and Youth Services Review*, 33: 2512–2518. https://doi.org/10.1016/j.childyouth.2011.08.028

World Health Organization (2014) *Preventing suicide. A global imperative. Executive summary.* Available from: https://www.who.int/publications/i/item/9789241564779

World Health Organization (2021) *Suicide worldwide in 2019: Global health estimates.* Available from: https://www.who.int/publications/i/item/9789240026643

12

Getting by and getting ahead in Australia: a conceptual approach to examining the individual impact of informal social capital on care-leaver transitions

Jacinta Waugh, Philip Mendes and Catherine Flynn

Introduction

Positive social capital or social support plays a significant role in smooth transitions to adulthood for young people leaving care. Different types of statistical modelling and analyses have been used to measure social capital (see Greeson et al, 2015; Okpych et al, 2018) and inductive, thematic analytical approaches have been mainly employed in qualitative studies (see Rogers, 2017, 2018; Mann-Feder, 2018). Building on this knowledge base, the lead author developed a conceptual and analytical framework by drawing on the social capital and social support literature (distinguished in Figure 12.1). Adapted from Bourdieu and Wacquant (1992: 119), social capital refers to resources a care-leaver gains through their network. Canavan et al (2016) define social support as actual or perceived assistance provided by others. Using the conceptual framework, we explore how social capital and social support interact to support young people leaving care. We also anticipate that the framework can contribute to better understanding how the informal relationship between the care-leaver and their nominated, unpaid support person works. This is done by bringing the lenses of social capital and social support concepts together to explore this relationship in detail. This conceptual lens was advocated by Canavan et al (2016) in understanding family support. The study seeks to contribute knowledge more broadly to care-leavers' transitions and how informal relationships can improve the likelihood of a more gradual transition.

Study foundation and conceptual framework

The framework facilitates examining the interaction of social capital and social support in the informal relationships between young care-leavers and

Figure 12.1: Integrated conceptual framework

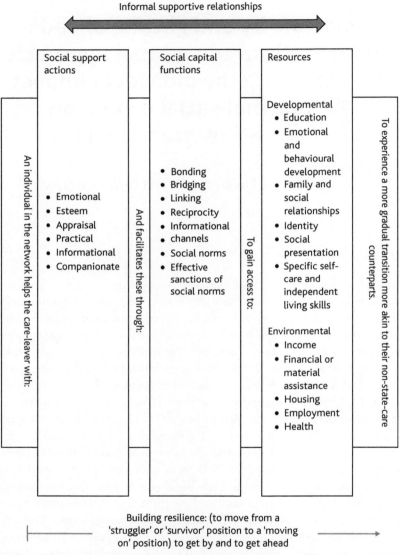

Source: Compiled from Bourdieu, 1986; Coleman, 1988; Putnam, 2000; Wills and Shinar, 2000; Woolcock and Narayan, 2000; Mendes et al, 2011; Torche and Valenzeula, 2011; Stein, 2012; Canavan et al, 2016; Kenny and Connors, 2017; Okpych et al, 2018; DFFH, 2019

their support people. Consequently, the study offers an explicitly theoretical perspective. The conceptual framework draws from understandings of social capital (Bourdieu, 1986; Coleman, 1988; Putnam, 2000; Woolcock and Narayan, 2000) and social support (Wills and Shinar, 2000; Canavan et al, 2016; Okpych et al, 2018), to consider the meeting of care-leavers' developmental and environmental needs (Mendes et al, 2011; Stein, 2012; DFFH, 2019). The study is also positioned within relevant concepts drawn from youth to adulthood transition (Elder, 1998; Coleman, 2011), and particularly Stein's typology of care-leaver resilience (Stein, 2012).

We outline these concepts separately in what follows, but simultaneously illustrate how they work together to form the conceptual framework that seeks to examine in what ways informal, supportive relationships may assist in a gradual transition for care-leavers, as depicted in Figure 12.1.

Youth to adulthood transition

A 'life course' perspective (Elder, 1998) takes account of the structural drivers of young people's transition to adulthood and the adversity they may encounter. It acknowledges that the transition to adulthood is characterised by overlapping and multiple changes (Stein, 2012).

Those with adequate resources are given the time and space to prepare psychologically for their transition (Coleman, 2011) and supportive relationships can help them succeed as they age. Care-leavers, however, often lack secure family and community support to ease their transitions (Mendes et al, 2011; Stein, 2012). Moreover, they can have extended transitions that end abruptly (Stein, 2014) while others experience transitions that are compressed and accelerated (Stein, 2012). Regardless, both transitions result in an 'instant adulthood' (van Breda et al, 2020: 2) in which care-leavers can arrive at their notional independence ill-prepared for its challenges. This means they face multiple challenges simultaneously with minimal assistance. Among these challenges are obtaining housing, employment, education and income. Learning independent living skills, maintaining health, and looking after emotional and psychological wellbeing are also necessary. There is an association between a sudden transition and adverse outcomes for care-leavers (Mendes et al, 2011; Stein, 2012). Therefore, care-leavers require resources that better meet their developmental and environmental needs and that support a gradual transition (Mendes et al, 2011; Stein, 2012).

A typology of care-leaver resilience

Stein's (2012: 170–172) typology frames care-leavers as belonging to one of three groups – 'moving on', 'survivors' and 'strugglers' – indicating the degree of resilience they may possess at any given time. Care-leavers in the 'moving on' group tend to have stable placements, secure attachments and solid support networks. They are highly resilient and welcome independence. Young people in the 'survivors' group experience significant instability, poor relationships, and bouts of homelessness and unemployment, and favourable outcomes are associated with the effectiveness of aftercare support. Pre-care trauma and problematic placements are most common in the 'strugglers' group. They have few connections, experience the poorest relationships with people and suffer severe social and emotional problems. While still essential, aftercare support is unlikely to relieve all these difficulties (Mendes et al, 2011; Stein, 2012).

Stein describes resilience as 'overcoming the odds, coping and recovery' (2012: 165). A broad definition but apt because it refers to the typical challenges faced by care-leavers and the qualities necessary to overcome them. According to van Breda (2015), rather than a static trait, resilience is more of a process that manifests over time. Factors in the social environmental develop progressively to help build a person's resilience (van Breda, 2015). Specifically, research shows that supportive relationships buffer stress and help people thrive, and that this interpersonal process unfolds over time (Feeney and Collins, 2015). Fostering supportive relationships is clearly a critical protective factor for care-leavers, helping them to become resilient. Moreover, as illustrated in his typology, Stein's research suggests that care-leavers in the 'moving on' group share positive relational characteristics associated with secure attachments, maintaining contact with and support from former carers and having strong social networks (2012: 170). Therefore, this study's conceptual framework uses Stein's resilience typology to capture a care-leaver's transition trajectory.

Concepts of social capital and social support

In this study, social capital is best understood to include elements of social relations, access, facilitation and functions (Bourdieu, 1986; Coleman, 1988; Putnam, 2000; Woolcock and Narayan, 2000). How these concepts are applied in this study is noted here:

- *Social relations*: social relations (Coleman, 1988) in this study are considered as the simple network between the care-leaver and a person they nominated as important to them.
- *Access*: Bourdieu (1986) describes social capital as the ability to efficiently help individuals to access resources through other people in the network. Here, the access dimension refers to the nominated support person providing the care-leaver access to developmental and environmental resources.
- *Facilitation*: Coleman (1988: S98) argues that a significant function of social capital is its capacity to 'facilitate certain actions' of individuals 'within the structure'. In this study, the actions of nominated people investigated are support focused. Table 12.1 provides definitions of social

support actions. However, sometimes these actions can also be performed by young participants.

- *Functions*: Coleman (1988), Putnam (2000) and Woolcock and Narayan (2000) identify specific functions of social capital that facilitate 'Access' (outlined previously). These functions consist of bonding, bridging (Putnam, 2000) and linking processes (Woolcock and Narayan, 2000) – which all include facilitating social connections, having social norms of expected standards of behaviour, as well as sanctions, reciprocity and providing informational channels (Coleman, 1988; Putnam, 2000; Torche and Valenzuela, 2011). Table 12.2 provides the definitions of these social capital functions.

Developmental and environmental resources

A range of research (for example, see Mendes et al, 2011), as well as practice guidance have indicated that developmental and environmental resources are critical for helping care-leavers navigate transitional difficulties (Okpych et al, 2018). These are the resources necessary for a more gradual and sustained transition to adulthood. Table 12.3 provides key definitions.

Integration of concepts to achieve the study's aim

Figure 12.1 illustrates the framework which seeks to examine how informal, supportive relationships may assist in a gradual transition for care-leavers.

Table 12.1: Definitions of social support actions

Social support action	Definition of social support action
Emotional	Being present, caring, listening and showing empathy. The young person feels heard or understood and has a person to talk to as they need.
Esteem	Showing genuine interest in the young person's wellbeing, providing reassurance of worth and enhancing self-esteem.
Appraisal	Providing positive and constructive feedback on achievements or behaviour in any given situation.
Practical	Meeting financial, material or accommodation needs, helping to complete tasks, or responding to emergencies.
Informational	Providing good advice and information about how to handle commonplace situations or do specific tasks. Offer opportunities to learn social skills, or where information can be gleaned through positive role-modelling.
Companionate	Spending time with the young person and doing activities together.

Source: Definitions are adapted from Wills and Shinar (2000), Canavan et al (2016) and Okpych et al (2018)

227

Table 12.2: Definitions of social capital functions

Social capital function	Definition of social capital function
Bonding	People who know each other well and have strong connections.
Bridging	Horizontal connection to different people and different sources of information and knowledge.
Linking	Vertical connection to people who have strong access to resources and power.
Reciprocity	Social dynamic in which individuals give, receive and return.
Informational Channels	Efficient way to acquire information via social relations which are maintained for other purposes.
Social norms	Belief about the acceptability of behaviour.
Effective sanctions	Correcting and/or approving another person's behaviour to uphold the expected behaviour and standards.

Source: Definitions are adapted from Coleman (1988), Putnam (2000), Woolcock and Narayan (2000), Torche and Valenzeula (2011) and Kenny and Connors (2017)

Table 12.3: Defining developmental and environmental resources

Developmental resources	Definition of developmental resources
Emotional and behavioural development	Internal resources of the young person that manifest in responses to other people and the world around them, as reflected in their feelings and demonstrated through their actions.
Family and social relationships	Social network of meaningful, stable, appropriate and affectionate relationships with family, peers and other important people.
Identity	Possession or construction of self-worth, an understanding of why the young person has been in care and of their place in family, community and culture.
Social presentation	Capacity to care for appearance, social behaviour and personal habits to influence how other people perceive and treat the young person. The young person develops knowledge on how to be responsible for their actions.
Specific self-care and independent living skills	Knowledge and skills in looking for accommodation and work; managing a domestic situation, health, education and training, and finances; organising oneself for work, and other skills such as driving a car.
Environmental resources	**Definition of environmental resources**
Income	Access to a living wage or to income support payments.
Housing	Access to affordable, secure and safe accommodation.
Health and wellbeing	Access to decent physical and mental healthcare.

Source: Definitions are adapted from Mendes et al (2011), Stein (2012) and DFFH (2019)

The social support actions named in the framework are active behaviours that indicate the presence of social capital rather than being a component of it (Beaudoin, 2007). These supportive actions are facilitated by the social capital functions within this social structure of the care-leaver and their nominated support person. Putnam (2000) explains that bonding capital assists people to 'get by', while bridging and linking capital assists people to 'get ahead'. As illustrated, all the social capital functions can help care-leavers to 'get by' and 'get ahead'. The notions of 'getting by' or 'getting ahead' are conceptually suggestive of building care-leaver resilience and helping them progress to a 'moving on' position (Stein, 2012). Formal specialist workers are essential for care-leavers to assist them in attaining developmental and environmental resources. However, care-leavers cannot always obtain these formal supports when needed (Hiles et al, 2013). Consequently, this study is particularly interested in what informal, supportive relationships can offer in facilitating care-leavers' access to these developmental and environmental resources to assist in a more gradual transition to adulthood. A framework integrating these concepts is presented in Figure 12.1.

Methodology

The research is grounded in the experience and expertise of care-leavers, seeking rich and individual data via interviews, to examine how social capital and social support intersect in the transition process. The researcher mainly used non-government organisations staff to mediate access to care-leaver participants. The unpaid support person was recruited through the care-leaver nominating this person to be interviewed if willing and available to participate. Ultimately, eight care-leavers and six nominated support people participated in semi-structured interviews. The researcher sought information about the nature and characteristics of their relationship and the support given.

While data collected from care leavers about their informal support is a relatively common investigation, data collected from informal support people is rare in leaving-care research. Integrating both matching sets of material is rarer still. Hence, this chapter intends to illuminate the benefits of such relationships. Rather than overviewing all eight relationships here, three case studies are featured to illustrate the benefits emanating from social capital and social support interactions. This 'deep dive' is effective in showing the interactional variation. The case studies exemplify the role of informal social capital and social support in addressing fundamental needs.

The conceptual framework brings a deductive analytical method that follows a top-down process by applying predetermined codes to the data (Crabtree and Miller, 1999). As they originate in and are created from the literature, the social support actions, the social capital functions and the developmental and environmental resources, as defined previously, are utilised as sets of predetermined codes. The deductive analytical process involves identifying passages in the transcripts of each care-leaver and support person participant, searching for these concepts and finding relations between them. Then this information is evaluated for what developmental or environmental need is being met. NVivo software was used to categorise and code the data as it helped organise and structure the text-based information (QSR International, 2021). Some independent coding of de-identified excerpts of data was carried out to strengthen trustworthiness (Patton, 2015). The study received ethical approval from the Monash University Human Research Ethics Committee.

Introductory description of each case

The researcher gave each study participant a pseudonym to protect their anonymity. The three cases presented are Trudy and Peter, John and Amy, and Leroy and Helen. Information about the nature and character of these dyadic relationships are provided as case vignettes.

Trudy and Peter

When interviewed, Trudy was 18 and lived in the south-eastern suburbs of Melbourne (the capital city of the State of Victoria) with her ex-foster carers and their family. In primary school, Trudy became involved with child protection because of child abuse. She was placed in foster care at age 11 with Peter, Louise, and their three daughters. Peter, a person she nominates as essential to her, has provided her with a stable home. Peter is a highly educated and accomplished man with a well-paid job in a senior position. Trudy and Peter characterise their relationship as father and daughter: they see, talk or text each other daily.

John and Amy

When interviewed, John was 20 and living in community-based youth accommodation west of Melbourne. He entered state residential care at the age of two after suffering severe mistreatment. At 11, he entered long-term foster care without his siblings and remained there until he was 16. He also moved into two other placements before eventually, at 18, moving into a house with his mother and sister. He is then linked to the youth accommodation where he lives when interviewed, an arrangement that will last for at least 12 months.

Amy was nominated by John. Amy is tertiary-educated and works in the welfare sector. Amy and John have known each other for 14 years. They met when John was six, when Amy acted as his respite carer. Their relationship developed through frequent and regular contact, mainly John's monthly weekend stays with Amy. Throughout John's shifting living circumstances, Amy's marriage to Matthew, and their children's births, this pattern continued. In between the monthly visits are phone calls and other incidental contacts. Both report they do not see each other regularly now since John moved across the city to find accommodation. They currently communicate mainly via Facebook, private messaging and texting. Amy and her family still celebrate John's birthday and spend Christmas together. Amy and John intend to continue their relationship.

Leroy and Helen

When interviewed, Leroy was 25 and living in an inner suburb of Melbourne. Leroy described suffering from 'psychosis' at 15 and later being diagnosed with clinical depression. Leroy entered state care voluntarily at 16, describing the home environment as emotionally traumatic. Over the next two years, Leroy had three, highly variable, foster care placements. When Leroy completed Year 12 and turned 18, the carers officially lost their carer payments. After an argument with these carers, Leroy returned to the parental home to live, which lasted only seven days before Leroy's mother called the police to remove Leroy from the home. Then started a period of struggle with acute bouts of mental illness, homelessness, and intermittent periods of employment and study. During this time, Leroy connected to a non-government mental health service which played a critical role in recovery. Leroy was also assisted by various informal supports and nominated Helen as the most important.

Helen is 27 years old and a very close friend of Leroy's. Helen also has a history of abuse and indicates that she cannot rely on her family as a supportive network. When they were teenagers, Helen and Leroy met for the first time at an organisation that works with people under 18 who identify as gender or sexually diverse. In their teens, their relationship matured via attending social events such as under-18 dance parties and helping each other through what Leroy describes as 'tough times'. Their friendship rapidly developed through the support they gave each other. They mostly see each other at social events such as Leroy's birthday, and sometimes they catch up for a meal or coffee. They keep in contact via social media, regular phoning or texting. The meaning of their relationship is significant because they both indicate they have given each other warmth and encouragement to be brave. They see their friendship as lasting.

Findings: the role of informal social capital

The findings are presented in two parts. In applying the conceptual framework, the first part identifies how developmental and environmental resources are accessed through the social support actions and social capital functions in these three sets of relationships. The second part discusses the themes that emanate from this conceptual analysis.

Accessing developmental and environmental resources

This section employs relevant quotes to illustrate the utility of the various combinations of developmental and environmental resources accessed through the interaction of social support actions and social capital functions.

Social relationships

Social relationships are built through companion support that is facilitated through bonding capital. Each relationship pair bond over a shared experience. This aspect of social capital made available to these young individuals through their nominated support seems acutely felt.

'I normally go and get the meat with him (Peter) every Saturday for dinner … like he shouts [buys] me every now and then some roll or something from the bakery … it's fun.' (Trudy)

'It's usually dinner at theirs [Amy and Matthew], home-cooked meal and that, which is nice.' (John)

'We [Leroy and Helen] used to go on like trips and all that kind of stuff, like as in social gathering, have a coffee or whatever.' (Leroy)

Emotional and behavioural development, social relationships and health

Leroy's case illustrates both Leroy and friend, Helen, reciprocally benefiting from the comfort they give each other. Helen gives emotional support to Leroy through bonding capital.

'She's [Helen] gone through way more than what I've gone, but she's always there to offer support. That to me is – there is no one like that in the world, you know what I mean?' (Leroy)

Leroy develops behavioural maturity by providing Helen with the emotional support facilitated through bonding and reciprocity capital. These interactions help maintain their friendship but also, through this peer relationship, Helen provides Leroy, perhaps unknowingly, the opportunity to access the resource of emotional and behavioural development.

'He [Leroy] was very much there for me, especially around my ex, Stacey, in terms of the leaving and cheating, and the loss of the relationship. ... So yeah, he was there with me after the breakup, and listened to me, and cried with me. ... But yeah, he was incredible.' (Helen)

Helen also provides practical support to assist Leroy's mental health through linking capital. It illustrates how linking young people up to more authoritative assistance can be achieved by peers and is not necessarily the sole domain of adult support.

'I've had times when he's been suicidal and he's called me, and I've contacted help lines, and gotten police and things involved.' (Helen)

Family-like relationships and identity

Through multiple interactions between different social support actions and social capital functions, young participants gained access to the developmental resources of family and social relationships. Esteem support is facilitated through bonding capital for both Trudy and John. As the data suggest, esteem support – in being treated as if they were family – reassures young people of their worth and enriches the resource of belonging to a family identity.

'He's [Peter] like a dad, he's a dad-figure.' (Trudy)

'I know that they're [Amy] basically like family to me.' (John)

Amy further provides esteem support by bridging John to her children and allowing him to bond with them. Companionship is a supportive action that John reciprocates. It has the effect of John maintaining his relationship with the children and possibly encouraging a positive self-identity:

'Oh, my children love him [John]. I mean he was around before my children. So, he gave them bottles and saw them grow up, and so they don't know life without John really. ... I think he feels quite connected with my kids. He often rough and tumbles them and tickles them and throws them around. It's quite terrifying, but it's quite normal. It's what an uncle would do.' (Amy)

In the following passage, companionate support is likely facilitated through bonding, reciprocity and social norms capital. Peter expects that Trudy, like Peter's biological daughters, will visit Peter and Louise when they are older. Reciprocation is a norm in many families where grown-up children want their children to have a relationship with their grandparents.

'Yes, she'll [Trudy] be one of the daughters who visits us. I think that's what I expect will happen because I think she'll will want to belong to a family ... and we will be the grandparents. I think that's how she will see it and I reckon that's what will happen.' (Peter)

Peter's words in the following extract illustrate esteem and emotional support through bonding and bridging capital. The relationship must have a firm bond for Trudy to trust Peter to start bridging her to her biological father. Peter plays a critical role in Trudy's birth family identity.

'So, in a weird kind of way she [Trudy] wants him to know about her but she doesn't want to have any contact with him but through me she can kind of say to him that I do remember you and I care for you and I'm going to send you some photos so, that was kind of the idea, as much as she could handle.' (Peter)

Specific self-care and independent living skills, income and identity

As evident in the quotes presented next, the developmental need being met for both Trudy and John is the beginner's need for self-care skills. Through the social capital function of the informational channel, their informal supporters are teaching Trudy and John how to navigate bureaucratic systems. The environmental need being met for Trudy – a critical one – is the need for a basic income. The need being met for John is learning how to obtain a crucial identification document – his birth certificate. Trudy and John are linked to institutions that have the power to address fundamental income security and identity needs. Peter and Amy's information and practical support actions assist in having these needs met.

'With Centrelink [income support government department], when I had to get Youth Allowance, he [Peter] obviously googled everything and gave me a debrief[ing] of it when I asked him ... that really helped because I had no idea what Centrelink was. ... And then we got the documents, and then we just drove to Centrelink like 8 o'clock, first thing the next day, and I got my Centrelink.' (Trudy)

'And if he [John] needed something we talked about how we could find that and sometimes I would write out step by step what he would do to achieve something. Like he needed his birth extract [abridged birth certificate] once ... so I'd just write down okay you need to go to this address, and do this, and say this, and kind of guide him through it, like I could from afar, in a sense.' (Amy)

Housing, family relationships, identity

Different housing needs are being met for Trudy and John through the actions of their informal supports. Trudy knows she can stay with Peter and his family once the guardianship order has ceased. She has this as a secure base if she wants to try living independently for a while. Trudy will not be turned away if she missteps and needs to return. This passage indicates both esteem (as she is 'family') and the necessary practical support of being provided shelter.

> 'But look my sister moved out and she moved back in home ... the same thing would apply to me if something does happen and if I didn't have anywhere to live they [Peter and Louise] would definitely [allow Trudy to return home].' (Trudy)

On the other hand, John has not been able to stay with his foster carers and has tried his luck living with his mother. It did not seem to be working well for him, but fortunately, he has such a good bond with Amy he can ring her to ask for the practical support he needs to keep his housing and not be evicted.

> 'When he [John] lived with his mother in the private rental they were struggling with that and there was often the landlord saying, "If you don't do this, we'll evict you." And so, he would ring us and say, "The landlord is saying if I don't mow the grass or get the gardens under control we're going to be kicked out. Can you come and help me?" And so, we'd bring over a lawn mower and the whipper snipper and we'd go and sort out the garden.' (Amy)

Emotional and behavioural development and social presentation

Both Trudy and John benefit from the social capital functions of bonding, social norms about expected behaviour and the effective sanctioning of such behaviour. These functions of social capital interact mainly with information and appraisal support. These interactions help access the developmental resources of emotional, behavioural development and social presentation.

> 'Like, two weeks ago she [Trudy] went out late ... she had a late night, Saturday night, another late night, Sunday night, and then Monday and Tuesday she was sick and missed TAFE [Technical College] ... we kind of talked about that later in the week and said, I wonder if there's a connection between two all-nighters drinking ... and not being able to make it to TAFE. And she said, "Yeah, I think I definitely should

235

only ever go out one night on the weekend and not two." "Okay, that's a good conclusion to draw".' (Peter)

'John is quite avoidant of conflict. … He's a real pacifist and will often just kind of go, "Well, that doesn't matter. I'll just do this instead". But we have had discussions about when that's healthy to do and when that's not healthy to do.' (Amy)

Themes

This investigation of care-leavers accessing developmental and environmental resources draws attention to the fundamental roles of informal social capital and social support in their lives. The analysis is further refined into two major themes that will be discussed now.

Theme 1: Informal social capital and social support are valuable to all care-leavers

The positive interaction of social capital and social support are valuable to all care-leavers because through these they develop meaningful relationships, normative social experiences, resilience and positive self-identity.

Meaningful relationships: The young participants had different levels of need and functioning. Thus, they called on divergent forms of social support to meet their needs, each identifying people who would support their priorities. Social capital is experienced on a continuum rather than being either positive or negative. Asymmetric access to informal social capital contributes to uneven acquisition of resources required for a smooth transition to adulthood.

Despite this, the social capital functions of bonding and reciprocity help build informal, meaningful and trustworthy relationships over time. In the study, people who provide support are present for the ordinary challenges and opportunities of everyday life, and when sensitivity and companionship are needed. The young participants reciprocated in distinct ways. Leroy gives emotional support to Helen, John entertains Amy's children and Trudy could potentially return social support to Peter when he is older. Bonding and reciprocity are needed for trust to be built. Once trust is present, other social capital functions can take effect. For example, bridging a young person to their birth family or linking them to a health or government service.

Normative social experiences: Social capital as an unconscious phenomenon (Bourdieu, 1986; Coleman, 1988) in a personal relationship is particularly significant when working with young people with a state care background. Paradoxically, they are likely to be overly conscious of lacking the kind of relationships that confer these invisible relational advantages. The invisible advantage is relevant when examining the opportunities for 'normal' social experiences for young participants. For instance, the information channel (Coleman, 1988) is a significant component that allows access to 'normal' social experiences. Compared to its linking capital partner, the information channel is more subtle. While Peter and Amy were overtly linking Trudy and John to government services, the needs for income and proof of identity were obviously being met. In contrast, role-modelling how to apply for a payment or a birth certificate is a less recognised form of social capital. Trudy and John have understood the role-modelling information imparted through the informational channel. They are now aware of such services, which deepens their knowledge of engaging with such organisations to meet their needs successfully. Information channels are just as crucial as linking capital for the transition of care-leavers. It helps meet the need to learn independent living skills.

Resilience and positive self-identity: Through investigating how these numerous social resources interact in the lives of these young participants, there is an observed difference between emotional and esteem support. Nonetheless, both types of support are essential for young people to develop resilience and identity.

Bonding and emotional support enable young people to self-regulate and 'get by' psychologically by having a reliable ally who cares for and understands them. It confirms literature relating constructive social relationships to care-leaver resilience (Dickens and van Breda, 2020). This association is crucial because the young participants' trauma backgrounds originate in relationships with people (mainly biological parents) they trusted to be their reliable allies and caregivers. Broken trust and internalised shame underscore the importance of providing emotional support to young people in and leaving care.

Nevertheless, the enduring need for unconditional positive regard is distinct from emotional support for these young participants. While Trudy, John and Leroy do not explicitly mention esteem support, it is implicitly reflected in the data. Identity development, a significant developmental resource, can be depleted by stigma or enhanced by bonding capital. In these relationships, bonding is observed by the companionate time spent together. Having dinner, coffee or shopping together naturally strengthens their connection. Equal enjoyment of each other's company builds a personal and mutual relationship. It is especially so for Trudy, who nominated a former foster carer (Peter) and John, who selected a former respite carer (Amy). For Peter and Amy, these expressions of companionship may imply forgoing their official role. Peter views Trudy, and Amy views John, simply as people rather than defining them through their care-leaver status. The relationships evolve from state-engineered to something more personal and elusive. It is not something to be underrated. Spending time doing activities together seems to help Trudy and John develop a broader identity other than their care-leaver status.

Theme 2: Informal adult support is crucial for care-leavers

This theme emphasises the significance of informal adult support that assists with progressive responsibility. The informality of these relationships is critical because it can help in ways that formal adult support cannot. Progressive responsibility may help decelerate the transition.

The importance of the informality of the relationship: A formal statutory relationship can easily evolve into an informal relationship over time. Trudy and John's relationships with Peter and Amy quickly developed into family-like interactions. In no small part, Peter and Amy's success in being nominated is due to the considerable skills and life experiences they bring. Even if these qualities are present in the formal professional workers caring for these young people, the same outcome cannot be guaranteed. These relationships provide ongoing informal social capital that is more available than what workers can provide. It is particularly exemplified in the housing, family relationships and identity passages. Stability is created, and a gradual transition has a better chance of being realised. The success of this depends on the availability and continuity of caring adults. The formal system lacks these elements.

Progressive responsibility: Through adult assistance, Trudy and John have also benefited from the social capital functions of social norms about expected behaviour and the effective sanctioning of such behaviour. These functions of social capital interact mainly with information and appraisal support. Having a bond allows the adult to discuss what is expected of the young person. As Peter and Amy give Trudy and John constructive feedback in different situations, we see effective sanctions working.

As a result of combining these social resources, Trudy and John learn how to behave and present themselves. The final two excerpts illustrate how young participants learn progressive responsibility (Smith, 2011). In general, 'progressive responsibility' involves reinforcing social norms that express what young people are commonly expected to do as they become adults. Moreover, social norms, bonding and sanctions help create the incremental, socially typical experiences needed to teach progressive responsibility. By applying the term 'progressive' in this sense, we mean that they are improving their learning and moving forward. Thus, the notion of 'progressive responsibility' can be considered a characteristic of a gradual and managed transition. It is not a feature of the accelerated transition experienced by many young people from state care, in which multiple 'responsibilities' come simultaneously and rapidly (Stein, 2012).

Getting by and getting ahead

While this study contributes to a better understanding of care-leavers' informal social capital, the data are limited by interviewing the participants once and focusing on one relationship. Additionally, there are variations in the young participants' reporting of how their support person helps them. A major strength of this study is that it fills in the little-known details of how social supports and social capital work together to help care-leavers access vital resources. Detail illustrates how these young participants can both 'get by' and 'get ahead' (Putnam, 2000).

As in Trudy's case, the more varied combinations of social resources a young person has, the more likely they are to experience a gradual and managed transition. According to Stein's (2012) typology of resilience, Trudy belongs to the 'moving on' group. With so much social support and social capital in place for Trudy, her transition to adulthood is similar to many of her peers who have sufficient family support and social networks. Her gradual transition to adulthood has been facilitated by Peter's sustained support, allowing her not only to 'get by' (Coleman, 2011), but also to 'get ahead' (Putnam, 2000).

John, who had severe pre-care trauma, had consistent support from Amy from a young age. While his needs are not being met in the same way as Trudy's, Amy has undoubtedly helped his transition be more gradual. John relies on specialist support for his housing and training needs. However, Amy has provided him with stability and the necessary esteem support to help him 'psychologically get by'.

Trudy and John both cite caring adults as their most significant relationships. Hence, it is not surprising to see appraisal support and social norms combined as part of their transitional social resources. These resources gradually help Trudy and John become increasingly responsible for various aspects of their lives.

Leroy has moved on (Stein, 2012). A good job and renting privately are indicators that Leroy is not unlike many other young people. Still, Leroy has struggled with mental health issues, and has been homeless and unemployed. Leroy's transition was compressed and accelerated because of having to deal with these simultaneously. However, Leroy has been resourceful in getting by and getting ahead (Putnam, 2000). While specialist assistance was pivotal for Leroy in getting housing and mental health needs met, Helen's emotional and esteem support was critical to slowing Leroy's transition. Significantly, Leroy reciprocated the emotional support. Interdependence has been crucial for managing the transition.

Conclusion

Bonding, bridging and linking are the typical social capital functions commended as paramount to a person's accrual of resources in their network. However, there are clear advantages delivered by the lesser-known social capital functions of the informational channel, social norms regarding expectations and effective sanctions when identifying resource gaps in a young person's network of informal personal relationships. These social capital functions significantly contribute to the young person's normative experiences and developmental and environmental needs. They are indispensable to the young person learning about and gradually undertaking responsibility. This knowledge must underpin the policies on extending care and developing young people's positive informal relationships while still in the state's care.

Peter, Amy and Helen have likely deliberated on how they support their respective young participant. Their support actions can also be automatic responses to what is occurring in the moment. It may sound clichéd, but the ordinary actions people can take can have extraordinary effects in mitigating stigma and enhancing wellbeing. The conceptual framework used in this study allows close observation of these everyday moments. It helps in seeing more clearly the benefit of social resource interaction. We have a deeper understanding of what needs to be replicated for those who leave care with poorer informal relationships.

Therefore, policy makers and practitioners must elevate the importance of identifying and working on the young person's positive or potentially positive relationships in their social network before leaving care. Working on young people's adult and peer relationships while still in care must be built into the transitional care plan. Specialists could work on the young people's relationships with family members (immediate and extended) when safe to do so. They could identify and help young people consolidate natural mentors in their social circle before they leave care. Investment in sporting, cultural and community activities is needed for young people to build and maintain positive social networks. We want the formative benefits of the unacknowledged, incremental, informal support for young people in care and to have them established and settled when they reach the sharp end of their transition from care to adulthood.

References

Beaudoin, C.E. (2007) 'Mass media use, neighborliness, and social support: Assessing causal links with panel data', *Communication Research*, 34(6): 637–644.

Bourdieu, P. (1986) 'The forms of capital', in J. Richardson (ed) *Handbook of theory and research for the sociology of education*, New York: Greenwood, pp 241–258.

Bourdieu, P. and Wacquant, L.J.D. (1992) *An invitation to reflexive sociology*, Chicago: University of Chicago Press

Canavan, J., Dolan, P. and Pinkerton, J. (2016) *Understanding family support: Policy, practice and theory*, London: Jessica Kingsley Publishers.

Coleman, J.C. (2011) *The nature of adolescence*, 4th edn, Hove: Routledge.

Coleman, J.S. (1988) 'Social capital in the creation of human capital', *American Journal of Sociology*, 94: 95–120.

Crabtree, B.F. and Miller, W.L. (1999) *Doing qualitative research*, 2nd edn, Thousand Oaks: SAGE.

DFFH (Department of Families, Fairness and Housing) (2019) *Child Protection Manual: Looking After Children*, Document ID number 2742, Version 3, 20 June 2019, accessed on 27 July 2023. https://www.cpmanual.vic.gov.au/advice-and-protocols/service-descriptions/out-home-care/looking-after-children#h3_0

Dickens, L. and van Breda, A. (2020) *Growth beyond the town: A longitudinal study on youth leaving care; resilience and outcomes of South African Girls and Boys Town care-leavers over the first six years out of care*, Girls and Boys Town South Africa in partnership with the Department of Social Work and Community Development, University of Johannesburg.

Elder, G.H. (1998) 'The life course as developmental theory', *Child Development*, 69(1): 1–12.

Feeney, B.C. and Collins, N.L. (2015) 'A new look at social support', *Personality and Social Psychology Review*, 19(2): 113–147.

Greeson, J.K.P., Garcia, A.R., Kim, M., Thompson, A.E. and Courtney, M.E. (2015) 'Development and maintenance of social support among aged out foster youth who received independent living services: Results from the Multi-Site Evaluation of Foster Youth Programs', *Children and Youth Services Review*, 53: 1–9.

Hiles, D., Moss, D., Wright, J. and Dallos, R. (2013) 'Young people's experience of social support during the process of leaving care: A review of the literature', *Children and Youth Services Review*, 35: 2059–2071.

Kenny, S. and Connors, P. (2017) *Developing communities for the future*, 5th edn, Melbourne: Cengage Learning Australia Pty Limited.

Mann-Feder, V.R. (2018) '(You gotta have) friends: Care leaving, friendships, and agency intervention', *International Journal of Child, Youth and Family Studies*, 9(1): 154–167.

Mendes, P., Johnson, G. and Moslehuddin, B. (2011) *Young people leaving state out-of-home care: Australian policy and practice*, Melbourne: Australian Scholarly Publishing.

Okpych, N., Feng, H., Park, K., Torres-Garcia, A. and Courtney, M.E. (2018) 'Living situations and social support in the era of extended foster care: A view from the U.S.', *Longitudinal and Life Course Studies*, 9(1): 6–29.

Patton, M.Q. (2015) *Qualitative research & evaluation methods: Integrating theory and practice*, 4th edn, Newbury Park: SAGE.

Putnam, R. (2000) *Bowling alone: The collapse and revival of American community*, New York: Simon & Schuster.

QSR International (2021) NVivo. Available from: https://www.qsrinternational.com/nvivo-qualitative-data-analysis-software/home/

Rogers, J. (2017) '"Different" and "devalued": Managing the stigma of foster-care with the benefit of peer support', *British Journal of Social Work*, 47: 1078–1093.

Rogers, J. (2018) 'Preserving and memorialising relationships: Exploring young people's experiences of foster care through the lens of social capital', *Adoption & Fostering*, 42(2): 176–188.

Smith, W.B. (2011) *Youth leaving foster care: A developmental, relationship-based approach to practice*, Oxford: Oxford University Press.

Stein, M. (2012) *Young people leaving care*, London: Jessica Kingsley Publishers.

Stein, M. (2014) 'Young people's transitions from care to adulthood in European and postcommunist Eastern European and Central Asian societies', *Australian Social Work*, 67(1): 24–38.

Torche, F. and Valenzuela. E. (2011) 'Trust and reciprocity: A theoretical distinction of the sources of social capital', *European Journal of Social Theory*, 14(2): 181–198

Van Breda, A.D. (2015) 'Journey towards independent living: A grounded theory investigation of leaving the care of Girls & Boys Town South Africa', *Journal of Youth Studies*, 18(3): 322–337.

Van Breda, A.D., Munro, E.R., Gilligan, R., Anghel, R., Harder, A., Incarnato, M., Mann-Feder, V., Refaeli, T., Stohler, R. and Storø, J. (2020) 'Extended care: Global dialogue on policy, practice and research', *Children and Youth Services Review*, 119 (105596): 1–14.

Wills, T.A. and Shinar, O. (2000) 'Measuring perceived and received support', in S. Cohen, L.G. Underwood and B.H. Gottlieb (eds) *Social support measurement and intervention: A guide for health and social scientists*, Cary: Oxford University Press.

Woolcock, M. and Narayan, D. (2000) 'Social capital: Implications for development theory, research, and policy', *The World Bank Research Observer*, 15(2): 225–249.

Conclusion: Going over the edge

*Adrian D. van Breda, Veronika Paulsen, Inger Oterholm
and Samuel Keller*

Introduction

This book has aimed to present research about edgy facets of leaving care – understudied groups of care-leavers, fresh methodological approaches and innovative theories. The research has been conducted and chapters written by authors from across the world who are, mostly, on the edge, transitioning between postgraduate student and scholar. It is our hope that the book opens fresh perspectives and angles on care-leaving research and inspires continued innovation in this field. In this concluding chapter, we draw together key findings regarding these three facets, highlighting what has been learned collectively through this project. And finally, spring-boarding from these new insights, we attempt to imagine what leaving-care research will look like in the future and where the new edges might be. We draw attention to the many gaps and edges that remain and suggest possibilities for ongoing research that pushes the boundaries yet further forward.

Groups of care-leavers

Much of the research on leaving care has focused on care-leavers as a single, homogeneous group, and less focus has been given to the particular characteristics, challenges and needs of specific groups within this larger group. The edgy contribution in this book is thus to give attention to groups that have not been visible in previous research and that potentially could have different challenges and needs in transitioning to adulthood from care. Together, these chapters point out that in future leaving-care research we need to differentiate the group 'care-leavers' to get a more nuanced understanding of care-leavers' different trajectories into adulthood.

Studying groups of care-leavers that have been given little attention brings new perspectives and understandings, which are also relevant for understanding care-leavers' transitions and trajectories in general. For example, by studying unaccompanied minors, the gaze is set on networks in a different way and their findings bring in a new perspective on social support, when highlighting the importance of integrating young migrants' families digitally. Unaccompanied migrants, compared with their peers, show higher levels of satisfaction with their families, with whom they were able to maintain contact through phone and online messaging. These insights, together with previous research that underlines the links between social support, and outcomes and wellbeing in adult life, make visible a dimension of social network and social support that has been under-focused in care-leaving research: the possibilities of digital contact as a source of social support. This edgy finding broadens the view on what social networks are and where and how young people leaving care could find sources of social support. This can affect both further research and practice with care-leavers in general, not only with unaccompanied minors. It also makes visible that research needs to consider how society changes and thus affects people's lives. For research to be 'up to date', we need constantly to be aware of the social context that young people live in.

Another understudied group in leaving-care research is young people who identify as LGBTQIA+. The chapter explores how theories of minority stress, life course, resilience and anti-oppressive frameworks may be used to help conceptualise how experiences of discrimination impact the health and development of these youth over time, and develop research, policy and practice approaches that are theoretically grounded in strengths-based perspectives. In particular, the author discusses the need to integrate critically based practice with structural approaches to provide a more culturally responsive and effective platform for increasing the health and wellbeing of these youth. The chapter highlights that more research is needed to gain a better understanding of the needs, experiences and outcomes of LGBTQIA+ young people. While research highlighting adversities is integral to understanding the experiences of LGBTQIA+ youth in foster care, it is also important to identify and promote the ways in which this population may be resilient to these risks and challenges.

Another group that has been given little attention is care-leavers living on the streets. One of the chapters focuses specifically on young people ageing out onto the streets in Bolivia, though the findings are also relevant for young people with street experience in other countries, care-leavers in general and young people in general. The chapter also raises the edgy question of who should have the power to define what are 'good outcomes' and that 'good outcomes' also are connected to experiences in the past. For the group of young people interviewed in this chapter, being homeless or living on the street is not merely a negative 'outcome', as it is in most care-leaving research, but a return to an ecology that they had experienced prior to coming into care. The researcher discusses that 'outsiders' may have thought that care-leavers with a street-connected past would avoid life on the streets, but the reality for those in this study is that life on the streets is the only or a preferred solution, as the streets became the most familiar and preferred place to be when they were turfed out of care. This also makes visible how adults' and societies' views on what is a 'good life' and 'good outcomes' are not always in line with the views of the young people themselves.

Another chapter, located in South Africa, similarly considered care-leavers who had come into care from the streets, but who had not transitioned out onto the streets. This chapter considered the resilience processes that these young people mastered on the streets and how these shaped their lives in care and after care. This chapter brings new insight by showing that while on the streets, participants reported building safe, collaborative family relationships with other street-connected children – this approach to building fictive kin relationships continued in and after care. They also show how life on the street taught the young people to identify and mobilise meagre resources for survival, which they reported continuing to do after leaving care. And they cultivated a reflective, self-aware approach to life on the streets, which helped them after care to navigate towards young adulthood. These narratives point to long-term growth through resilience and the drawing forward of learnings across multiple life phases and social contexts.

The edgy chapters on specific groups of care-leavers make visible that there are many similarities when it comes to challenges and needs of young people leaving care: the feeling of being dumped out of the care system, abrupt transitions, no aftercare system and lack of family and social support. What is especially interesting in the studies of specific groups is that they help us see the importance of paying attention to and recognising each unique person's life story and identity, whether it is identifying with the LGBTQIA+ community, living on the street, being an unaccompanied minor, or simply having been in care. The chapters make visible how the experiences of coming into, living in and leaving care continue to ripple through their lived experience and social connectedness and are relevant in how they approach and experience the transition to adulthood. This shows us the importance of paying attention to young people's life stories prior to entering the care system and the importance of recognising the young people's own perspectives of what is 'safe' and 'a good life'.

Research methods

A wide range of methods have been used in the book. Even though there are more qualitative than quantitative studies, the qualitative studies draw on a variety of designs, including different types of interviews (both open and more structured), longitudinal and cross-sectional studies, fieldwork, mixed methods and studies with an emphasis on theoretical approaches. Several of the chapters also combine different approaches.

The four chapters with a particular methodological emphasis highlight important themes that are relevant for developing new knowledge about diverse groups of young people ageing out of care. These chapters thematise how to involve hard-to-reach groups in the leaving-care population, the importance of expanding the concept of research ethics and conducting research in a caring way, reflections around being an insider researcher with care experience and how to access the institutional aspects of the care-leaving experiences. Overall, this contributes to edgy methodological themes. They raise questions about who are included in research, and ways to include the variety of the care-leaving population, as well as questioning who the researchers are and institutional aspects that are rarely addressed.

In order to generate valid knowledge about young people ageing out of care, research must include the breadth of the population, including those who are hard to reach. Excluding them or other disengaged young people weakens the rigour of the research. An important topic in the book is how to design research that involves groups that are under-researched, such as disabled care-leavers, early parents and homeless youths. If these and other groups are not included in care-leaving research, there is a risk of overlooking their perspectives and important knowledge about their situation, consequently not recognising what kind of support they need.

There could be several reasons why young people do not participate in research. Young people with a care background may have traumatic experiences that give them reason to be sceptical of researchers. Furthermore, they may feel stigmatised as care-leavers and wish to distance themselves from this part of their background. Three of the chapters give important examples, reflect on ethical and scientific methodological questions and outline practical thoughts and suggestions for how to overcome these challenges. The book chapters highlight the importance of creative and trauma-informed research designs with the goal to avoid, or at least minimise, tokenism or the re-traumatisation of participants, while maximising reach and impact. Across the chapters, practical advice is given based on the experiences from research in different countries with different groups of care-leavers. Overall, the themes highlight how important the research design is, regarding how groups are categorised, how recruitment is done, the value of inclusive research tools, and how to respond to the individual needs of the young person while avoiding the risk of paternalistic, disablist or age-inappropriate approaches. One of the chapters also presents an adaptive participation model to identify several key considerations for choosing approaches that are suited to engage young people on the edge of different fields in research. Together these methodological innovations bring concrete examples of how to conduct research that can open up experiences from new groups of care-leavers and also research in more ethical ways.

Following a hermeneutic understanding, all researchers bring with them preconceptions that influence how a situation is understood. Being reflective and self-critical is important. Several of the chapters argue for participation by care-leavers in the entire research process, from conceptualisation to dissemination of findings. Having a care background gives one another position, raises other questions and challenges power differentials. Another example of how lived experience can inform research is institutional ethnography. Within this approach, lived experience is used as a starting point of inquiry into the institutional context of leaving care. This framing of research is less developed in care-leaving research. The chapter on institutional ethnography uses the standpoint of both care-leavers and social workers, to show how individual experiences of receiving or providing aftercare support are shaped by institutional forces.

Beyond traditional ethical questions, like avoiding harm and ensuring caring conduct, the chapters highlight the importance of young people benefiting from being involved in research. This is related to the impact of the research itself, to the research process being conducted in a caring way and to what young people learn from being part of the research process.

While rigorous research education and training as a researcher is vital, being both a trained researcher and a care-leaver adds to these layers of insider–outsider competence. For research to be transparent, researchers with a care-experienced background face other questions which they have to decide upon. Of particular edgy interest are the complex decisions these researchers must make regarding whether, when and how to disclose their care history to research participants; and of how they are perceived and judged by their peers in terms of their so-called 'objectivity' as researchers.

The edgy themes of these chapters about methodology foreground the extent to which all knowledge is situated, contextual and partial and not universal. They show the importance of bringing forth knowledge diversity and presenting multiple and varied stories that are both connected to and different from each other. The dialogue between these stories highlights the importance of including different participant groups and researchers with different competencies and backgrounds. What makes knowledge situated includes who is doing the research, what theories inform their research, with whom they do their research and how they do their research. Even though these methodological issues are raised in the methodological literature, they are not often debated in care-leaving research. Following up on the methodological issues in this book can give more in-depth knowledge of the care-leaving process and experiences of different groups of care-leavers that is important to improve practice and policy.

Theories of leaving care

The central epistemological interest here is to define forward-looking theses thanks to 'edgy' theoretical backgrounds or combinations. As a theoretical conclusion, future leaving care research needs to take into consideration the following challenges and tasks: owning one's blind spots as an 'edgy' starting point, going 'on the edge' of established concepts, and broadening theoretical understandings of care-leavers' experiences. What we should pay attention to when following the research discussed will be presented here.

Overall, research on leaving care presented in this book has brought together different theories that have shaped the 'edgy' research questions, design and/ or discussion: we read about theories with more person-oriented focus, such as theories on minority stress, resilience, positive self-identity or theories of life course, and, as a consequence, on concepts of trauma-informed research. Further, some authors discussed theories with a more social focus, such as the theory of social capital and social support, social ecological theory, or habitus theory linked to instability. Others combined theories to differentiate specific issues, like the combination of the Interpersonal-Psychological Theory of Suicide and theories on transitions, or relational bridging of classic dualistic concepts such as micro-meso-macro or agency-structure. Several authors also used power-critical theories to criticise research's (mis-)use of power, the absence of culturally adapted instruments or so-far empty claims in leaving-care research that we had moved towards postmodern thinking. These theories invite the development of anti-oppressive frameworks, self-critical questioning and re-conceptualisations or re-operationalisations of concepts like 'stability', 'relationships', 'family' and 'resilience'.

Blind spots as 'edgy' starting points: critical reflections on well-established frameworks and concepts

Almost all theory contributions in this book have, as their starting point for the presented research project, an irritation: a questioning or a critique of established terms, concepts or theories. It was even part of some researchers' visions to contribute to a paradigm shift, well knowing that it is not possible to achieve a complete shift within a single study. Authors questioned, for example, the use of continuity in out-of-home placements as an operationalisation of stability or the abbreviated definition of stability. From these critical points of view, too many previous studies used theories that labelled care-leavers as living unstable lives or as making short-term choices that limit their options for life course planning. In one sensitive field of research – care-leavers' suicide risks – the author's criticism is all-encompassing: previous research on care-leavers' suicide risk has largely neglected existing theories of suicide which led to blind spots.

Other critical reflections as a starting point of an empirical study contribute to a better theory-based understanding of care-leavers' needs in general or specifically of so-far overlooked groups' needs. For example, studies started by worrying that the relevance of informal relationships might be overlooked due to a dominant theoretical focus on formal relationships; or by worrying that simplified and colonialist views of research are responsible for misunderstanding street-involved children's specific context of living and needs.

'On the edge' of concepts: reconceptualisation of theoretical framework by proposing new aspects

As a next step after irritations and criticisms, all authors presented how they either re-conceptualised their research-designs in advance – based on theories with potential to change terms, assumptions or paradigms – or they wrote about their different ways of interpreting the data, thanks to mindset-changing theoretical frameworks. We read, for example, about re-conceptualisations or re-operationalisations of 'stability', 'relationships', 'family' and 'resilience'. Others present supportive theoretical concepts that help researchers to take an alternative perspective: concept of a habitus of instability, theory of social capital and social support, social ecological perspective, or connecting suicidology to concepts of leaving care.

These different uses of theories led to new understanding of what contributes to placement stability or to new understanding of how care-leavers position themselves in relation to experiences of instability. Other theories allowed new perspectives on the impact of meaningful and trustworthy relationships over time, on resilience and positive self-identity, or new perspectives on mismatching normative concepts of family and participants' sources for resilience in building family-like connections in the streets. And key factors of the Interpersonal-Psychological Theory of Suicide could be found again in concepts of specific experiences when leaving care. Thus, it is not only about new theories, but also about new combinations of theories or new combinations of theories and specific research fields.

'Over the edge': extension of theoretical understanding of care-leavers' experiences to strengthen the value and impact of research

In conclusion, it became apparent how theories support research designs and discussions to recognise, define and understand resources, as well as the needs of children living in and leaving alternative care around the globe. This is an important base – for children, practitioners and researchers – to create safe and collaborative alternative care and aftercare settings. The complexity and dependence on circumstances of this research field require more than repeating well-established theoretical frames that prescribe how to look at and talk to and about children and youth. Nevertheless, questioning established concepts does not inevitably have to falsify or discredit them. Rather, questioning allows us to take over new perspectives and new understandings of different perspectives on leaving care. And it allows one to develop clear, ethical and theoretically grounded applications for research, policy and practice approaches. Of course, a coordinated critical discussion is also a central prerequisite for being able to transcend established knowledge in favour of new research paradigms.

But if we take this metatheoretical conclusion seriously, it also means that the theoretical concepts highlighted in this book, which led to new insights and knowledge, should also not become static or fixed. Rather, they also need to be questioned in future dialogues as they have been questioned here. And since they made their theoretical framing clear, this will be quite possible – as opposed to imprecise definitions of terms or theoretical embeddings. A dialogical research discourse finally supports ethical and participative culture in child- and youth-oriented research and practice around the globe.

Reaching into the future

This book has aimed to address some of the edgy, understudied or marginalised facets of leaving-care research, with a focus on three themes: theories and conceptualisations of leaving care that could generate new insights into care-leaving; groups of care-leavers who need greater attention; and methods of care-leaving research that are innovative and could generate fresh data. We, the editors, have framed the book as 'living on the edge', because we see those leaving care as living in the liminal space or on the edge between care and post-care, between childhood and adulthood, between dependence and independence (or rather interdependence). In addition, we have used the notion of 'living on the edge' because most of the authors are working at the liminal space between student and researcher, junior and senior academic. And, third, we have drawn on the term 'edgy' to emphasise our collective effort not to do 'more of the same' (repeating what has already been published), but to find fresh, innovative and contentious facets of care-leaving research.

As much as we have emphasised the liminal, transitional spaces between past, present and future in the lives and work of care-leavers and leaving-care scholars, we have also been mindful of the liminal space between the present and future of leaving-care scholarship itself. Where is leaving-care research going? What are the unacknowledged, uncomfortable and even conflictual edges that we should focus on in future?

First, edgy care-leaving researchers need to consider the tensions between focusing on small sub-groups of care-leavers versus focusing on care-leavers as a collective. Traditionally, care-leaving research has tended to aggregate care-leavers into a unitary group. There is value in disaggregating care-leavers into more nuanced groups; and even then, to recognise the diversity within these groups, so as to recognise and validate the edges between care-leavers. Not all care-leavers are the same: their histories, personalities, family constellations, life experiences, cultures, contexts, identities and sexualities are different (along with numerous other differences, as with other people). While we caution against disaggregating to such an extent that each young person finds themselves in a group of just themself, and while we advocate the value of interconnectedness between collectives of diverse care-leavers, we do also recommend that, going forward, leaving-care scholars give greater attention to the diversity of care-leavers. This book has helped to open new insights into some of the most understudied care-leavers, such as those with a street-connected history, those in the LGBTQIA+ community, those who are unaccompanied migrants, those who are disabled, and those who are early parents and/or are suicidal.

Groups that we could not include in this book, but believe warrant more attention, are, for example, Indigenous peoples, those who experienced abuse or neglect while in care, and those from countries where no known leaving-care research has been conducted. In practice, researchers should continue to study aggregates of care-leavers – there is value in such studies, particularly with large samples. But we do recommend that such studies provide more information about the profile of these groups and that, where relevant, disaggregated analysis be conducted on key demographic and life variables. In particular, actively identifying sub-groups that are large enough to do meaningful quantitative, qualitative or mixed-methods research on and with, could assist in focusing in on groups with distinctive care-leaving experiences.

Second, there are tried-and-tested research methods and methodologies that are and should continue to be used: grounded theory, longitudinal studies, surveys, case studies, mixed methods, and so on. These methodologies are known to generate useful insights into life experiences. But the chapters in this book have raised up several less widely known methodologies that could significantly enrich the kind of data collected and the sense made of that data: institutional ethnography, methods for including disabled care-leavers, techniques to engage hard-to-reach young people, trauma-informed designs, greater attentiveness to issues of power and care, consideration of the gap between researcher and researched, challenges and opportunities for care-experienced researchers, and interviewing a young person's social network and ethnography. Other methodologies that we consider worth more attention are discourse analysis, interpretive phenomenological analysis, visual methods and Indigenous methodologies.

Most studies on leaving care tend to rely on a small number of methodologies. We envisage a future in which leaving-care scholars explore less-well-used methodologies and even create new methodologies that are tailored to this population, and where the cultural appropriateness of methods is critically considered. We also aspire to a future in which the engagement of care-experienced young people as researchers, field workers, advisors, data analysts and writers or presenters becomes the norm, as part of a broader ethic of care. We do recognise that resources may significantly constrain the ability to make use of these methods, particularly for those in the Global South. Finding creative solutions to collaborate in egalitarian ways across better- and less-resourced contexts is something that should be high on our agenda.

Third, in 2006, Mike Stein famously called out the tendency at that time for leaving-care research to be overly empirical and lacking theoretical framing. At the time, he recommended three theories – attachment, focal and resilience – the first and particularly the third of which have become prominent, while the second almost invisible. While leaving-care scholarship is far more theoretically informed and driven than in the past, and while we agree that not all research needs to be theoretically grounded, this book introduces or revitalises some important theoretical frameworks: the conceptualisation of 'stability', the habitus of instability, Joiner's Interpersonal-Psychological Theory of Suicide and trauma theories. In addition, more familiar theories are sometimes taken from a fresh angle, such as a social ecological approach to resilience, rather than the more familiar psychological and individualistic approach, and fresh considerations of social capital. Other theories that could expand our insights into leaving care include minority stress, interactional resilience, anti-oppressive frameworks, feminism, and decolonial and postcolonial theories.

Conclusion

As we draw this book to a close, we highlight the tensions and benefits between continuity and discontinuity in scholarship, between what is known and what is edgy and fuzzy. In many ways, as we move into the future, we wish to build on the legacy that has been left to us by our predecessors in the scholarship of leaving care – much has been learned over a relatively short time (in relation to how long 'care' has been a feature of societies around the globe). But in other ways, which this book has explicitly set out to accomplish, there is a need to carve out new facets of scholarship. These may confirm what we have already learned – that is good. And these may generate revolutionary new insights into the provision of care, the process of transitioning from care and the 'outcomes' experienced over the course of adulthood. This is, in our view, a worthwhile, albeit sometimes uncomfortable, adventure.

An important theme going forward is which terms are used by researchers when writing about care-leaving research. Which concepts are experienced as inclusive, ethical and not stigmatising may differ between groups of care-leavers, contexts, countries and languages. Deciding which terms are used is a sensitive and complicated topic that needs to be addressed to a greater extent than before and researched in an open and respectful way, allowing for diverse contributions and conclusions.

Another important edge in care-leaving research is the experience and challenges faced by care-experienced researchers, particularly professional, academic researchers. While all care-leaving researchers bring a unique set of life experiences to their research, which often includes working in children's services, the experiences of researchers who grew up in care are surely distinctive. Given the findings about the questioning of the legitimacy, bias and rigour of care-experienced researchers' research, this is an edge that needs further voicing.

We wish to emphasise, also, the need to recognise and bring to the centre the experiences and discourses of care and care-leaving from the Global South, through building closer power-conscious partnerships between North and South, including with Indigenous peoples living in Global North countries. Nevertheless, not all dividing lines go between the Global South and Global North. There are still countries within the Global North that have little knowledge about young people ageing out of care, while some countries in the Global South have more research.

Finally, greater interdisciplinarity in a field that has been largely dominated by social workers may introduce fresh methods and theories – social geography, political science and policy, anthropology and youth studies (in sociology) spring to mind as potential candidates. And the global histories and discourses of racism and patriarchy, and heteronormativity and gender dichotomy, also need far more attention as we move into a future that is diverse, inclusive and caring. There will always be edges in research on care-leaving, and we hope that scholars will continue to engage with and push forward at these edges.

Index

Page numbers in *italic* type refer to figures; those in **bold** type refer to tables.